Teaching Critical Religious Studies

Also Available from Bloomsbury:

All Religion Is Inter-Religion
Edited by Kambiz GhaneaBassiri and Paul Robertson

The Critical Study of Non-Religion
Christopher R. Cotter

Interreligious Resilience
Michael S. Hogue and Dean Phillip Bell

Teaching Critical Religious Studies

Pedagogy and Critique in the Classroom

Edited by
Jenna Gray-Hildenbrand, Beverley McGuire,
and Hussein Rashid

BLOOMSBURY ACADEMIC
LONDON • NEW YORK • OXFORD • NEW DELHI • SYDNEY

BLOOMSBURY ACADEMIC
Bloomsbury Publishing Plc
50 Bedford Square, London, WC1B 3DP, UK
1385 Broadway, New York, NY 10018, USA
29 Earlsfort Terrace, Dublin 2, Ireland

BLOOMSBURY, BLOOMSBURY ACADEMIC and the Diana logo are
trademarks of Bloomsbury Publishing Plc

First published in Great Britain 2023
This paperback edition published 2024

Copyright © Jenna Gray-Hildenbrand, Beverley McGuire, Hussein Rashid,
and contributors, 2023, 2024

Jenna Gray-Hildenbrand, Beverley McGuire, and Hussein Rashid have asserted
their rights under the Copyright, Designs and Patents Act, 1988,
to be identified as Editors of this work.

For legal purposes the Acknowledgments on pp. xiv–xvii constitute an
extension of this copyright page.

Cover image © Saul Gray-Hildenbrand, Practicing Disappearing - 35"x 35" - oil and lit
gunpowder on canvas (2019)

All rights reserved. No part of this publication may be reproduced or transmitted
in any form or by any means, electronic or mechanical, including photocopying,
recording, or any information storage or retrieval system, without prior
permission in writing from the publishers.

Bloomsbury Publishing Plc does not have any control over, or responsibility for, any
third-party websites referred to or in this book. All internet addresses given in this
book were correct at the time of going to press. The author and publisher regret any
inconvenience caused if addresses have changed or sites have ceased to exist,
but can accept no responsibility for any such changes.

A catalogue record for this book is available from the British Library.

Library of Congress Control Number: 2022933172

ISBN:		
	HB:	978-1-3502-2841-2
	PB:	978-1-3502-2845-0
	ePDF:	978-1-3502-2842-9
	eBook:	978-1-3502-2843-6

Typeset by Integra Software Services Pvt. Ltd.

To find out more about our authors and books visit www.bloomsbury.com
and sign up for our newsletters

Dedicated to those of you who made it this far.

Contents

List of Figures ix
Notes on Contributors x
Acknowledgments xiv

Introduction: Under Pressure *Hussein Rashid, Beverley McGuire,
 and Jenna Gray-Hildenbrand* 1

Part One What is Religious Studies?

1 Bringing the Introduction to Religious Studies Course to Its
 Senses *Katherine C. Zubko* 17
2 Pre-bracketing: Embodied Questioning in the Introductory Religious
 Studies Classroom *Jenna Gray-Hildenbrand* 31
3 Grief and Joy in the Religious Studies Classroom *M. Cooper Minister* 42
4 Students' Emotional Labor in Religious Studies Courses:
 Toward Greater Instructor Intentionality *Jeremy Posadas* 53
5 Reorientation: Teaching Theory and Method to Future Faculty
 Jill DeTemple 65

Part Two What are Religious Traditions?

6 Mustafa: Teaching Beyond the Five Pillars *Hussein Rashid* 83
7 Pedagogical Strategies for Critically Examining the
 Consumption of Asian Religions *Beverley McGuire* 95
8 Telling the Story of American Religions: Responding to
 Protestant and Pluralist Paradigms *Martha Smith Roberts* 105
9 Teaching Critical Religious Studies in the World Religions Public
 Sphere *Henry Goldschmidt* 115

Part Three Is There Religion Outside of Religion?

10 Who and What's Included?: Teaching Religion and Science
 Benjamin E. Zeller 133

11 Using Sports to Tackle the Problem of Defining Religion
    Annie Blazer   148
12 "I Want to Break Free": Abolition and Full Participation in the
    Religious Studies Classroom *Joseph L. Tucker Edmonds*   162

Notes   174
Bibliography   202
Index   222

Figures

5.1	"No Weasels" Cookie Cake, 2016	67
5.2	Communication Agreements, 2019	70
5.3	Playlist Capture, 2019	78
9.1	K-12 teachers Lavie Raven (left) and Aaron Bible explore the Bronx Lourdes grotto at the 2017 Religious Worlds of New York summer institute for teachers	123
9.2	Brooklyn rabbis Avi Lesches (left) and Heidi Hoover speak on a panel discussion at the 2012 Religious Worlds of New York summer institute for teachers	125
10.1	Goals of Religious Studies Venn Diagram	144

Contributors

Annie Blazer is Associate Professor of Religious Studies at William & Mary in Williamsburg, Virginia. Her courses cover religion in America from the colonial to contemporary period. In particular, her courses investigate the relationships between religions and American culture, paying attention to race, class, gender, and sexuality. Her first book was *Playing for God: Evangelical Women and the Unintended Consequences of Sports Ministry* (2015). The book is an ethnographic exploration of the religious experiences of Christian athletes in the United States.

Jill DeTemple is Professor of Religious Studies and, by courtesy, Professor of Anthropology at Southern Methodist University. She also serves as Academic Associate at Essential Partners, a nonprofit dedicated to strengthening communities through dialogue. Her research interests include faith-based economic development, Latin American religions, Pentecostalism, and the use of dialogue in classrooms to promote intellectual humility, conviction, civic engagement, and deep learning. She is the author of *Cement, Earthworms and Cheese Factories: Religion and Community Development in Rural Ecuador* (2012) and *Making Market Women: Gender, Religion, and Work in Ecuador* (2020).

Henry Goldschmidt is Director of Programs at The Interfaith Center of New York, where he develops programs for religious and civic leaders, K-12 teachers and students, social workers, police, and other audiences. He also works as a cultural anthropologist, community educator, interfaith organizer, and scholar of religion. Henry received his Ph.D. in anthropology from the University of California at Santa Cruz and has taught religious studies and anthropology at Wesleyan University and elsewhere. He is the author of *Race and Religion among the Chosen Peoples of Crown Heights* (2006) and other publications on American religious diversity and religious studies pedagogy.

Jenna Gray-Hildenbrand is Associate Professor of Religious Studies at Middle Tennessee State University. She has published articles on Christian serpent-handling, the spirituality of hula hooping, embodied religious practice, religious experience, and the scholarship of teaching and learning. Her current book project examines three interconnected features of the Christian serpent-handling tradition: religious beliefs and practices, media engagement, and legal consciousness. So, when she is not in the classroom, you may find her doing ethnographic research in the mountains of Appalachia in Sign-Following churches.

Beverley McGuire is Professor of East Asian Religions at the University of North Carolina Wilmington. Her book *Living Karma: The Religious Practices of Ouyi Zhixu* (2014) examines the karmic worldview of an eminent Chinese Buddhist monk and his practices of divination, repentance, vows, burning, and bloodwriting. She has published articles on Buddhist board games, Buddhist blogs, karmic memes, and Buddhist and Christian responses to natural disasters. She has also published about undergraduate teaching in Buddhist studies, online learning, experiential learning, and digital privacy, digital ethics, and digital literacy.

M. Cooper Minister is Associate Professor of Religion at Shenandoah University. They are the author of *Rape Culture on Campus* (2018) and *Trinitarian Theology and Power Relations: God Embodied* (2014), the coeditor (with Sarah Bloesch) of *Cultural Approaches to Studying Religion: An Introduction to Theories and Methods* (2018) and *The Bloomsbury Reader in Cultural Approaches to the Study of Religion* (2018), and the coeditor (with Rhiannon Graybill and Beatrice Lawrence) of *Rape Culture and Religious Studies: Critical and Pedagogical Engagements* (2019). Their most recent work is on transmuting illness, time, and death on the dancefloor.

Jeremy Posadas is Associate Professor of Religious Studies and Director of Gender Studies at Austin College (on the Texas-Oklahoma border) and a co-chair of the American Academy of Religion's Class, Religion, and Theology unit. A social ethicist, he has recently published essays on reproductive justice, worker justice, and, in the volume *#MeToo and Literary Studies* (2021), pedagogies for dismantling rape culture. He is currently at work on an eco-queer economic ethics and is also the creator of the "United Regions of America" map, a county-based delineation of US regions that calibrates common perceptions with ecoregions and land-use patterns.

Hussein Rashid, Ph.D., is an independent scholar and founder of islamicate, L3C, a consultancy focusing on religious literacy. His research focuses on

Muslims and American popular culture. He co-edited a book with Jessica Baldzani on Kamala Khan/Ms. Marvel, *Ms. Marvel's America: No Normal* (2020). He is currently co-editing *The Bloomsbury Handbook on Muslims and Popular Culture* with Kristian Petersen and another volume with Huma Mohibullah on Islam in North America. He was the content expert on the Children's Museum of Manhattan's exhibit "America to Zanzibar: Muslim Cultures Near and Far."

Martha Smith Roberts is Assistant Professor of Religious Studies at Fullerton College. Her teaching covers all aspects of religion in culture and the diversity of religious traditions around the world. Her research and writing focus on North American religious diversity and pluralism, race and ethnicity, new religious movements, and religious studies pedagogy. She has written articles on hula hooping, communities of practice, antiracist pedagogy, and religious diversity and pluralism in the United States.

Joseph L. Tucker Edmonds is Associate Professor of Religious Studies and Africana Studies at the Indiana University School of Liberal Arts at IUPUI (Indianapolis). His research interests include alternative Christianities in the Black Atlantic, Black embodiment, and the role of scripture in Black religious traditions. His first book, *The Other Black Church: Alternative Christian Movements and the Struggle for Black Freedom*, was released in 2020, and it explores the role of the Black body in twentieth-century Christian movements. He currently serves as an editor of *Religion and American Culture: A Journal of Interpretation*.

Benjamin E. Zeller is Associate Professor and Chair of Religion at Lake Forest College (Chicago, USA). He researches religious currents that are new or alternative, including new religions, the religious engagement with science, and the quasi-religious relationship people have with food. He is the author of *Heaven's Gate: America's UFO Religion* (2014) and *Prophets and Protons: New Religious Movements and Science in Late Twentieth-Century America* (2010), editor of *Handbook of UFO Religions* (2021), and co-editor of *Religion, Food, and Eating in North America* (2014) and *The Bloomsbury Companion to New Religious Movements* (2014). He serves as co-general editor of *Nova Religio: The Journal of Alternative and Emergent Religions*.

Katherine C. Zubko is Professor of Religious Studies and NEH Distinguished Professor of the Humanities (2018–23) at the University of North Carolina

Asheville. Her areas of expertise include aesthetics, ritual, performance, and embodied religion in South Asia. Zubko is the author of *Dancing Bodies of Devotion: Fluid Gestures in Bharata Natyam* (2014) and the general editor of the journal *Body and Religion*. Current research interests include exploring the role of embodied gestures of compassion and hospitality in performances on conflict transformation and inclusive, interdisciplinary curriculum design as part of the scholarship of teaching and learning.

Acknowledgments

Our desire for this volume is that as you read it, you feel like you joined an ongoing conversation of teacher-scholars. A conversation among friends, familiars, and people with whom you have always wanted to talk. Hopefully, it is also a conversation in which you want to take part, even just as an active listener. It is one that each of us in this volume is continuing to have with one another, our peers, and most importantly our students.

This conversation has its origins at the Wabash Center for Teaching and Learning in Theology and Religion, to which is our first thanks. The three of us first met there in the 2017–18 Colloquy on Writing the Scholarship of Teaching in Theology and Religion, and the seeds for this volume were first planted. We were encouraged and guided in our work by the leadership team of Tom Pearson, Eugene Gallagher, and Kwok Pui Lan. We were well supported by Beth Reffett and her team, including the student workers.

As the seeds were germinating, we received funding from the Wabash Center for Teaching and Learning in Theology and Religion to bring together scholars to cultivate conversations on pedagogy and disciplinary critique. The funding, provided under the leadership of Nadine Pence and Paul Myhre, allowed the seeds to sprout into this volume. Through the opportunity to engage with our peers, we were pushed to imagine a much more comprehensive project than we had initially farmed.

Our next round of thanks is to our contributors. They have worked with us, pushed us, and each other, been generous to the community, and have built something we are proud to share. Not everyone who has engaged with us is included in this volume, and we are grateful for what they gave, and we hope they see their impact in the final product. Coordinating group meetings with all contributors and editing a volume during a global pandemic presented challenges none of us editors imagined. We are glad that everyone we worked with in this volume has been understanding, honest, and transparent with their struggles and successes, so we could support each other.

This generosity and understanding extend to our wonderful editors at Bloomsbury, Lalle Pursglove and Lily McMahon, who have kept us on track, and been kind when we were not there. They saw the impact of what we were proposing and organized productive reviews that helped this volume.

D. Jamil Grimes, at Middle Tennessee State University, has been with this group since we received funding for the cohort. He has been a diligent notetaker, copy editor, and a critical eye on the work that we are doing. His contribution to this volume has been instrumental in getting it to the point that it is in now. We hope he learns as much from these essays as we learned from him.

Thank you to our students. You inspire us. You frustrate us. You challenge us every day to perfect our craft. We contributors worked together for thirty months, and we were always trying to understand each other's institutional contexts, to give better feedback. The thing we kept coming back to was how we entered this profession to teach and to be better teachers. It is the students who galvanize us. Even with our institutional and regional differences, our students' needs were consistent: make it real.

Finally, we have to thank St. Freddie of Mercury. During our first meetings, we discovered one of the editors of this volume was unfamiliar with the band Queen. The other two editors quickly went about rectifying this significant gap in knowledge, and in explaining all the ways in which Queen was important, we began to relate their impact to the structure of the volume.

Beverley

I have immense gratitude for my co-editors, Jenna and Hussein, who kept me feeling connected, grounded, and sane during an incredibly overwhelming and isolating time. Their humor and collegiality made our collaborative work fun – so fun that my children would inevitably be drawn by our laughter into my office where they would then Zoom bomb our meeting! Our shared commitment and concern about how we might fully engage our students in the classroom, and how we might improve teaching in Religious Studies by drawing from the Scholarship of Teaching and Learning, has generated many fruitful conversations and pedagogical insights over these past four years. It has been inspiring and energizing to co-create a learning community with them.

I would also like to thank all of the contributors for their mutual support, constructive feedback, and collective vision. Together we have created a volume that shares pedagogical possibilities for our field in the hopes of transforming the way that we connect with our students and our discipline in our classrooms. Across differences in our subfields and institutional contexts, we imagined and implemented new ways of teaching critical Religious Studies in the hopes of inspiring others to do the same.

I would like to acknowledge those whose teaching inspired me to follow in their footsteps, including Bob Gregg and Lee Yearley at Stanford, and Anne Monius, Rob Gimello, Michael Puett, and Shigehisa Kuriyama at Harvard. The late Anne Monius was particularly influential in modeling a holistic concern for her students. She gave so much of her time to us that her office felt like home, and I miss our annual dinner reunions at the American Academy of Religion.

Finally, I want to thank my husband Michael, my daughter Haley, and my son Connor for all of their love and support. Although Michael teaches his students how to operate video cameras and fix audiovisual issues, rather than how to analyze religious texts and practices, he similarly connects with and cares for his students as whole people. Our joint commitment to education means a great deal to me.

Hussein

I would like to begin by thanking my wife, who helps me in innumerable ways to get my work done. Our relationship is a good reminder that academia is not life, and home is what we make of it. My kids are my first audience. It is to them that I explain what I am doing to know that I have an idea worth developing.

I also need to thank Martin Nguyen from the colloquy for listening to the ideas that would work their way into my chapter. Martin also arranged for a Wabash Peer Mentoring Cluster grant on "Racialization and the Study of Islam: Navigating Teaching and Service," where the conversations among Martin, Hussein, Arshad Ali, and Sylvia Chan-Malik were influential on my work. Some inspiration came from the retreat of that cohort to Easton's Nook, where we spent time talking about how we teach.

Our contributors in this volume have been equally influential. Our check-ins, draft reviews, and one-on-one conversations always had me thinking in new ways about everything we were doing. I have a whole new bibliography of things I want to read based on working on this book. It is like taking my comprehensive exams all over again in the best possible way.

Of course, in the "last, but not least" category are my co-editors. Like the vast majority of my faculty peers, I am precarious faculty, what is euphemistically called "adjunct," or "independent scholar." At a certain point, I realized I cannot perform for a system that does not care about me, but I love research and teaching. As a result, I decided to only do work that stimulated me, rather than work that I "had" to do because it could potentially lead to an imaginary position. I have been fortunate to find comrades not just among other precarious faculty but among the 1 percent of faculty, including Jenna and Bev, who understand that my mind works differently about projects, since I am not as conditioned by the inherent conservatism of academia. They understood that references to *qawwali*, Queen, *The Aeneid*, were not just throwaway lines, but deep intertextual work that belonged together. It was also wonderful to work with people who had complementary skills, and who gladly stepped in to help without question when needed. These were good people to work with and become friends with and spend time with during a pandemic. I can think of no higher compliment, except maybe organizing the sequel to this volume, Religious Studies Strikes Back.

Jenna

It will be very difficult to match the academic rigor, mutual respect, and fun that I have experienced working with my co-editors. Who has the experience of working with two exceptional colleagues on a project like this and by the end everyone is still enthusiastic, laughing, and completing one another's sentences? And, this all took place during the COVID-19 pandemic. Thank you, Bev and Hussein, from the bottom of my heart.

I want to thank each contributor to this volume for helping me grow as a teacher, a scholar, and a person. This learning community was a respite during a very difficult time to be a teacher and person in the world. Our meetings were a place to be present—not stuck in the pre-pandemic past or hoping for a COVID-19 free future. As this volume represents, our conversations, for me, were a place to be present in an embodied space where we pushed one another to think critically in solidarity. The conversation continues.

I would like to thank Eugene and Jennifer Gallagher for feedback on ideas and the best self-imposed writing retreat weekend I have ever had. In addition, the support of the MTSU staff, Terri Ferrell and Joe Driver, who helped manage grant funds and contracts has been an asset during the course of this project. Also, I am indebted to my colleague and friend Rebekka King for years of productive conversations about pedagogy, curriculum, and O-Net.

Finally, I want to thank my spouse and child for all their love, support, and advice throughout this project. Saul's writing advice to overcome perfectionism and writer's block: "Get it down; then, get it right later." As well as, Jerome's sage advice, "Mama, you are funnier when you don't try." Both pieces of wisdom have gotten me out of a pickle in various situations.

Introduction: Under Pressure

Hussein Rashid, Beverley McGuire, and
Jenna Gray-Hildenbrand

The word "saint" is a useful word to enter into the framing conversation of this book. It emerges out of Christian contexts to refer to those with a special proximity to God. Eventually, it is used for figures in phenomenologically similar positions in other religious traditions. It becomes a gloss, and later a synonym, for *rishi*, *wali*, *tzadik*, and *bodhisattva*, among numerous other terms for spiritually elevated individuals, regardless of the religious tradition from which they emerge.

The ways in which Religious Studies is dominated by Christian, particularly Protestant Christian, understandings of religion are exemplified by the word "saint." The bias for understanding religion through Christian complexes is so strong in the discipline that historically using theological language from Christianity to describe non-Christian traditions is normalized.

Culturally, in the United States the language of Christianity is further entrenched through secularization, which seeks to neuter the theological impact of words like "saint."[1] However, such flattening only reinforces the Christian understanding of the term, because it treats the word as having no valence of its own, and it can be used across religions, with no consideration of differences in how proximity to God is understood in those traditions. It is a sign of privilege, and an act of epistemological violence, to articulate one understanding of religion as providing the natural neutral language for all religions. Language cannot so easily be divorced from meaning.

When the three editors of this volume, Beverley, Hussein, and Jenna, met at a writing colloquy at the Wabash Center for Teaching and Learning in Theology and Religion, we realized we were each working on issues related to religious literacy, pedagogy, and the World Religions Paradigm. We knew that in academia the World Religions Paradigm bias had been named and challenged within the last generation, but as we wrote together, we understood that there is a gap between the theories of our field and our practices in classrooms. There are two distinct bodies of literature that attempt to unravel the presumptive normalcy of Christian theological thought: critiques of the World Religion Paradigm and critiques of secularization.

We began to consider how the work each of us was doing related to each other. Since we were coming from different content perspectives, and distinct methodological backgrounds, we started talking in analogies. We all engaged with pop culture in various capacities and settled on music as our way to think together.

Within our conversation spaces, we recognize the role the secularized "saint" has to play in both our theorizing and teaching. St. John Coltrane inspired a church, drawing on the religious marketplace of the United States, before finding a home in the African Orthodox Church, which was formed in response to the racism of the Episcopal Church in the United States.[2] These religious groups offer ways to think about how religions come together, interact, and generate new ways of understanding religion as a category. With these more contemporary religious identifications, it is easier for scholars to more easily integrate questions of race, gender, sexuality, ability, and class.

With this understanding of the contemporary, secularized saint, we could not help but adopt as our "patron saint" Freddie Mercury (d. 1991) of the band Queen. Freddie Mercury, born Farrokh Bulsara, is symbolic of the type of problems we see in the Study of Religion. He was born to a Parsi family, Iranian Zoroastrians who migrated to Gujarat, India. The family went to Zanzibar, a crossroads of South Asian, Swahili, and Omani culture. So Mercury becomes the symbol of natural cultural, including religious, flows, eventually ending up in Dear Old Blighty. The name Blighty comes from the English corruption of the Perso-Urdu word, *vilayeti*, or the imperial center. Of course, he goes there because England is the center of Empire, and India and Zanzibar were both English colonies. With Queen, he partners with David Bowie, the symbol of an adaptive, open culture based in power. However, most people know their collaboration through the sample of a hack, who reduces their music to the most simple understanding that serves the purposes of late capitalist power centers. Freddie is Lived Religion and Vanilla Ice is Religious Studies.

As we engaged in such analogies and connections, the idea of crafting a volume around these themes became more attractive to us. We started the call for chapters focusing simply on the relationships among the World Religions Paradigm, the scholarship of teaching and learning, and student learning.

However, we quickly realized, both in the initial submissions and subsequent group calls with our contributors, that this volume would move beyond just the World Religions Paradigm. The group of writers who generously gave of their time and knowledge to this volume were interested in the same questions the editors were asking about the limits of the Study of Religion, but they were coming at it from different perspectives. If we take seriously the idea that the Study of Religion is linked intimately to *imperium*, then our contributors were pushing us to think about other exercises of power embedded in the Study of Religion. Our volume reflects the input of these brilliant minds.

While using the World Religions Paradigm as a starting point, our volume moves beyond that specific consideration of power and considers how knowledge is constructed, not just in theory but in practice. A common theme in our contributor conversations was the way the Study of Religion theorizes against power but also teaches acquiescence to power. The authors are speaking to a disjunct between theory and pedagogy. These observations are connected to pedagogy and student learning. Therefore, the volume is about practical approaches to teaching religion, not about theoretical approaches. The volume is working to bridge theory into practice.

State of the Fields: Bohemian Rhapsody

The theories we start with come from critiques of the World Religions Paradigm. Tomoko Masuzawa skillfully outlines how understandings of Protestant Christianity inflect the study of so-called "world religions."[3] Paradigmatically, simply removing Christianity from the category of religions of the world signifies that Christianity is a special case of religion. Comparative Theology, the precursor to the Study of Religion, leveraged this status of the special case of Christianity to establish it as the teleology of religions. The comparative aspect established that other religions were deficient compared to Christianity, particularly forms of Protestant Christianity.[4] Since Christianity was the true religion against which other religions were measured, most scholars examined these religions as though they were structured and functioned as failed forms of Christianity. Our framing and examples are stark in order to illustrate the strictures and structures against which we catalyzed our thinking. Our goal is not to offer a nuanced and complex history of the Study of Religion, but instead to start a conversation for the future of the field.

Taking Islam as an example, historian Farhad Daftary argues that the use of Christian terminology and biases structured Shi'ism as a "heterodoxy" and "heresy" within Muslim traditions. Sunni Islam was presented as the "orthodox" form of Islam.[5] This division neatly mirrored the Protestant-Catholic divide in Europe, where Shi'ism was paralleled to Catholicism because of the strong central leadership inherent in both traditions. Since Catholicism was understood to be a "heresy," Shi'ism also had to be a "heresy." The language of "sect" and "heresy" is theological and problematic as analytic descriptors in the Study of Religion. It is even more troublesome when used outside of the Christian context, as it connotes different types of division than are emic to the religions in question.[6]

As sociologist William Barylo argues, "Using terms and concepts rooted in Latin and Greek languages to describe spiritual systems which are not native to them, holding to Eurocentric concepts and visions and performing a binary segregation between what is 'religious' and what is not, puts research at risk of major simplification."[7] The very use of language, like Greek and Latin, to describe religious phenomena among communities who do not speak those languages automatically curtails a complete understanding of those phenomena.[8] Yet, despite these critiques, there is still an emphasis on teaching the "Five Pillars of Islam," which reinforces the bias of Sunni Islam as "orthodoxy" and other conceptions of Islam as "heterodoxy." Even though many scholars of religion do not work on Comparative Theology, the field of Study of Religion has inherited the prejudices of the disciplines from which it descended.

Using Hinduism as another example, the typical reference to Brahma, Vishnu, and Shiva as equivalent to the Triune God suggests an equivalency that glides over substantial differences in cosmogony and worldview. The so-called "Hindu trinity" identifying Brahma as creator, Vishnu as sustainer, and Shiva as destroyer of the universe captures only one way of understanding these Hindu deities. For Shaivite devotees, Shiva plays all three roles as he creates, maintains, and destroys the universe himself.[9]

It is with the inherent biases of Comparative Theology, and the subsequent limits imposed by these biases on truly understanding non-Christian traditions, that Comparative Religion emerges. The goal for this discipline, like Comparative Theology, is not actual understanding of religion, but domination and control for the service of Empire. David Chidester focuses on the relationship between the Study of Religion and domination by empire.[10] In one of his works, Chidester makes a direct connection between the construction of religion by the *imperium* and the justification for *imperium*, in ways that are particularly relevant for the Study of Religion in the United States. He writes:

> European explorers, traders, and merchants in West Africa used [the word *fetish*] to denigrate African religions for their lack of any "authenticity" that might provide a stable system of values. In the work of W. E. B. Du Bois ... the fetish posed a crucial problem for understanding the role of religion in American culture. Initially, Du Bois tried to rehabilitate African fetishism from its European denigration, but eventually he realized that the very notion of fetishism was a European invention. Accusing Africans of worshiping objects, Europeans masked the actual workings of slavery, which turned living human beings into objects, into commodities, for the transatlantic slave trade.[11]

In this short passage, Chidester moves from the religious fetish, as a European invention to diminish the religious lives of West African people, to commodity fetishism. The denial of interior lives of enslaved peoples is part of the process of turning those people into products that only have capitalist value. If we follow the logic of Comparative Theology that all religions are deficient except Christianity, then it is possible for Comparative Religion to judge certain people deficient because of their religions. While this example of the transatlantic slave trade is striking, it is not unique in how Comparative Religion and *imperium* were conjoined. The enslavement of people also illustrates how race and religion are intertwined.

This narrative is only one of many that connect race and religion. In the context of the United States, there is extensive literature on how these two are intertwined and used to enforce white supremacy.[12] Within this literature are also analyses of how religions are used to challenge and subvert statist structures of domination, as well as fulfilling the religious needs of those communities.[13] The broader narrative arc of the connection between race and religion illuminates that the dominating aspect of religious categorization is not unidirectional, but that the dominating aspect informs much of the discipline of the Study of Religion. Chidester implicitly critiques the idea of simply using emic terminology as a liberatory act in understanding religious traditions. He points out that the use of one language or term in another language automatically unmoors it from its meaning in its original context.[14] The introduction of a term like *tabu* or *totem* can enrich the Study of Religion by pushing boundaries. The terms can also be co-opted to serve Empire, or neutered of any religious meaning and become fully commodified.

David Hicks, writing about museums, argues that anthropology and institutions of material culture are not composed of things given to the field. An easy comparison can be made with the Study of Religion, and the methods and vocabulary used in this field. He says, "compared with giving, we have no such fine nuance in the vague vocabularies of booty, desolation, wasting, ravaging, depredation, plunder, pillage, confiscations, desecration, trophy-taking, spoliation, enslavement, loot, *elginisme*, relics of war."[15] In the variety of words we have for taking, there is no escaping the implicit and explicit violence in them. There are edifices, buildings and disciplines, dedicated to moral and physical crimes, which seek to replicate the same reprehensible acquisition of information. Ironically, Hicks does not include the term "loot" in his litany of ways knowledge was taken from other people. It's of Hindi origin, looted by the British, along with many objects that inform the imperial understanding of India.[16]

Similar to linguistic hybridity, dominant languages co-opt discourse from communities they seek to dominate. That absorption, neutering, and transformation are based on power dynamics. And, as linguistic hybridity gives rise to cultural hybridity, looking at broader questions of power, production, and consumption, we editors found ourselves needing to move beyond just looking at critiques of the World Religions Paradigm. It was simply a manifestation of deeper structural power issues in the Study of Religion. The World Religions Paradigm was about exercising control over other people's religions. This control was in the service of colonialism, linked to the so-called "civilizing mission" of the Enlightenment, itself bounded by anti-Semitism and what we would now call Islamophobia. However, the question of control included questions of gender, sexuality, class, ability, as well as race.[17] At its core, we conceive of the Study of Religion as being grounded in a history of domination and control.

Informed by these critiques of the Study of Religion, and recognizing that we are embedded in this same system, it is Diane Moore who offers a potential way out of this morass, without burning it all down and salting the earth. She melds religious literacy with cultural studies to raise questions of power, to consider the contexts of time and location, to center adherents' understanding of their own religions, and to integrate praxis as a form of interpretation.[18] Moore's intervention focuses on the teaching of religion, and while not all of the authors in this volume subscribe to her method, they are committed to the idea that pedagogy and theory are in a dialogic. Therefore, by focusing on teaching in the classroom, we make the theory and critique of the field real for the students, and impact the ways in which we collectively, as educators and learners, reshape the field of Study of Religion.

The Scholarship of Teaching and Learning (SoTL) offers a practical bridge for many of our contributors between teaching the Study of Religion and theory. SoTL focuses on effective, equitable ways to design learning for students.

A widely accepted approach is "backward design," in which instructors first identify their learning goals, then articulate what would count as evidence of learning, and finally plan learning experiences and instructional activities that help students meet those goals.[19] In order to address inequities and improve underserved students' success in higher education, the Transparency in Learning and Teaching project (TILT)[20] encourages instructors to make clear the purpose, tasks, and criteria for their assignments, explicitly stating the transferable skills they will develop through the assignment, detailing the steps they should take and obstacles they should avoid when completing the assignment, and providing a checklist or successful assignment example for students.

Other evidence-based principles include activating relevant prior knowledge, targeting appropriate levels of challenge, giving frequent feedback, and attending to the social, emotional, and intellectual climate of the course.[21] Scholars emphasize the value of developing our students' capacity to inquire, ask questions, and draw on their innate sense of curiosity,[22] arguing that students learn best when addressing questions that they care about or goals that they want to reach.[23]

In Religious Studies courses, students come in with particular expectations that impact their motivation to learn. As Barbara Walvoord has observed, students typically hope to grow spiritually or religiously, while their instructors seek to develop their critical thinking skills; however, if we can overcome this "great divide," we can create the opportunity for deep learning.[24] Our institutional context impacts the degree to which our students can engage in contemplative learning, with those at private or church-affiliated universities typically having greater leeway than those at public universities.[25] However, experiential learning can provide an opportunity for students to reflect on their personal experience as they visit religious sites[26] or engage in activities analogous to religious practices.[27] By connecting our course material to their interests and showing the relevance of their learning to their present or future lives, we can motivate our students.[28]

Another ongoing pedagogical conversation in the field has centered around religious literacy.[29] Religious literacy includes both basic information and critical thinking skills to help the student examine how religion allows people "to orient themselves in the world, express their individual and communal self-understanding, and give their lives direction and meaning."[30] While these conversations lay a foundation for teaching religious studies content and skills, they do not unpack how religious literacy skills can align with disciplinary critiques of religion (as a social, cultural, and academic category) to foster the human connections many millennials and post-millennials identify as important. We want our students to bring their full selves into the classroom, and to consider their relationships to religious texts, traditions, and histories.

This student-centered approach encourages us to be present and responsive to the way students show up in our classrooms. We start with their assumptions and preconceptions about religion, meeting our students where they are by using accessible and familiar metaphors, and then guiding them into more complex terrain (Blazer, McGuire, Rashid, Roberts, Zeller). The ability to integrate the Study of Religion with our students' prior knowledge is especially useful for "one and done" courses that many of us teach within general education programs, but it can also prompt critical self-reflection among undergraduate and graduate students in our field, encouraging them to determine what they want to "replicate, change, or discard" as scholars in the academy and citizens in the world (DeTemple).

In our volume we also draw on critical, engaged, and transformative pedagogy such as that of bell hooks, Paolo Friere, Henry Giroux, and others who adopt a collaborative approach to learning where students and instructors co-create and construct knowledge together (DeTemple, McGuire, Minister, Roberts, Tucker Edmonds, Zubko). Recognizing that our embodied selves are structured by inequality, we also draw attention to the power effects of knowledge (Goldschmidt, Gray-Hildenbrand, McGuire, Posadas, Tucker Edmonds), and the way we might "reduce the carcerality" of our classroom and teaching (Tucker Edmonds). This encourages us to be vulnerable and receptive alongside our students (McGuire, Minister, Tucker Edmonds). We incorporate Reflective Structured Dialogues into our classes, which create spaces for deep listening and speaking, build trust, allow for vulnerability and risk, and encourage personal and intellectual growth (DeTemple, Gray-Hildenbrand, Minister). When working with community partners, we adopt a public, civically engaged approach that fosters an empathetic understanding of other people's religious lives by having religious leaders tell stories about the role of faith in their personal, professional, and social activist lives (Goldschmidt).

Not only do we facilitate a democratically engaged, participatory classroom, we make space for affect, emotions, and feeling in our classes (Gray-Hildenbrand, Minister, Posadas, Zubko). Instead of prioritizing the cognitive over the affective dimension, we make space for and name the affects that arise within the classroom (Minister). Building on the scholarship of embodied learning and sensory education, we encourage our students to use their sense of smell, taste, hearing, and touch as a lens for understanding religious experience (Zubko). Drawing on the work of feminist and disability scholars, we have our students "practice interdependency" in the classroom, helping each other learn in more accessible, clear, and relatable ways (Gray-Hildenbrand).

Gaps and Thinking with Them: Invisible Man

When critical theory in the Study of Religion is brought into dialogue with best practices in the Scholarship on Teaching and Learning, a transformation takes place in the classroom enriching the student, the instructor, and the academy. Contributors to our volume demonstrate work within the classroom (when taken seriously and critically) that can destabilize problematic structures, definitions, and institutions that inhibit student success because these are the very things long critiqued within our discipline. It is time we practice what we teach.

The contributors propose several ways of practicing what we teach. Two main themes stand out. The first theme is that we must adjust the starting point of inquiry in our classrooms, focusing on the first weeks of the class when we set the tone and direction as well as acknowledging power dynamics and disciplinary methods. This approach impacts the entire semester and beyond, informing the place from which our students live, embody, feel, and digest their studies. The second theme challenges us to tackle the primary tensions, assumptions, and misconceptions dominant within the course topic. Contributors address these challenges by designing courses that scaffold foundational ideas throughout the semester to aid students in their journey to identify, interrogate, relate to, and deconstruct the topic at hand.

Teaching Critical Religious Studies is organized into three sections, with each section examining a broader category of disciplinary critique in the Study of Religion. In the first section, "What is Religious Studies?", the authors engage disciplinary critiques by reconceptualizing the starting point for the Study of Religion. In this way, scholars of religion practice what we teach in the classroom by presenting a more authentic glimpse of how scholars of religion engage with and examine our object of study.

To begin this conversation, Katherine Zubko argues that belief-centered approaches to the Study of Religion fall short and demonstrate a Protestant Christian legacy in Religious Studies. She asserts a shift is needed toward embodied religious knowledge. Building upon the turn toward the body and affect in Religious Studies, Zubko structures her introductory religion course around sensory content. She concludes that this approach brings students closer to the "how" and "why" of lived religion.

Jenna Gray-Hildenbrand argues that bracketing is not an essential starting point in the introductory Religious Studies classroom. Rather, she presents an alternative approach that strengthens students' understanding of lived embodiment by scaffolding academic questioning. Gray-Hildenbrand outlines a pedagogy of embodied questioning that is informed by Feminist Disability Studies, Religious Studies, and the Scholarship on Teaching and Learning. By focusing on developing embodied academic questions in the Religious Studies classroom, students better understand the experiences they bring to the course material and how they shape the questions about religion which they will find interesting and valuable.

M. Cooper Minister forces us to face the unfolding crises, threats, and traumas we and our students carry into the classroom and shift our focus toward transformative reflectiveness by making space for affect in the classroom. Minister argues that religious affects have been removed from the Religious Studies classroom by way of bracketing. According to Minister, this cleansing is misguided, because paying attention to our students' affects, naming them, and integrating them into the classroom learning process is essential to creating a space where both teachers and students are fully present in the learning process.

Similarly, Jeremy Posadas challenges readers to bring pedagogical intentionality and respect to the emotional dimension of learning. Every cognitive task, Posadas asserts, is concomitant with an emotional task. This chapter provides a detailed example of this approach in the classroom. Posadas challenges the reader to draw upon and elevate ethical and professional standards within our discipline. He presents ten commitments to promote greater emotional agency in the religious studies classroom.

Jill DeTemple focuses on the graduate theory and method seminar, rather than the introductory undergraduate classroom. Like the other chapters grouped in this section, DeTemple aims to change the focus and direction of these courses which, through rote repetition, have grown as dull as an over-rehearsed patriarchal grad school drama. DeTemple asks if we might do better by challenging our students to think of their relationship to the texts, traditions, histories, and one another as a community of scholars. DeTemple demonstrates how this works in her seminar through the use of various teaching techniques.

In the second section, "What are Religious Traditions?", the authors address disciplinary critiques about the creation, commercialization, and narration of religious traditions. They also examine how scholars reify religious boundaries and the dissonance between those constructed boundaries and teaching lived traditions. Through teaching tactics, assignments, and panels, these chapters demonstrate that practicing what we teach energizes the classroom and connects students' lives to the course material. These approaches reveal the misconceptions and contestations that exist in topics students may previously have taken for granted.

Hussein Rashid challenges the practice of using the Five Pillars to teach students about Islam. Teaching Islam in this way perpetuates Orientalist depictions of Muslims, flattens the rich diversity of lived Muslim experiences, and denies Muslims any sense of agency in their own religion. Students enter our classrooms with incomplete knowledge of Islam, Rashid explains, and educators should work with that incomplete knowledge. Using scholarship on religious literacy and cultural studies, he asks students to investigate their own assumptions about Islam using a variety of teaching techniques, particularly the arts.

Beverley McGuire pushes instructors to tackle theoretical critiques of consumption and commercialization of Asian religious practices in introductory religions courses. Using data collected from her own courses, McGuire demonstrates the need to address prior knowledge and misconceptions about Asian religions. McGuire finds that having students engage in personal reflection and analyze their participation in the consumption of religion, such as through yoga classes and meditation apps, improves their critical thinking abilities.

Like other chapters in this section, Martha Smith Roberts problematizes the ways pluralism informs the assumptions, forms, and content of American religion courses. Roberts demonstrates the underlying neoliberal humanistic, white supremacist, and Protestant hegemonic bases of the unexamined pluralism narrative. She argues for teaching students about pluralism rather than teaching students to be pluralists. She presents American religious history as one centered on narrative and myth making, providing students with the understanding that history is contested, constructed, and dependent upon the narrator.

Henry Goldschmidt examines the dilemma of how one teaches critical Religious Studies in the public sphere outside of academia. Developing religious diversity education programs with the Interfaith Center of New York, he grapples with the same types of tensions we do in our college classrooms. He has to negotiate the students' expectations for fixed and easy definitions of religion and religious groups and what we know to be the reality of the diversity within and among the very religious communities. To address this concern, Goldschmidt balances Religious Studies critiques of the World Religions Paradigm with a contextualized empathetic understanding of lived, local religious experiences.

In the final section of *Teaching Critical Religious Studies*, "Is There Religion Outside of Religion?", the authors examine disciplinary critiques that juxtapose religion with something else: science, sport, or carceral spaces. These juxtapositions make the familiar unfamiliar, thus providing space in the classroom to practice what we teach by critically examining tensions and assumptions regarding the course topic.

Benjamin Zeller identifies the challenges instructors face when students enter the classroom with certain assumptions about what constitutes religion and science. Problematizing these definitions brings to the surface long-standing disciplinary critiques about the influence of colonialism, sexism, racism, and elitism on both science and the Study of Religion. Zeller argues it may be easier to ignore students' underlying assumptions, but it is bad pedagogy. He adopts a pedagogy of teaching controversial topics by carefully curating the material to provide alternative narratives that disrupt commonly held assumptions about the relationship between science and religion.

Annie Blazer acknowledges the struggles students encounter facing the multiple definitions of religion within the Study of Religion. This multiplicity can be confusing, but she asserts it is necessary to present essential theoretical approaches because definitions are arguments. Blazer presents an avenue to address this complexity by way of something familiar—religion and sport.

Joseph Tucker Edmonds describes the university classroom as a carceral space and asks what it would look like to transform the classroom into a democratically engaged space. He proposes a shift to explore Religious Studies through the pedagogical intervention of abolition. Tucker Edmonds begins his course with abolition and the recognition that spaces of higher education have not been liberating for all people. Here, the very logic of the university—its surveillance, discipline, and control—is critically examined for the common good. Once this work has been addressed, then the work of Religious Studies in the classroom is pursued.

Each of these chapters offers insight as to how the authors use pedagogy to engage with theory in their respective environments. These essays are not universal "how-to" manuals. Context plays an important role in how each author is constructing their class. Conceptually, these essays are not a move toward decolonizing Religious Studies, the syllabus, or even the classroom. That project is far different and far larger than what anyone in this volume proposes. However, each essay makes explicit different power dynamics of the Study of Religion, exposing various methods of domination and control. By bringing in the tools of the Scholarship of Teaching and Learning and Cultural

Studies, these essays are not using the same tools that were used to build the discipline.

At the same time, there are obvious gaps in the work these essays are doing. All of our contributors are based in the United States, and write from US-based educational perspectives, although we do hope readers elsewhere will be inspired to grow this work. None of the essays actively addresses ideas of diaspora and how diasporic identity shapes and frames religious thinking and identification. Without consideration of diaspora, this volume does not adequately address African diasporic religions, nor transnational connections through diasporic flows. Despite the impact of Karen Brown's monumental work *Mama Lola* on many of the contributors of this volume, teaching the type of work that she did is absent in the essays here.[31] Relatedly, transnational influences, outside of diasporic connections, are another important area that is absent from this volume. Without this analysis, it is tempting to explain certain violent movements emerging out of religion as *sui generis*, rather than the Enlightenment project repackaged without state support or dominant narratives.[32]

Naming gaps is both a way for us as editors to hold ourselves responsible for what is not in here and an invitation for others to build on this work. Part of the structure we hope to disrupt is the idea of the lone scholar working independently of other people, who is not indebted to anyone else. Our ethos is informed by the way we want to work, with commitments to transparency, accountability, and collaboration. These commitments are true not just for our co-learners in the classroom but also for our co-learners in academia.

Conclusion: The Prophet's Song or Let Me Entertain You

This volume started as a conversation among the editors at a writing program. While drawn together by our overlapping work in critiquing the World Religions Paradigm, we thought of bringing together other people who were doing similar work. In speaking to those colleagues, we realized our focus was too narrow.

The World Religions Paradigm is only one tool in the Study of Religion used to minimize the humanity of the subjects of our study. If the Humanities, at its core, is about exploring and expanding the human experience, then this volume had to bring that perspective to the Study of Religion. Therefore, every essay brings a new focus to the humanity of our subjects, or our students, or both. It is, in fact, possible to offer dignity to our students and our field without taking dignity away from the people about whom we are teaching.

A discipline that cannot fully consider, understand, or present the humanity of people is fundamentally flawed and deficient. It not only denies the value of the people we are talking about, but it denies the value and humanity of scholars who come from marginalized positions. If we as scholars are told by disciplinary practice that we are not worth our full being, our options are to deny ourselves, or find new ways of building a discipline, to become the center. The essays in our volume not only critique the present state of the discipline, but also offer methods to build a future.

We also believe that it is important to recognize the conditions in which the volume came together, because the authors are embodied and subject to the affect of the world in which we live. Our first gatherings were at the end of 2019. Very early on we had to contend with a global pandemic and the new national conversations catalyzed by the murder of George Floyd. Our contributors felt the impact of these events, and many others, throughout the course of putting the volume together, and some of the thinking is reflected in the essays.

Our core premise and our core learning are that the human being has to be centered in our work. The human being who is our subject; the human being who is our student; the human being who is us. If we cannot center being human, then we have become the widget that late-stage capitalism demands. Be human.

Part One

What is Religious Studies?

1

Bringing the Introduction to Religious Studies Course to Its Senses

Katherine C. Zubko

"What is a mandala?" I ask, as I pull up a slide with a kalachakra (wheel of time) Tibetan Buddhist sand mandala depicted. A student notes, "It is a focus for meditation practice. Buddhists stare at it to quiet their mind." This statement is followed by silence in the way that students sometimes signal that the right answer has been given and nothing needs to be added.

"Good start. Let's hear some of the things that we see or notice about the mandala." The first few students to speak offer observations such as the geometrical circles and squares, colors, and repeated motif of wheels, but then another student adds, "What are those things around the outer edge of the mandala? Are they letters or words? If we knew what it said, and what all those symbols meant, we would know what a mandala is." Several other students nod their heads in agreement.

"Instead of focusing on those letters or finding meaning in symbols for a moment, let's try a slightly different approach. How do you think people interact with this sand mandala as a religious practice? What are they doing with their bodies in relation to this mandala?" I show a video clip of a sand mandala being made and dismantled.

The observations and questions begin to shift, as the students begin to see through different embodied perspectives various devotional possibilities: the mindful attention of the nun who is placing sand into the mandala, the role of chanted sound, stylized movement, and colorful crowned attire of monks embodying bodhisattvas who protect the space and dwell in the mandala, and the slow intentional walk of attendees to the nearest body of water to disperse the sand at the end. We move from earlier assumptions of an externalized, stationary visual tool for mental focus to a discussion about interactive embodied possibilities that disrupt student ideas about meditation as a cognitive activity somehow separate from a still, quiet body. To add one further perspective, I show students a three-dimensional rendering of a sand mandala as a multi-level physical palace that practitioners enter into to meet with and practice becoming the bodhisattvas and buddhas who dwell within to help students question what types of relationships are being assumed about mind and body as part of powerful transformative possibilities. By this point in the class, the habituated track of students privileging words, symbolic interpretations, or seeking discursive meaning that began the class is fully and successfully derailed.

Students, and many faculty, still head toward words and assume this language will serve as the code to unlock what religion or a religious practice means, as it is very entrenched in the European enlightenment paradigms of intellectual thought and the logos-centric, unmediated biblical word of God in Protestant Christian foundations of Religious Studies as an academic discipline. Shifting from the "what" of religion to "how" helps decenter written and verbal discursive analysis to focus on the multiplicity of embodied interactions that often shed light on what moves people to engage in various religious practices, or the "why" of it all. What is created in those interactions defies the appearance and centrality of monolithic, neatly bounded belief systems that loom large in textbooks, syllabi, and tests, and gets closer to the complex pluralities of lived religious multi-sensory lifeworlds[1] that many of us want to forefront for our students, but often do not do so until upper-division courses, like Religion and the Body, or a unit within Theories and Methods, allows the body, at least in theory, back to the table.

This chapter reviews in brief some of the history and aspects of the disciplinary critique around textual, belief-centered approaches to the study of religion, and then seeks to use the critique to center embodied ways of knowing in an introductory level course. Studies on embodied pedagogy have pointed to several benefits in K-12 and adult education, or higher education, contexts that I will discuss, before also noting how embodied pedagogies have made some inroads into Religious Studies' classrooms.

Inviting embodied learning in the study of religion is not without special challenges, especially within public educational contexts that must adhere to lines of separation between religion and state, namely avoiding religious, confessional, or devotional practices within state contexts in ways that would advocate for or engage in a particular religion.[2] I propose a careful restructuring of the introductory course around sensory-focused case studies paired with a parallel trajectory of both unlearning the habits of cognitive dominant ways of knowing while inviting embodied knowledge to inform a more blended, multimodal style of learning. This moves students more into the "how and why" inquiry mode, raising important questions about how we know what we know, diversifying epistemological toolboxes, resisting a dominant overemphasis on text and belief, and building community to create vulnerably productive spaces to deepen collaborative inquiry into the study of religion from the very first class.

Bodiless Religion and the Interdisciplinary Embodying of the Study of Religion

The largest context for the problem at hand is the ongoing bracketing of what scholars have known for decades now about the history of and reasons for the body's disenfranchisement within the study of religion. Several scholars beginning to write in the 1980s and 1990s examined some of the roots of the separation between mind and body, or sometimes soul and body, with the mind or soul presumed to be superior, as exemplified in European Enlightenment and Christian written and artistic artifacts. This foundational duality was also discussed in light of the tremendous impact on academic disciplinary ideological structures and inquiries that have defined not only what counts in religion, and the study of it, but also the ways of knowing and lenses of analysis.

These insights into the biases of the field are rehearsed in many studies that begin to shift the focus to explorations of embodiment from various disciplines.[3] Historians of Christianity Caroline Walker Bynum and Peter Brown are early forerunners in the late 1980s with their attention on embodiment in antique and medieval primary sources,[4] while other scholars of religion begin to incorporate theories by sociologists Marcel Mauss and Pierre Bourdieu on embodied habitus,[5] philosopher Merleau-Ponty's "lived body,"[6] philosopher-historian Michel Foucault's disciplined body,[7] and ideas from *Metaphors We Live By* (1980), a short text by George Lakoff and Mark Johnson, who combined their interests in philosophy, linguistics, and cognitive science to argue for the pre-cognitive bodily basis of this form of symbolic language. As they note, "no metaphor can ever be comprehended or even adequately represented independently of its [direct physical] experiential basis."[8] The inclusion of cognitive, and later neuroscientific approaches in the study of religion gained steam, as exemplified by Ann Taves's *Religious Experience Reconsidered*[9] which claims a central debt to cognitive sciences in Religious Studies.

Out of all the interdisciplinary strands coming together, the role of anthropology may be the most substantial in supporting this shift to body and embodiment. Michael D. Jackson's article "Knowledge of the Body" (1983) is one of the earliest that argues for placing bodied experience, without assuming it is symbolic of an idea or verbal formulation, at the center of analyses of culture.[10] A significant application to the study of religion came through cultural anthropologist's Talal Asad's critical dissection in *Genealogies of Religion* (1993) of how Protestant Christian ideological assumptions shaped analyses of religion, including an often-cited section on what "ritual" is. While starting out as a term to refer to a liturgical manual, when eventually also used to identify bodied practices, "ritual" continued to be framed as a text and keyed to representations of beliefs in problematic ways, demonstrating the stubbornness and valuation of dominant ideological legacies.[11] These critiques bear out in early studies of religions like Hinduism, in which the intellectualized preferences for the oldest "texts" led to the *Vedas*, especially the philosophical portions of the *Upanisads*, and the *Bhagavad Gita*, to be considered the best representative sources of the religion. In addition to this textual focus is a monotheistic overlay of what is considered sacred, for example, the outsized focus on Brahma as a singularly special creator god because of its familiarity to Christian structures.[12]

Other anthropologists, as well as more historically or textually trained scholars of religion adopting anthropological methods, began to carve out trajectories under the larger umbrella of embodiment, including studies on "practice" and "experience."[13] They also developed or contributed to the fields of performance studies, ritual studies,[14] and case studies and theories on materiality,[15] migratory religion,[16] sensorium/sensation,[17] emotion,[18] and, most recently, affect. In these queries, scholars, such as affect theorist Donovan Schaefer, keep moving toward the blurry, shifting messiness and dynamic potentialities of what is happening in the in-between that captures much of what is powerful for practitioners in lived religion. As Schaefer writes, "religion, like other forms of power, feels before it thinks, believes, or speaks."[19] In calibrating the study of religion toward the mechanisms of affect, it works to further disrupt the written and verbal discursive and belief-centric biases as well as tendencies toward overly simplified categories and binaries.

Many of these directions also interact with lineages of feminist and gender studies, such as Judith Butler's work on the citationality of the body as part of gender performativity, as well as queer, race, ethnic, and disability studies[20] which often focus on varying aspects of bodied epistemologies and ways of being that scholars of religion engage. Those whose perspectives have often dwelled in the in-between in relation to dominant categories—gendered and racialized others of the global majority, people with disabilities, and queer perspectives—are central leading voices in productively disrupting disciplinary canons and structures, often through emphatically embodied analyses. And yet, many of these voices have also yet to make their ways into the center of introductory class materials, but are considered present if tacked on in the "week of others" at the end of the semester.

While a comprehensive overview is not the aim of this section, I hope that in even attempting to mention some of the primary disciplinary threads, as well as only a handful of the many influential scholars and those bringing these threads to bear on the study of religion in relation to body and embodiment over the past several decades, it will be evident that this disciplinary critique of centering embodiment is mainstream, with many active tributaries, and exemplifies the breadth of interdisciplinarity that defines the field of religious studies' scholarship currently. The ways that introductory courses do not mirror this significant focus on embodied religion reveal a huge dissonance between the discipline that has worked to make the embodied non-discursive (not spoken or written)[21] ways of knowing more visible, even as scholars ply their trade in discursive presentations and publication, and our entry-level classrooms.

The institutional context also factors into the ongoing centrality of bodiless religion and disembodied pedagogical approaches, especially in public educational contexts. In public schools, teacher-scholars justifiably want to avoid any perception of the "practice" of religion due to constitutional lines of separation between religion and state, which often leads to avoiding embodied activities as part of courses on religion. It also perhaps leads to eschewing content on bodied religion as it might open up students to their own bodied experiences in ways that teachers do not know how to affirm and integrate into learning processes effectively. Private religiously affiliated institutions often have more leeway, but bodiless religious content still figures prominently due to Christian values of private, internalized, intellectualized religious formation.

For scholars who are aware of the dynamic sense of the field, the contrast to introductory course content can be jarring, and for students who are "one and done," taking care of a general education requirement, the rote approach often does not ignite a reason to come back for more. Embracing the disciplinary critique is overdue and necessary to align and add vitality, especially within departments struggling to spark interest, as noted in the national overall decline in interest in humanities majors, and specifically a 31 percent drop in Religious Studies bachelor degrees completed between 2013 and 2018.[22] In this chapter I will focus on public educational contexts by noting strategies of how to avoid the perception of "practicing" religion and provide models for inviting bodied knowledge into a blended multimodal learning process.

Reembodying Scholars and Students: Embodied Learning in Religious Studies

To remedy the disciplinary reliance on "linguistic tools (structuralist to interpretive) to *translate* symbolic *texts* (whether books, art, doctrine, ritual, etc.) into *verbal* forms (texts, talks, and teaching),"[23] philosopher-dancer Kimerer LaMothe calls for "a sensory education that can complement and enrich our text-based disciplinary training … [and] provide conceptual resources that afford us a better grasp of the bodily dimensions of religious life."[24] Based in an understanding of humans as "rhythms of bodily becoming," creating "self-and-world through patterns of sensation and response," LaMothe's approach creates a shared bodily basis for getting into what she notes as "productive proximity" to what moves people within their religious lives through raising awareness of the bodily sensations of our own scholarly inquiries. As she describes,

> Becoming a scholar of religion is not a mental process of learning how to collect facts and methods and then match the two; it involves educating our senses to "religion." We learn to pay attention, to notice nuances, subtleties, and contrasts and reflect upon them. As we do, we create and become patterns of sensing and responding. The sensory impressions that a given phenomenon makes give rise to questions and interpretive perspectives. We draw on what we know and have experienced in the past to guide us in responding to our own sensory impressions. Over time, we continue to elaborate and refine these patterns, cultivating both our vulnerability to shocks of insight and our ability to categorize and connect these moments with others we have sensed and thought. Our task in becoming scholars, then, involves learning to create and sustain relationships of productive proximity with the ongoing life of what we find ourselves studying. It involves creating *and becoming* the patterns of sensation and response that enable us to navigate the double movement towards and away from what appears to us as "religion."[25]

Critical thinking, presenting an argument, analytical framing, and use of evidence are not feats carried out by mental capacities alone. Instead, LaMothe suggests a more inclusive and bodily based understanding of the scholarly processes that lead to insights and the analyses that we develop about religion that parallels the disciplinary critique about the central role of body and embodiment in the religious lives of those we study. Inviting more attention to our own bodily sensations and responses creates a bridge that supports a more robust, blended learning process. It also makes more visible how knowledge is created and brings to the surface queries into how we know what we know.

Embodied Learning and Its Benefits

What LaMothe argues for in her call for sensory education into one's own patterns of sensation and response may be connected to what is often referred to more broadly as "embodied learning" as utilized by teachers in K-12 and adult, or higher education. Embodied learning overlaps with or is related to active, transformational, experiential, place-based, feminist, anti-oppressive, liberatory, and culturally responsive learning strategies, to name a few.[26] It involves identifying and inviting assignments that attend to movement, sensory information, physical-emotional responses, and might include artistic or theatrical activities such as drawing, body sculpting, and role play (especially, but not limited to non-verbal) and other ways to decenter discursive and cognitive analytical habits, language, and approaches. At its most expansive, embodied learning can be dynamic in its capacity for creating open explorations of underrepresented ways of knowing, while at its most limited, can end up mapping discursive knowledge onto bodies as a way to further predetermined cognitive outcomes, without room for the shifting that can happen during multimodal engagement.

As Diana Gustafson delineates it, the body is placed as a central epistemological site of knowing, but does not remain as the only site. For her, embodied learning becomes one of many ways of knowing that are integrated into a blended learning process that "contests the primacy of androcentric, Eurocentric, institutionalized knowledges" as the only ones that count.[27] Like the iceberg model of what informs how we engage with and navigate the world and communicate in response, embodied stimuli, sensory experiences, emotions, and other aspects often remain below the surface of what we are aware of at a cognitive, conscious level and yet make up a significant percentage of what informs our interpretations, responses, and analyses.[28] By engaging with embodied knowledge, it allows for the possibility of new insights to rise to the surface and inform our interpretations more intentionally, diversifying our epistemological tools.

Much of our bodied knowledge is informed by culture, family, and the experiences related to our identities, and so making embodied knowledge welcome in the classroom can also signal the value of students' diverse backgrounds and cultures, inviting their whole embodied selves to their learning.[29] Diversifying epistemological toolboxes supports inclusivity as well as becomes a communal practice in holding multiple truths, as "the insights produced from embodied experiences will be as diverse as the participants in the room."[30] At the same time, it is common for dominant perspectives to go unmarked, appear as "the norm" in relation to others framed as different (different from what?), and thus not a subject in need of inquiry. Exploring embodied knowledge also works to level these power dynamics by making visible embodied ways of knowing that inform whiteness, Protestant Christianity, and white supremacy.[31]

Studies on embodied learning also point to several other benefits besides tapping into a multimodal blended learning through diversifying epistemologies and creating agency in knowledge creation, especially for students whose ways of knowing are undervalued. One other outcome worth highlighting is the impact on community-building in the classroom.[32] Exploring and sharing in bodied experiences can create a level of bonding and increase capacities for risk-taking and vulnerability. Edward Brantmeier and Maria McKenna define vulnerability in their edited book, *Pedagogy of Vulnerability*, as education that values "mutual self-disclosure and *not knowing* as a central component of their and their students' learning processes."[33] When students trust enough to self-disclose, are willing to share their observations, and become curious about how we know what we know and don't know, it often leads to a depth in discussions and inquiry.[34] There are also many pitfalls to inviting embodied learning and vulnerability that I will address as part of the next section due to the specificity of issues in teaching about religion.

Embodied Learning in Religious Studies

Embodied learning has already made inroads into the teaching of religion. The primary form of embodied learning that people may be familiar with is the site visit to places in which religion is practiced. Three common reasons for site visits include ways to complicate or extend on textbook narratives, to engage questions of space and materiality, and, depending on whether a "tour" during a time of inactivity or an observation of ritual, ceremony, or service, to contribute to or contextualize knowledge about lived religion and practice. Professors agree that for the site visit to be effective, it cannot be tacked on, or freestanding without adequate preparation before, including explaining the pedagogical purpose, and reflective, integrative work after.[35]

When not done well, visits can perpetuate a colonizing voyeurism that can further exotify religions and indulge in one-sided takeaways if there is not a reciprocal relationship sustained with the community. In order to focus student attention, tools that invite sensory observations, such as this one developed by Becky Kraft,[36] can guide students during the visit and their processing after to integrate their embodied knowledge. While acknowledging the potential for brief, superficial encounters in unfamiliar site visits, Henry Goldschmidt sees the primary benefit centered in the "opportunity [for students] to fashion a new sense of self or personhood—a chance to become, through the encounter itself, a more deeply engaged member of their religiously diverse society" by "being there."[37] In this way, students experience LaMothe's patterns of sensation and response in relation to neighbors' bodily becomings. Embodiment is a communal act.

Besides site visits, embodied learning has entered into the study of religion through contemplative practices. While there is a wide range of activities,[38] several use the body for first-person inquiry and reflection. Contemplative practices are often human practices typically employed by religious practitioners to achieve religious goals. In public university contexts, these human practices are framed to support academic learning processes and outcomes. Many practices are already found in secularized forms. Silence, centering, journaling, deep listening, storytelling, and creating "rituals" are the most common, including the example provided by Jennifer Oldstone-Moore on her semester-long asceticism assignment that supports learning about religious disciplinary practices.[39] In addition, the sustained use of movement systems such as yoga, aikido, and tai chi and chi gong is also a popular strategy.[40]

The incorporation of contemplative practices is not without important critiques around issues of cultural/religious appropriation, the perception by students of "practicing religion" or an unintentional advocacy for a religion through its practice,[41] and possibilities of instigating student self-absorption. In the case of practices with strong roots in Asian religious contexts, there can also be an erasure of histories and supporting conceptual structures with explicitly religious frameworks, even when that is also happening in other secularized contexts.[42] As Kathleen Fisher also adds, critical thinking includes examining "how" we know and is "not a dispassionate, cerebral activity," but one that uses "attentive reading and reflective writing to engage both mind and heart."[43] The call for embodied ways of knowing thus can feel overly dichotomized.

Steven Geisz also notes the potential for embodied practices to exclude students, handling this with explicit discussions around intellectual and physical risk-taking, and why the latter is unusual in academic contexts. He also employs a variety of framing strategies around safety, creating staggered-level and alternative choices, helping students take ownership of their bodies and choices, and most importantly stating why he is asking them to engage their bodies in these activities, if they are physically able.[44] Beverley McGuire productively uses the framing strategy of "analogous activities" to pair with the study of different religions to shift students away from assumptions about the prominence of belief. For example, she creates opportunities for students to engage in the daily singing of a song of their choice while learning about the Sikh *Adi Granth*, and engaging in nonviolent communication practices with roommates or others as part of studying *ahimsa* as a way to parallel embodied activities while avoiding religious practice.[45]

Bodied activities can trigger students who have experienced bodily forms of trauma, and may not work for every student or class, to the same extent that other pedagogical strategies sometimes fall flat or cause unintended outcomes. It is worth experimenting with if your pedagogical goals match the benefits that embodied learning can bring to align one's teaching with the discipline and enhance the study of religion. Framing, choice, and reflective integration matter.

A Model for Sensory and Affective Education: Structure and Tactic

Another way to incorporate embodied learning is to take seriously LaMothe's charge in incorporating opportunities for a sensory education in the study of religion. As a dancer, it is not a surprise that she recommends movement as a type of sensory education, however for an introductory level course, I recommend an even more basic building-block approach than other more extensive embodied learning activities discussed. By breaking down the sensory education into its simplest components, it may also be a way to further avoid the perception of religious practice and other framing issues.

The strategy I took was to structure the introduction to religion course on sensory content, paired with activities that ask students to raise awareness of their own experiences around the sense being used as a lens for content. When working with smell, students also engage in a smell observation exercise in relation to response, memory, and physical-emotional reactions. We read, listen to, and watch materials on case studies focused on Chinese incense offerings, Indigenous smudging ceremonies, and evangelical Christian use of aromatherapy. The insights raised through their own olfactory inventories become the basis for asking questions of the case studies. For example, I had students who were inspired to go work in the campus garden and smell the herbs and plants growing. In reading about sweetgrass and sage being bundled and burnt, it led to questions about the different smells between fresh plants and burning plants—when is it pleasant or not, for whom, and in what contexts? How does fire transform the experience and what is created when people interact with smoke? What are the different ways that plants are a part of religious practices and what does engaging with plants create for practitioners?

Before we explore different sensory lenses, the first week of class involves delineating the disciplinary critique and making a case for studying bodied religion, while also engaging in a twofold parallel process of (1) "unlearning"—understanding why we habitually rely on analytical inquiry in our learning and have downplayed our own embodied forms of knowing—and (2) "inviting"—figuring out how to access our own embodied knowledge and integrate it into a blended learning process. This takes small steps and practice, as well as time to process what might be uncomfortable and awkward about bringing our bodied knowledge into our learning environment. I also have students go through an embodied knowledge inventory to help identify contexts for when they do engage their own embodied knowledge and what forms it takes.

An additional framework that students found helpful in engaging with the "how" of bodied religion is Elizabeth Pérez's attention to "micropractices" as part of her ethnographic method on Afro-Caribbean religions. Pérez defines micropractices as "routine and intimate sequences of operations that can be broken down into more minute units of activity" that "sustain religious formations," "organize space, time, and intensities of affect for participants," and "implicate their performers in the material and conceptual worlds of religious authorities."[46] An example of how she engages micropractices is the way she pays attention to details around how practitioners of *regla de ocha* prepare ingredients and dishes for the *orixa*, including how knife cuts are made, how people learn techniques for splitting coconuts, and the power dynamics involved in kitchen negotiations, all of which happen before dishes are covered and sent as finished offerings to the altars. Through paying attention to the knife cuts on chicken, Pérez transferred her own embodied insight into noticing where initiates are touched on their own bodies by their spiritual elder in a similar pattern, indicating how initiates are being prepared in ways akin to raw food that will be infused with power (*aché*).[47] Instead of focusing on the finished or cooked products, whether food or successful initiate, micropractices direct observations toward bodied actions, insights, and negotiations related to power, and I would argue, closer to what moves people affectively to participate in these religious practices.

To begin to combine different forms of sensory information, in the latter part of the semester I have students put their micropractice lens to use by developing a meal for a god/deity/spirit. Individuals, partners, or small groups (depending on the size of the class) are asked to research the foods and tastes of a particular god or spirit. They should also research the characteristics and qualities of that being as a way to discern their potential preferences. The task is to come up with a three-dish/item meal menu, with an explanatory cooking video or infographic as to the choices made around taste, smell, and visual components. It is important to include the strategies of preparation of the food (step-by-step recipe style), as well as what happens to any "leftovers" or disposal, instead of just giving a list of fully prepared foods or meal items. Reflections on sensory choices guide the inquiry. If resources are available, I encourage experimenting with preparing foods to bring their own bodied understandings to the assignment.

One group who focused on Amterasu, the sun kami in Shinto traditions, made mirror glaze rice cakes. This connected the use of the mirror in bringing Amaterasu out of the cave she was hiding in, as well as acknowledged rice as a central cultural outcome of creation. The rice cakes admittedly did not taste that good due to students being more concerned about the texture rather than flavor, but in creating the glaze, the patience and multiple attempts it took to get the ingredients to blend smoothly and turn shiny led to discussions about attentiveness, discipline, and determination as embodied values related to religious aesthetics of texture.

Another group created a meal for the Hindu goddess Durga (and Kali) that included rice-krispie treats shaped as skulls strung together as a garland, buffalo wings to mark the slaying of the buffalo demon Mahisa, and skewers shaped as the different weapons of the gods—trident, bow, mace—with red fruits (watermelon, strawberry, raspberries) on them. Students noted that they thought the goddess would appreciate how the rice-krispie heads provide a satisfying crunch that blended morbidity humorously with sweetness to entice her into a food coma after her violent battle. In general, these embodied insights related to affect, aesthetics, and sensory engagements were transferred into inquiries about other religious practices, including some of their own, as well as understandings of the sacred in relation to practitioners' embodied actions instead of focusing on beliefs.

In introduction to religion courses, I have seen small group "religious festival" presentations, and students often have included a list of foods as an add-on after giving the usual bullet points about who, what, when, where, and why. By placing food (and food preparation) at the center of the project, it allows those questions to still be explored but grounded around a practice that gives insight into underrepresented but central activities to understanding how religious relationships are cultivated. It also changes how students understand divine beings in comparison to and interaction with humans' needs, desires, and aesthetic pleasures related to food. Students often find websites and chat with bloggers/vloggers who give advice on recipes that they make, creating an avenue for having low-risk conversations with practitioners of religions that does not involve physically visiting a possibly more daunting fieldsite. Online classes have adapted this strategy well—and can involve actual or just planned cooking demos.

While the typical five senses can create plenty of structure for a semester course, there is also room to explore other senses, including spatial orientation, wonder, pain/pleasure, and desire—all with case studies in abundance.

Concluding Alignments

Centering sensory content and exercises that invite students' sensory awareness as the guiding structure of an introduction to religious studies course is a way to respond to the decades-long disciplinary critique that has moved body and embodiment into a primary position in the field. Bodies matter, not only in terms of what we focus on in religious phenomena, but also in how we know what we know about religion through our own embodied learning, or as LaMothe calls it, rhythms of bodily becoming.

The disciplinary critiques that drive toward a centering of embodiment are well supported by scholars of pedagogy like Megan Watkins, whose research on affect in the classroom demonstrates the impact of working with bodied learning as part of creating interest, curiosity, and connections with what is being studied.[48] In conversation with these ideas on pedagogic affect, Elspeth Probyn notes, "ideas and theories [and practices], especially about embodiment, cannot be divorced from their affective connections. How can one possibly teach concepts concerned with bodies without acknowledging ways in which bodies are inhabited?"[49]

By inviting sensory awareness in our students, it can help expand their epistemological toolboxes, validate multimodal ways of knowing, create agency in understanding how knowledge is constructed, and bring more of students' selves to their learning processes. In some ways, embodied learning is an expansion of the close observation skills we already typically teach in relation to the analysis of religious texts,[50] by asking students to practice those observation skills in relation to their own sensory engagements. By creating opportunities for sensory education, students have opportunities to utilize their embodied insights to explore what moves people to act and be religious in a variety of ways that align much more closely with the most powerful analyses being offered in the discipline today.

2

Pre-bracketing: Embodied Questioning in the Introductory Religious Studies Classroom

Jenna Gray-Hildenbrand

"That is so weird!" Ashley exclaims. "That is an incorrect interpretation of the Word of God," Brett confidently informs our introductory religious studies course. Similar discussions erupt around the class. It is week two of Religion & Society, and we are discussing religious studies fieldwork. I am using my own fieldwork in Appalachian serpent-handling churches as an example of Christian religious rituals, and my class has veered off track. "Wait a second!" I wave my hands over my head in an effort to get their attention. "What did we learn last week about the academic study of religion? And the differences between prescriptive and descriptive statements about religion?" "But, professor, they drink poison—IN CHURCH!" I scan the room. While Ashley and Brett are ready for a theological debate, many of the other students' bodies tell a different story ranging from complete disinterest, to discomfort, to annoyance.

My students' comments and reactions show the pedagogical limitations of the religious studies principle of bracketing. Bracketing is explained differently depending on which textbook you are using. However, it typically involves an introduction to the way Religious Studies scholars speak and think about religion by suspending judgment and exercising critical empathy. This goal is to facilitate student understandings of diverse religious traditions, many different from their own. Over the years, however, I have come to question whether bracketing does this work in my introductory courses.

Of course, every teaching experience varies based on institutional context. I teach at Middle Tennessee State University (MTSU) in Murfreesboro, Tennessee. Religion hangs in the air like the summer humidity, it coats your teeth like the sugar in your iced tea, and it gets tangled in your hair like the cicadas who seem to not realize, or care, that I was standing here first. Whether my students attend religious services or not, they have knowledge of religion based on their lived experiences. Since most undergraduate students at MTSU grew up in Middle Tennessee, these are Southern experiences of religion. MTSU established its Religious Studies Major in 2017 and created its introductory religious studies course, Religion & Society, four years earlier.[1] For many of my students, this is their first experience discussing religion from an academic perspective. Our introductory religious studies course also counts as social science general education credit. Therefore, in addition to majors and minors in Religion & Society, there are students from a variety of different majors. The goal of the class is to provide all these students with a basic religious literacy to help them succeed wherever life takes them.

I have used a variety of introductory textbooks in my religious studies courses, and many include a skills lesson on bracketing.[2] Bracketing is broadly defined in the religious studies literature, but it often involves articulating the differences between prescriptive and descriptive language and the suspension of moralizing judgment. The goals of these initial language lessons are to frame appropriate classroom discourse and to differentiate religious studies from theology. The assumption is it is difficult to proceed (if not frustrating and potentially unconstitutional if one is in a public institution) if everyone is making theological claims.[3]

Bracketing is commonly described as a commitment to the nonjudgmental, descriptive, and academic study of religion. But, how do we teach bracketing in the classroom? What are the values or skills students must cultivate in order to bracket successfully? And, what is at stake if they do not? The American Academy of Religion numbers among the skills acquired by attention to religious literacy: "Distinguish confessional or prescriptive statements made by religions from descriptive or analytical statements."[4] This juxtaposition between theological positions and academic ones opens up conversation around additional binary oppositions: theology and religious studies, insiders and outsiders, and critics and caretakers.[5] The idea being that pedagogically we must position our students in a place where they should, for the time they are in our classes, cultivate within themselves the skills to understand religion in a certain way. In my institutional context, many of my students find this quite jarring. I use the metaphor of glasses. I tell them that I am not asking them to remove their worldview/religious/personal "glasses" completely. Rather, I am asking them to develop Religious Studies bifocals for the purposes of seeing the religions of others more clearly. As a woman who has bifocals myself, I understand how dizzying these new lenses may be. I tell them not to fear! They may really like the world they see once they get used to them. But this analogy falls short. I *need* bifocals in order to see. And, I *chose* the academic study of religion as my career. Why should they pick up these lenses and use them? Why should they bracket?

Personally, I have found that teaching bracketing in my institutional context at times feels like gate keeping. While many students quickly grasp bracketing as a skill and are onboard with the academic enterprise, others remain silent or resistant. I appreciate the impulse to begin religious studies textbooks with a discussion of how we discuss religions academically. We cannot proceed if students are speaking different languages, or are not speaking at all due to confusion or complete lack of intellectual investment. That being said, it may be time to review, once again, whether bracketing is the best starting point in all institutional contexts.

Problematic Aspects of Bracketing in the Classroom

From a pedagogical perspective bracketing creates roadblocks to learning. In Barbara Walvoord's oft-cited research project investigating sixty-five introductory religion courses at both public and private colleges and universities, she found no matter the institutional context there exists a recurring disconnect between what students hope to receive in the class and what professors intend to nurture in their students. Students want to engage big questions that professors may feel are better suited for a religious or spiritual advisor, while professors intend to inculcate critical thinking skills.[6] Furthermore, Emily Gravett explains that bracketing can exacerbate this divide because "students may miss the opportunity to understand how critical thinking can inform or lead to—not compete or contrast with—spiritual/religious development."[7] Gravett also points to a second layer of bracketing, which can either confuse students or lead them to lose interest in the study of religion: "our field is populated by so many individuals who identify as religious themselves—who got into the field for the very same reasons that many students say they want to take religion courses—it seems disingenuous to urge students to bracket those same interests, values, concerns, questions, and commitments."[8] In effect, we are sending our students mixed messages by misaligning our pedagogy and content with disciplinary critiques and academic best practices in religious studies on the ground today. We need to stop.

The bracketing of certain values, concerns, and commitments in the classroom is echoed by Stephen Prothero's criticism of endless bracketing in the academic study of religion. Prothero made waves in 2004 when he wrote, "Belief Unbracketed: A Case for the Religion Scholar to Reveal More of Where He or She is Coming From."[9] In the short essay, Prothero asserts bracketing, or epoche, has long defined Religious Studies as a separate discipline from Theology. However, Prothero argues, "I have come to believe that the endless bracketing that I have always taken as my charge is viable only as long as our work exists in the splendid isolation of the Ivory Tower. In the rough and tumble of the real world, it is not possible, and likely not desirable."[10] He assesses "this hand-wringing about bracketing beliefs and suspending the ethical" as paternalistic and condescending to the subjects we study, and, then, by extension one may argue, to our students.[11] In other words, it is time for religious studies scholars to use their expertise to make informed judgments about religion.[12]

Stephen Prothero's statements sparked a debate. David Chidester responds that the type of moralizing judgments Prothero longs to make are simply opinions—"self-interested, self-indulgent posturing."[13] Chidester explains that it is through the "theoretically disciplined and methodologically self-conscious teaching and learning about religion, religions, and religious diversity" that Religious Studies maintained its integrity.[14] Where Chidester links bracketing with a theoretically and methodologically self-conscious approach to the study of religion, R. Marie Griffith sees bracketing as "the well-developed, highly nuanced stance of critical empathy."[15] For Griffith, when done well, "empathy is a strategy of concentrated encounter that leads to intelligibility and mutual recognition."[16] Scholars do not convert to the position of the other, but engage in a form of listening and observation that enables them to better present their position. Robert Orsi also asserts the suspension of judgment as vital to "a disciplined attitude of attentiveness to the other" identifying this as central to the relationship Religious Studies scholars develop in the field and in the archives.[17] Orsi identifies this as a vulnerable position. The scholar must be open to a disorienting reality of the other. This does not mean ignoring power structures or fear for safety. It does mean, however, an acknowledgment that judgment may serve as a safeguard protecting the scholar from taking seriously their own biases clouding their research.[18]

While these conversations are important and vital to our work as scholars, we need continued discussions on how to do this work in the classroom. Who decides what judgments are bracketed? Who establishes the terms of the dialogue between the interlocutor (in the field or in the archive) and the scholar? Whose questions, concerns, and values are investigated and in what manner?

There is power involved in the management of these categories and the manner by which our students bracket. Voices are silenced. I want to be clear that when I am discussing bracketing, I am not discussing the silencing of speech that is otherwise prohibited by university guidelines (hate speech, violent speech, etc.). Bracketing is a tool used in religious studies to achieve a specific type of disciplinary scholarship. However, one wonders not only what is lost when we force our students to bracket specific values and judgments in the introductory religious studies classroom but also how marginalized students feel when, once again, their lived experiences are silenced. The management of bracketing in the classroom may tell us more about the preferences of the professor than the discipline of religious studies.

It is a privileged position to bracket with ease in the classroom. Instructors should not take this for granted. Asking students to bracket may be requiring them to lower a defense mechanism that sustained them in racists, sexist, ableist, Christiancentric, heteronormative, discriminatory environments. For many who are constantly having to explain the value of their existence and, then, negotiate the size of their very being in that space (large enough to be seen, but not too big as to appear offensive, dangerous, or inappropriate) to enter the classroom and be required to bracket that self is oppressive. And, as this essay will demonstrate, it is unnecessary.

Let us ask ourselves: How do we *do* religious studies? How do we identify, observe, describe, and analyze our object of study? Thomas Tweed urges us to first recognize where we stand. He explains, "No interpreter has hovered; no interpretation has been ungrounded. All interpreters stand here—in a particular place—in every one of them. The difference? Some interpreters have said so."[19] Tweed's locative approach has consequences for our conversation on bracketing, for even bracketed description is situated and constructed through a lens of interpretation. As scholars of religious studies, we cannot teach a binary between prescriptive and descriptive language as if one is rooted in judgments and assumptions while the other hovers above such human limitations.

There Is Another Way: The Pre-bracketed Questioning Body

One solution is to readjust our students' points of entry into Religious Studies. The starting point is not the tool or the disposition (as with bracketing), but the question of inquiry or the problem to solve. I do not pick up a hammer and then go looking for something to pound. I have a task at hand that upon observation and inquiry leads me to the conclusion of which tools, skills, and dispositions will help me best achieve the outcome I desire. While bracketing may be a useful tool, it is not the starting point. The observations and questions are. And, it is here that I propose we begin in our introductory classes.

Questioning Bodies

Our students are not disembodied brains plopped on our classroom desks ready to be filled with knowledge and skills.[20] They are human beings with their own unique lives shaped by their embodied experiences. Feminist disability studies remind us we are bodies moving in and through cultural environments that ascribe meanings and value to our bodies' features based on social and material conditions.[21] These meaning-making discourses about the body construct identities and formulate common-sense understandings of the world and how it should be.[22] Categories like race, gender, sexuality, and disability can be understood as an assemblage, to use Jasbir Puar's approach, "events, actions, and encounters between bodies, rather than as simply entities and attributes of subjects."[23] These categories, often listed side by side, are nonetheless experienced with pronounced differences. As Ellen Samuels explains, "each may function to materialize norms and their constitutive others, but those functions are neither parallel nor discrete."[24] This is particularly the case for people whose bodies inhabit the encounters of multiple categories. Research in disability studies finds that stigma and discrimination associated with disability are multiplied when the person is already facing stigma and discrimination based on their race, gender, sexuality, and/or class.[25] Helping our students understand this is vital to their learning, understanding, and interpreting of religion and the experiences of religious peoples past and present.

Therefore, rather than introducing students to the academic study of religion through the skill of bracketing, an alternative entry point is to strengthen students' understanding of lived embodiment by scaffolding academic questioning. This pedagogical approach builds on Barbara Walvoord's discussion of the type of "voice" instructors decide to design throughout their courses. Walvoord discusses the questioner, the thinker/arguer, and the autobiographer.[26] Of the various voices utilized in introductory religious studies courses, Walvoord found "many highly effective faculty adopted for themselves and encouraged in their students was that of the questioner, who adopts a questioning pose toward the course material and toward his or her own beliefs, and who is centrally concerned with posing effective questions."[27] Courses designed to be question-centered help students construct critical questions. Walvoord outlines five possible ways instructors utilized the question-centered approach for their courses. First, the instructor constructs the entire course around questions. Second, the instructor assigns and rewards question-asking in the class. Third, the instructor generates informal spaces for students' questions, such as a journal or online discussion. Fourth, the instructor invites questioning in class discussion that redirects attention away from the instructor as lone authority on the topic. Finally, the instructor shares their own "life and career as a questioner."[28]

Key to the embodied question-centered approach is interdependency, a pedagogical practiced, articulated, and utilized by feminist disability scholar Kristina Knoll. In an interdependent classroom the students and the instructor are dependent on one another for a positive and productive learning community.[29] When students support one another in their learning by helping one another make the course more accessible, clear, and relatable this is referred to throughout the course as "practicing interdependency." The practice is incentivized in various ways appropriate to the institutional context. But is it possible to have enough time in the course to cover the required content, address student questions, and meet the learning needs of all students through a practice like interdependency? Knoll has a response, "I agree that it may be an impractical task, but this could mean that large lecture classes are inaccessible. However, when multiple individuals work together to make the environment accessible, it suddenly becomes significantly easier to meet all the various needs of the classroom, including the instructor's needs—which is rarely discussed or considered."[30] It is our job as teachers to ensure our classrooms and content are accessible to our students. This is particularly true in introductory classes where important threshold concepts are presented. Because of their significance, the manner in which threshold concepts—a core concept that, when understood, changes the way a student thinks about a topic—are introduced to students and the tools utilized to facilitate this encounter should not be oversimplified or superficially engaged. This can create a barrier to student learning because these concepts and skills are not mastered and left behind but continue to be relied upon for the duration of the student's coursework in Religious Studies.[31] This makes threshold concepts, and the skills used to understand them, paramount for laying the groundwork in our introductory courses. As Jan Meyer and Ray Land assert: Educators need to locate the troublesome "stuck" places— the "epistemological obstacles" blocking a transformed perspective.[32]

In the Classroom: Teaching Tactic

One way to implement embodied questioning in the classroom is to mark it as a priority from the beginning of class and scaffold the skill throughout the semester. The first unit in my introductory course is "Exploring, Inquiring, and Questioning Religion."

Class One (fifty-five-minute session): We begin the class period with my spin on a classic religious studies exercise, Alien Religion. The goal of this exercise is to get them to uncover the understanding of religion they bring with them into the classroom. On a sheet of paper I ask them to define religion in one sentence. Then, I ask them to itemize a list of five characteristics or qualities that all religions have in common. Once these two initial items are complete, I show the students four videos. For each video students write whether it is an example of religion using their definition and the five qualities of religion they outlined above. If they are not sure, students are asked to write questions they would ask to find out what they would need to know or observe to help them determine whether it was religion or not according to their previous answers.

I explain there are no "right" or "wrong" answers here. A central learning outcome of the course is that they can craft religious studies questions and apply religious studies typologies to the beliefs and practices they observe. The first case study show is of Buddhist monks chanting. Many students are familiar with Buddhism as world religion. However, for this assignment I ask students to pretend they are an alien from outer space—completely unfamiliar with various manifestations of religion on Earth. In other words, it does not matter to me, in this exercise, whether scholars of religion think what is playing in the video is a "religion"; what I am interested in is whether what students observe in these videos fits their definition and the five characteristics they outlined. My videos grow less familiar, and I end with a video of the playing of the national anthem at a University of Tennessee, Knoxville football game. By the end of the exercise, students reflect on the difficulty in defining religion and the subtle differences between religion/spirituality, religion/culture, religion/patriotism, and religion/sport.

With this exercise under our belts, the next class period begins with a reflective structured dialogue (RSD).[33] The goal of RSD is to "speak to be understood and listen to understand."[34] As the name suggests, the method begins with reflection. This type of reflection works best when it links a student's personal experience, their values, and the lesson material. I give them a series of reflection questions and then structure the time to help focus attention and facilitate the dialogue.

For this RSD, I ask my students to take out a piece of paper and a pencil and answer a series of questions. They have two minutes to write on each in silence. The first sentence is,

> Think of a time you had something important to communicate (or tell) someone and that person just wasn't listening to you. Or, somehow, misunderstood what you said. Where were you? How are you feeling? What are you doing to make your point? Who was the person? How are they feeling? What are they doing? How do you know they do not understand you?

Next: "As you reflect on this situation in the past, what is at stake for you? What values are important to you when you think about this?"
Third:

> Think of a time you had something important to communicate (or tell) someone and that person really listened to you. Where were you? How did you know they were really listening? How did it feel? What are you doing to make you point? Who was the person? How are they feeling? What are they doing? How do you know they do not understand you?

Finally: "As you reflect on this situation in the past, what is at stake for you? What values are important to you when you think about this?"

Because this RSD takes place early in the semester, I do not ask my students to share each response—in RSD students may always "pass." I do ask them to get into small groups and share what they learned about themselves in the process. They have two minutes for each student to share. Once we return to our seats, I hand out "Why 'Do You Believe in God?' Is at the Heart of Our Religious Problem" by Michael Jerryson and ask the students to read it.[35] In the essay, Jerryson discusses his terminal ALS diagnosis, and, ever the inquisitive scholar of religion, Jerryson used this embodied lens to revisit questions about religious people and institutions. "People are more willing to discuss their religious beliefs when they know you're dying; they're also very keen to learn about your own beliefs," Jerryson explains. He becomes increasingly frustrated with the theistic assumptions buttressing these conversations about his religious life as a Pedestrian.

Before discussing the article as a class, I ask students to take out a piece of paper and write a series of questions they would ask Michael Jerryson to better understand his religion. I ask them to honestly reflect on how his disability and terminal diagnosis inform those questions. I ask them how the RSD exercise informs the questions they would ask Dr. Jerryson. The students are placed into small groups and given two minutes each to share what they wrote with one another. We regroup as a class and discuss what we have learned. I put pictures of Michael on slides and remind students that we want to think about religion as "events, actions, and encounters between bodies, rather than as simply entities and attributes of subjects."[36] In this way Pedestrianism is more than an identity Dr. Jerryson has chosen, but a way he encounters the world around him and others encounter him as a body in the world.[37] We conclude the class by handing back their Alien Religion assignment and rethinking whether they would adjust any of their answers.

I see a marked difference in my students' approach to the course material when I begin the course this way. Rather than referring them back to bracketing if conversation veers off course, I refer them to the embodied experience of being misunderstood and understood. I encourage them to reflect on what they are experiencing, what questions they have for the material, and what questions they have for one another. I find their assignments are more critically engaged with the course material and the classroom discussions are dynamic and respectful.

Pre-Bracketed Embodied Questioning

This essay demonstrates some of the ways bracketing fails to serve students as a productive starting point in the introductory religious studies classroom. Anytime a student's voice is silenced it is our obligation as instructors and scholars to think critically about this act of silencing. We need to question whether this action is necessary to achieve our learning outcomes and whether this is the least restrictive means on student creativity and speech to accomplish this outcome. Finally, we need to think seriously about the consequences of the discipline of bracketing and whether this is detrimental to teaching and learning about religion in the introductory classroom. If bracketing alone is not the answer, then what is a possible option to better address these disciplinary and pedagogical criticisms?

Asking religious studies questions is central to our discipline. As a matter of fact, the bracketed descriptions of our subject matter are not our entry point into our research at all. Ongoing questioning is vital to religious studies. We move back and forth among the various pieces of information we collect and people we engage while simultaneously reflecting on our own embodied position as interpreters. It can be a dizzying, never-ending, frustrating, upsetting process. Robert Orsi describes this as an in-between space—"between confessional or theological scholarship" on the one hand and the moralizing judgment of "radically secular scholarship" on the other. This in-between space "is characterized by a disciplined suspension of the impulse to locate the other."[38] For Orsi, this "disciplined attitude of attentiveness to the other" is not a denial of self. Rather, "to stand in an attitude of open, disciplined, and engaged attentiveness to an other means to put one's own world in dialogue; to be open is to be vulnerable—to be vulnerable to the disorientation of seriously meeting a different reality."[39]

A pedagogy of embodied questioning highlights the contested and problematic nature of bracketing, description, and the suspension of impulse to other or judge to the introductory religious studies classroom in a way relatable to student experience. A pedagogy of embodied questioning begins with a conversation of who *we* are in this space—never assuming that there is one embodied student experience or approach that is more valuable. This process is essential to creating an accessible interdependent learning environment. This also helps students understand the interpretive lenses they bring to the course material and how these shape their understandings of religion and the questions about religion they will find interesting and valuable. Using their own experience constructing questions and engaging in the course materials together, they discover what Thomas Tweed states, "scholars are always situated, often at morally ambivalent sites, as they construct meaning and negotiate power in their interpretations."[40] It is once this threshold has been crossed that a student is best suited to avail themselves of the tool of bracketing.

3

Grief and Joy in the Religious Studies Classroom

M. Cooper Minister

In the fall of 2019, I wrote these words in the initial abstract for this chapter:

> Here are the plans for an essay I intend to write, plans which are different from the essay I thought I might write when I signed onto this project and plans which will be different from the essay I will write. Such is assumed in an abstract, but I name the assumption here because I am interested in exploring the conditions under which changes of plans occur, how plans change in the classroom, and how we swerve to accommodate these changes.

Reading those words now, I can hear the collective groan in my use of the word swerve, a word that became too familiar while constantly making new plans in relation to the COVID-19 pandemic. In the moment I wrote, I was swerving to accommodate two mid-semester lung surgeries to remove metastatic tumors in my lungs. Having undergone treatment for cancer mid-semester before, I knew that I would not simply veer off course before returning to the same trajectory, but I did not have another framework for how to think about making changes mid-semester. This lack of framework for making mid-semester changes was especially true for changes that seemed externally imposed instead of internally generated by emerging interests, concerns, or conversations.

In *The Shock Doctrine: The Rise of Disaster Capitalism*, Naomi Klein successfully describes how crisis is used to dismantle economic protections that stabilize markets and divert funding from public institutions.[1] This works, in part, because crisis produces a state of emotional overwhelm that makes it difficult to do anything other than survive. Psychologists and neuroscientists have many explanations for this from chemical overload in the prefrontal cortex to polyvagal theories about the nervous system. The rise of trauma and affect theories as areas of academic study also helps to explain these states of emotional overwhelm and how they can impact learning. These theories give us potential explanations for why learning is difficult in the midst of crisis or the wake of trauma and are often used to push back on the demands to carry on.

While I am not interested in pretending like we are not in the midst of crisis, I am also no longer interested in acting like I can only teach once crisis has been resolved. This may be true at an extremely basic level that I cannot teach well when under new and imminent threat, but the assumption that I can only teach once crisis has resolved fails to account for the ongoing nature of contemporary shared crises, from racial injustice to the pandemic and climate change, and for the ongoing nature of my own personal crisis of managing stage IV cancer. These are not simply punctiliar events which occur and then heal. Rather, they are ongoing and require continual negotiations that impact teaching and learning.

How do we carry on in the wake of tragedy? Is there a space between refusing to challenge ourselves and our students (the therapeutic approach) and attempting to return to normal or as normal as we can achieve? How do we shift ourselves and our students out of crisis mode? How can we allow tragedy and grief to shift our priorities and behaviors, our learning outcomes, and teaching tactics? How can we make space for a truly transformative reflectiveness? Perhaps especially pertinent for religious studies contexts, how do we create and inhabit this space in religious studies classrooms, classrooms that were created by wresting space from the faith-based approaches of theological education? I argue that religious studies classrooms must make space for affect without normalizing certain religious affects.

Normalizing Neutrality in Religious Studies

It seems that scholars of religion are concerned that allowing affect into religious studies classrooms might normalize certain kinds of religious affects such as Christian aversions to rituals of animal sacrifice or the orientalizing fascination with meditation and yoga. In response, many scholars attempt to adopt an objective stance, neutralizing any affects that might emerge, without realizing that neutrality normalizes affects produced by distance such as indifference and apathy with regard to specific religious practices. In the *Religious Studies Skills Book*, Eugene V. Gallagher and Joanne Maguire write,

In order to understand the complexities of religions, you need to adopt as neutral a stance as possible, at least temporarily. That allows you to openly consider alternative ways of viewing the world, to see how they make sense to other people. This also necessitates that you recognize your own biases and assumptions so you can factor them in as you think through an issue.[2]

This process of temporarily adopting as neutral of a stance as possible and then opening to different ways of viewing the world seems to work on a conscious level insofar as it is possible to do some self-assessment, try to understand the things you believe, and then attempt to control for those biases when teaching. Gallagher and Maguire continue,

One major difference between religious studies and other humanities disciplines is the place of prior commitment in a given classroom. You have learned about religion all your life, and some of that learning has resulted in fixed positions that can sometimes interfere with the kind of learning that college courses demand. Notably, the legacy of theological studies in religious studies departments and the complexities of student expectations can cause a divide between students' and teachers' understandings of the entire enterprise.[3]

The tension here results, in part, from the desire of students to ask big questions and consider their own answers to those questions in relation to the answers of others and the expectation of religious studies scholars that those desires must be bracketed in order to perform the discipline. This tension is related to a cluster of issues in the discipline including the so-called insider/outsider problem, the gap between religious studies and theology, the binary between teaching about religion and teaching religion, and concerns about academic objectivity.

In the context where I am currently teaching, I have experienced the limitations of bracketing and maintaining the tensions central to the discipline. Most of the students I teach take a course I offer in order to fulfill a general education requirement. Many identify as Christian, many more decide they are "nones" after reading Elizabeth Drescher's *Choosing Our Religion: The Spiritual Lives of America's Nones*.[4] In my attempt to do what Gallagher and Maguire describe, I have inadvertently offered students a label that describes their experiences, a label many decide to try on for themselves. In my attempt to teach students to bracket, I have so failed to account for what they need in the course that I am converting students (or, more generously, presenting students with an opportunity to take on a new label that helps them make sense out of their religious experiences)! And this is happening in the one and only religious studies class most of these students will take.

Based on this experience, I have three predominant concerns about the usefulness of the process outlined by Gallagher and Maguire for my context. First, such a process overlooks the ways in which we become knowable to ourselves in part through interaction with difference (for example, I did not know I was a Christian until I encountered someone who was not). If I have bracketed my assumptions during this encounter, those assumptions remain impervious to the new ideas I may encounter. Second, this process of temporarily adopting as neutral a stance as possible and then opening to different ways of viewing the world also neglects parts of ourselves that we do not know. I cannot control for biases I am not aware I have, and I can do my best to understand my biases but there will always be limitations to my self-awareness. Bracketing, therefore, is not a simplistic or watered-down glimpse into what scholars of religion do but, rather, expects something of students that scholars of religion cannot do. Worse is the thought that there are scholars of religion who believe they are transparent enough to themselves that they can account for their own biases in teaching and research. I cannot expect students to be knowable to themselves, to understand their biases and assumptions, because I am not knowable to myself and I won't expect something of my students that I cannot do myself. Finally, this aspirational ideal of religious studies forces the passionate histories of ourselves and our students out of the classroom. Such an expectation asks instructors to be gatekeepers of a classroom focused on honing the ability of students to describe something that they themselves do not believe or practice. Instructors teaching in this manner tend to assume that students bring in an inappropriate desire: to have an encounter between their own ideas and the ideas of others. We can study feeling only if we leave our own feelings out of it. What if, instead, we gave students what we think they want, namely a better understanding of both themselves and others? What if this understanding unfolded in relationship?

One of the fears I think such a proposal produces is the fear that we will be unable to control the affects that emerge from this process. We bracket and we ask our students to bracket because we do not feel prepared to engage the affects produced when we fail to bracket. We also bracket and ask students to bracket because we as scholars of religion believe in the history of the discipline as we've been taught it. But there are good reasons to question the histories we accepted in graduate school. Sarah Imhoff describes one such reason in "The Creation Story of Religious Studies, or How We Learned to Stop Worrying and Love Schempp." Imhoff states,

I argue that Schempp provides religious studies with a narrative of progress (one that says 'In 1963, Americans realized the difference between proselytization and the analysis of religion') rather than a narrative of conformity and political adaptability (one that says 'Universities participated in and capitalized on cultural notions of American religiosity and Cold War rhetoric'). The latter story replaces a tale of progress with one of political calculation and capitulation. It associates religious studies with a particular cultural moment—one which is mostly unappealing to contemporary scholars—while the progress narrative remains compelling because it can continue to provide an intellectual and social raison d'être for religious studies and serve a new cultural moment.[5]

According to Imhoff, the discipline of religious studies, especially the commitment to an analysis of religion that requires the kinds of bracketing Gallagher and Maguire describe, was created to conform to the political climate. If this is the case, our discipline and its commitments are, in fact, more adaptable than our graduate programs suggested.

The concerns about allowing affect into religious studies classrooms are laudable in their attempt to control and mitigate bias and emotional manipulation in the classroom. Rather than dismissing affects, however, we need ways to help students understand the relationship between their assumptions and affective responses. Making space for student responses to the material helps to create a learning environment with the potential to do something other than consuming and regurgitating information. Rather than ask students to bracket their feelings in order to adequately perform the discipline, I argue that we must make space for experiences of grief and joy in the religious studies classroom.

Making Space for Affect in the Religious Studies Classroom

We can follow scholars already doing the work of making room for affect in the classrooms of other disciplines. My own pedagogical inspiration derives, in part, from a course I took on Augustine and Rainer Maria Rilke with Mark Burrows, who introduced the class asking us to read Rilke's poem "Archaic Torso of Apollo":

> We cannot know his legendary head
> with eyes like ripening fruit. And yet his torso
> is still suffused with brilliance from inside,
> like a lamp, in which his gaze, now turned to low,

gleams in all its power. Otherwise
the curved breast could not dazzle you so, nor could
a smile run through the placid hips and thighs
to that dark center where procreation flared.
Otherwise this stone would seem defaced
beneath the translucent cascade of the shoulders
and would not glisten like a wild beast's fur:
would not, from all the borders of itself,
burst like a star: for here there is no place
that does not see you. You must change your life.[6]

Burrows ended our analysis with the final line of the poem, something that felt almost like a plea, "You must change your life." As a student, I could feel the desire for transformation emanating from the poem, from Burrows, and from some of the others in the class. This simple act of telling students what he wanted from us established the course of our semester. Rather than attempting to manipulate our affects, Burrows invited us into a process where learning and transformation were interchangeable. Those of us who also wanted transformation quickly got on board, and many others were convinced along the way, as demonstrated by changes in affect from disengaged to curious. In this section, I consider how to make space for affect in religious studies classrooms by following Stefano Harney and Fred Moten in refusing to call classrooms to order[7] and Eve Sedgwick in refusing to teach texts in a way that requires students to get behind and beneath them,[8] instead following Rahuldeep Gill in considering how to teach students to feel (not think) texts[9] and Joseph Winters in learning to become vulnerable and receptive to others.[10] These scholar-teachers challenge the practice of academic criticism, offering new modes for teaching, learning, and being in the classroom. They create room for inviting experience, particularly difficult experiences, into the classroom as part of the learning process.

In order to make space for affect, we first have to refuse certain classroom practices that seem to have been imposed upon us by the structures of the university. The first practice to refuse is the practice of calling the classroom to order. Moten says,

> What's totally interesting me is to just not call the class to order. And there's a way in which you can think about this literally as a simple gesture at the level of a certain kind of performative, dramatic mode. You're basically saying, let's just see what happens if I don't make that gesture of calling the class to order—just that little moment in which my tone of voice turns and becomes slightly more authoritative so that everyone will know that class has begun. What if I just say,

'well, we're here. Here we are now.' Instead of announcing that class has begun, just acknowledge that class began … every day that you go into your classroom, you have a chance not to issue the call to order, and then to see what happens. And the goddamn president of the university is not going to knock on your door talking about, 'how come you didn't issue the call to order?'[11]

That instructors have some amount of agency in how we choose to run classes is often lost in the dialogues about learning outcomes, assessments, end of the semester surveys, and observations. There is a recognition that these instruments are designed to do exactly what Moten says won't happen (the president knocking on your door), but while they are an approximation of the authority structures of the university, we continue to have space to maneuver around their demands. While these instruments are designed to force us to call the classroom to order, it is possible to subvert these demands and teach something different by teaching differently. This potential, in part, is why Jennifer Doyle refers to the classroom as the "university's soft flesh."[12]

Another practice that we have to refuse is the practice of paranoid reading. In "Paranoid Reading and Reparative Reading, Or, You're So Paranoid You Probably Think This Essay Is About You," Eve Sedgwick describes paranoia as a strong theory of negative affects. In contrast to paranoia, Sedgwick offers the practice of reparative reading. One of the key elements of reparative reading, according to Sedgwick, is the capacity to be surprised. If we always know what we are reading in advance, we are not reading in a way that lends itself to new possibilities. For Sedgwick, the surprising and pleasurable joys of queer intertextuality, camp in particular, result from a reparative impulse that becomes through addition. She states, "The desire of a reparative impulse, on the other hand, is additive and accretive. Its fear, a realistic one, is that the culture surrounding it is inadequate or inimical to its nurture; it wants to assemble and confer plenitude on an object that will then have resources to offer to an inchoate self."[13] To teach from this reparative impulse would require both admitting our pedagogical desires and fears and the affects produced by those desires and fears.

Rahuldeep Gill embodied his pedagogical desires and fears as he taught students to feel (not think) texts. In this method of teaching, Gill opened texts to students in a way that allowed texts to care for them in the midst of life's emergencies, from the shooting at the Borderline Bar and Grill that killed twelve and injured many students attending Gill's institution at the time to the devastating wildfires that had claimed so many homes in the area. Teaching into this context, Gill invited students to analyze Punjabi Sufi poetry that influenced Guru Nanak and concluded, "the horizon of death and the horizon of love are the same horizon—you are up against the same impossibilities. That's a beautiful thing. It's a thing to celebrate and to live for."[14] In this way, Gill made space for affect in his classroom by creating openings for students to identify with affects in the text. Textualists often worry about the risks of students overidentifying with texts that are quite different from them (as happens when students overidentify with a bible verse taken out of context, for example). Gill's approach recognized this risk and taught the history and context of texts while also using affect to create bridges between historical texts and contemporary readers.

These bridges must be wide enough to contain pleasurable affects, such as joy and love, and difficult affects, including melancholy and grief. In *Hope Draped in Black*, Joseph Winters argues that melancholy and remembrance are responses to grief and loss that remain receptive to others and ultimately hopeful. Winters states,

> A different set of possibilities, I have argued, open up when we think hope and melancholy together, when vulnerability to the suffering of others becomes a site for a different kind of future and imaginary … I have demonstrated how the work of sorrow, the breaks and cuts of literary jazz, the cuts, images, and sounds of film, and the fictional reimagination of race, gender, and national belonging can challenge, or at least expose, tendencies to forget, repress, displace, or explain away the tragic dimensions of race, sociality, and human coexistence.[15]

As these gaps expose what the dominant narratives omit, affect in the classroom has the potential to expose where the dominant classroom narratives fail and how we can transform the classroom in response. In order to do this, we have to be receptive to and curious about the possibilities that emerge when we meet: the frustrations about assignments, the eyerolls, texting, or turning the camera off in an online environment. Attending to and inviting expressions of these affects suggests that we should not attempt to avoid affects that we may find challenging but, rather, that we might invite these affects and change how we teach in response. Changing our narratives about these affects such as the narrative that students unworthy of time and attention disengage and complain creates opportunities to explore affects as a means of inviting more students into a transformative learning process. We can learn to listen not only to what students are saying but also to what they are not saying.

I hope that students walk away from a class with me with more than an ability to list the noble truths of Buddhism and the schools of Islam. I tell them I want them to learn how to talk about their differences, starting by talking to each other. One of the keys to this process is learning to see difference in places where students have been more inclined to see sameness, to paper over their differences in order to make everyone more comfortable. Another key is getting playful with these differences in a way that allows new things to emerge. This is a process of addition and accretion that adds through analysis and a recognition of difference, not by seeing sameness where there is, in fact, difference. This approach can transform our approach to the classroom. Instead of learning new things in a way where the accrual of new knowledge marks the accomplishments of the learning process and instead of requiring students to get behind and beneath texts, we can be with each other differently, asking questions without clear answers, and letting instructors and the authors we bring into the room speak as part of the conversation.

Teaching Tactic: Naming the Affective Responses I Observe

This is a strategy that I use in general education classes later in the semester, after meeting a group of usually entirely new students at the beginning of the semester and developing some amount of trust or at least familiarity with and among students. I have found it almost necessary to do on Zoom because Zoom has a way of mitigating some affects while intensifying others. In person, I move around the classroom a lot, using my physical presence to generate energy and excitement among the students. That affect is mitigated on Zoom. The affective changes on the faces of students, on the other hand, are intensified. Because of the proximity of the camera to the face, I am much more aware of the exhaustion and overwhelm in the eyes of students. That and other factors have contributed to the phenomenon of Zoom fatigue, which makes teaching and learning on Zoom difficult.[16] The purpose of this strategy is to reduce the impact of nonverbal overload, primarily on video-chatting technologies such as Zoom but also in the classroom.

When I started teaching on Zoom, I read these affects as a lack of engagement and was much more discouraged in my teaching, wondering how to get students out of crisis mode in order to engage in the teaching and learning process. I have learned to read things I used to read as disengagement as emotional overwhelm and I offer those interpretations to students. In this tactic, I reinterpret somatic movements such as a yawn, a big stretch, or a long period of silence and suggest how these may be responses to encountering difficulties in the course material. Rather than asking students to respond to the material differently, I attempt to name the affects I see, to acknowledge and make space for difficult affects as a way of helping students notice and even potentially shift those affects. This is different from continuing to encourage or demand a response from students, all parties becoming more disengaged and disinterested in the process.

In one example of how I used this tactic, I entered a breakout room on Zoom one where the students were discussing higher education debt as part of brainstorming a research project for town hall night, during which students from courses in different disciplines share how the perspectives and approaches in their class might respond to contemporary cross-disciplinary issues. When I entered the breakout room, I saw that some of the students had leaned back in their chairs, eyes open wide in what I interpreted as overwhelm. I acknowledged the sensations it looked like some of the students were feeling and asked for the students to confirm. Simply acknowledging what I was seeing allowed some of the students to lean forward and speak affirmatively, saying that they realized the importance of this discussion but that it was hitting a little too close for them to consider at the moment in light of their own student loans. The students who had been dominating the conversation received these cues and began to create more space for others as the discussion progressed. I am beginning to think of these simple moments in which we can acknowledge affect and through this acknowledgment make some kind of shift, as extremely important to what we are doing in the classroom.

While naming the affects I observe is not a complete solution to the problem of engagement on Zoom or in person, I am convinced that we have to name student crises in relation to the material in order to give students the opportunity to be challenged (even in the midst of crisis!) and to imagine something different. This is not a tactic that exists in isolation from a classroom devoted to dialogic approaches in line with what Jill DeTemple and John Sarrouf describe in "Disruption, dialogue, and swerve: Reflective structured dialogue in religious studies classrooms."[17] It is a tactic that can work in spaces where the contributions of students are normalized and encouraged.

Conclusion: Creating Space for Affect

Naming the affective responses I observe in the classroom after establishing a dynamic in which the contributions of the students are encouraged and affirmed contributes to the learning process by shifting difficult affects and allowing new forms of engagement to emerge. The practice of naming the affects I see provides a snapshot into a classroom where the relationships between the students, instructor, and the texts create opportunities for learning and for transformation. This classroom begins with the recognition that students bring experiences and information that can contribute to the learning process and, in light of this recognition, refuses to call the classroom to an order that centers what the professor knows or to require students to get behind and beneath texts. Instead, the experiences and affects of the students become part of the learning process. Naming affects that emerge in the learning process is one concrete pedagogical practice that creates space for the experiences of grief and joy in the religious studies classroom.

This approach centers learning outcomes such as listening, understanding multiple perspectives, reflection, and self-awareness. In my university context, these are learning outcomes consistent with courses I teach in programs such as first-year seminar and the navigating difference competencies in general education, which include cultural understanding and ethical reasoning. They are also consistent with learning outcomes in the religious studies program.

We do not have to choose between teaching content and teaching skills. We can offer students a rigorous engagement with content while also attending to their relationships to that content. To do this requires teaching students how to engage with difference not by bracketing their own beliefs and feelings but by learning how to listen and learn from others. This process must be expansive enough to contain pleasurable affects, such as joy, and difficult affects, including melancholy and grief.

4

Students' Emotional Labor in Religious Studies Courses: Toward Greater Instructor Intentionality

Jeremy Posadas

Acknowledging the Emotional Dimension of Learning

In this chapter, I offer a perspective on the emotional dimension of student learning that I hope fellow teachers will find encouraging for their own further reflection on this dimension, in order to better take account of it in planning courses, sessions, and assignments. By no means will this be a comprehensive account, nor is it intended as the final word on the matter. Rather, it is intended to invite deeper reflection on our teaching practices as well as to encourage new lines of inquiry about the role of emotions in learning. My assumption is that most readers already do engage the emotional dimension, but often do so intuitively more than intentionally: we teach because we care about our students' development, after all. I hope that this chapter gives fellow teachers some useful tools for more consciously recognizing how they approach the emotional dimension of learning, so that they can make choices about their approach with fuller intentionality. Moreover, I want to provoke ongoing collective discernment of ethical principles that should guide our pedagogical choices with respect to the emotional dimension of learning. To that end, I'm going to propose we understand students as performing emotional labor in our courses and invite us to consider how we can structure that emotional labor responsibly and thoughtfully.[1]

Before getting too theoretical, it will be helpful to call to mind some of the many emotional tasks that are inherent in the learning process.[2] While the following observations arise from my teaching context of undergraduate education in a small, residential liberal arts college, the emotional dynamics I am describing are common in many different teaching contexts. When, for example, we ask students to read a challenging text, one that stretches their thinking, we are asking them to feel initial uncertainty and possibly confusion or bewilderment; it can feel frustrating to have to reread phrases, sentences, or even whole paragraphs and in addition it can create feelings of self-doubt or worry about not being "smart enough."[3] At the same time we are also asking them to feel empathy toward another person, the author, whose perspective they likely have never encountered before. When we ask students to actively speak with one another in a class discussion, we want them to use tones and speech-patterns that convey respect if not also excitement for one another's ideas. Moreover, they have to do this while following unexpected turns of thought and, for many, confronting feelings of fear at public speaking. As for writing, probably the mere mention of it brings a flood of emotional memories to present readers' own minds.

Nor do the emotional tasks inherent in the learning process fall equally on all students: structures of inequity such as racism, patriarchy, poverty, disability, nationality, and so on shape every moment of the learning process.[4] On top of the emotional demands that all students must balance as they perform acts of learning, students who inhabit marginalized identities must often struggle against dominant societal messages of our communities' inferiority. And they must deal emotionally with what psychologists term "stereotype threat," the fear of confirming those negative messages if one does not perform perfectly, which only adds further stress to the learning process.[5] Women students must contend against expectations of female docility. Students of color must contend against stereotypes of laziness or lesser intelligence or of being capable only in certain domains of learning but not others. Working-class students bear "the hidden injuries of class" while learning in higher education contexts that are infused with professional-managerial-class proprieties.[6] Disabled students face myriad societally constructed barriers to participation in the learning process. Queer students must constantly police whether they are sufficiently conforming to heteronormative culture or else weigh the risks of transgressing it. Undocumented students have to maintain a positive attitude despite constantly facing demeaning messages about their families. And on and on: every marginalized identity a student claims adds a layer of disparate emotional burdens that can make the pains of the learning process much greater than its wonders.

While the observations above are only a fraction of the emotional tasks students must perform as part of a course, they demonstrate a central claim of this chapter: every cognitive task brings concurrent emotional tasks, that is, *every intended learning outcome is simultaneously an expectation of emotional output.*

Students do not have a choice to *not* experience various emotional reactions to the cognitive tasks assigned by their instructors. They can only choose how they will engage those emotional reactions—that is the core emotional task implicit in every cognitive task. Instructors, though, have many pedagogical choices to make as to how conscientious we are when it comes to the emotional tasks we are expecting (whether transparently or implicitly) students to perform and the tools we offer (if any) for such tasks. The pedagogical challenge, therefore, is to continuously grow more aware of and intentional about such choices and make them as thoughtfully and responsibly as we can in each iteration of our teaching. In the following sections, I will propose a particular way to conceptualize the emotional tasks we ask of our students, offer some illustrative examples of how I try to responsibly engage this dimension of my students' learning, and conclude with a call for fellow instructors to reflect further on the commitments they want to make to their students regarding this dimension.[7]

Conceptualizing the Emotions of Learning

Although the scholarship of teaching and learning in religious studies has not extensively thematized the emotional dimension of student learning, there is a moderate-sized pedagogical literature on it drawn from across other fields. In *How Higher Education Feels*, education researcher Kathleen Quinlan comprehensively surveys this literature and distills a cogent typology of seven distinct perspectives scholars have advanced on the role of emotion in education.[8] Quinlan's typology is useful not only for locating this chapter's argument relative to the broader scholarly conversation, but as an invitation for readers to consider which perspectives inform their own pedagogy.

Three of the seven perspectives (Quinlan calls them stances) focus on the relationship between emotions in learning and personal identity: "Emotions are the results of [self-]appraisals related to our goals" (stance 1); "Some emotions are the remnants of past, unresolved conflicts" (stance 4); "Emotional disorientation can catalyze changes in perspectives or identity. It is a natural and necessary part of the learning process" (stance 6).[9] Two stances frame emotions as themselves a target of a learning process: "Emotional intelligence is a set of personal success skills that can (and should) be developed" (stance 3); "Adults should be able to regulate and manage their own emotions" (stance 2).[10] Another stance questions whether too much emphasis has been placed on emotions: "Emotionalizing education is an unwelcome spread of therapeutic culture" (stance 7). Finally, one stance traces the social structures that evoke and naturalize emotional patterns in learning: "Students' (and teachers') emotions can (and should) be interrogated and critiqued as social-cultural phenomen[a]" (stance 5).

Before situating this chapter relative to these stances, I want to invite readers to take a moment and reflect on how they think about the emotional dimension of students' learning as a factor in course design. Which of the seven stances identified by Quinlan comes closest to your own approach? How did you arrive at this stance: was it modeled to you by one of your teachers, or does it derive from a specific conviction you hold about teaching or about human nature, or is it just what has emerged over the years of your teaching, or did you arrive at it some other way? What are some important pedagogical choices this stance influences you in? Which of the other stances are you intrigued by? Which do you feel negatively toward? Even by themselves, these stances and questions can encourage deeper intentionality about engaging student emotions in learning.

This chapter's primary impetus is stance 5, which recognizes that students' "emotional regulation is happening within a larger context that shapes how we … express emotion—and, even, how we feel."[11] In other words, this stance seeks to uncover the power-relations that shape possible emotional responses and attempt to channel each person's emotional energy in ways that are deemed socially acceptable. Quinlan notes that a few researchers have linked this stance to the concept of emotional labor, but this has not been developed extensively. The emphasis until now has instead been on the "implicit emotional rules" that govern which forms of emotional expression are acceptable in educational contexts.[12] However, emotional labor is a useful lens for perceiving the emotional tasks that we as instructors implicitly ask of students concurrent with the cognitive tasks we assign.[13] This points to an important qualification of this chapter's aims: I'm concentrating on the emotional tasks that arise in conjunction with or as a result of assigned cognitive tasks, a subset within the overall emotional dimension of learning.

Emotional labor is a concept first coined by sociologist Arlie Russell Hochschild to recognize how workers in service occupations, such as food service and personal care, have to self-govern their emotions so that their external expression conveys the emotions expected by their employer: for instance, smiling at customers, speaking in a way that makes them feel cared for, and similar actions.[14] In recent years, a number of social commentators have expanded the applicability of the term from paid work to unpaid domestic/relational tasks, although Hochschild has flagged concern at this expansion.[15] Regardless of how one comes down in this debate—and as a sometime labor studies scholar, I myself chart a middle path, upholding Hochschild's definition while also allowing it to be applied to core aspects of domestic labor, understood in socialist feminists' terms of social reproduction—I contend that the concept is nevertheless applicable to courses in higher education because it is a way of thinking about emotions that arise amidst tasks that one doesn't choose for oneself.

While most instructors do not think of the classroom as students' workplace (despite the multiple functional parallels revealed by a Foucauldian analysis and discussions of the neoliberal university), nonetheless when and insofar as instructors assign cognitive tasks that students are required to complete, we are simultaneously asking students to experience whatever emotions will arise for them as they perform those required tasks. Even in the most democratically organized courses, the instructor still sets the basic, initial parameters for the process by which students will co-construct the course, a set of cognitive tasks that elicit various emotional responses for students. And the majority of instructors still determine the structure of the readings, in-class activities, and written and other assignments students are required to do in order to pass a course. To whatever degree we exercise this power in a course, we need to recognize that we are asking students to perform emotional tasks concurrent with these cognitive ones, which they did not choose for themselves. That is what makes emotional labor apposite for understanding these emotional tasks. Whatever cognitive tasks an instructor assigns or requires, so long as it is the instructor who assigns or requires them—even if students have some options within them—the expectation that students will do emotional labor in the course cannot be eliminated. What instructors *can* do, though, is become as conscious as we are able about the emotional labor our assigned cognitive tasks ask of students and structure this emotional labor as responsibly as we can. In the next section I describe some of my own efforts to cultivate an ethos of responsibility with respect to students' emotional labor, to illustrate how it can be an additional toolkit for effective pedagogical design.

Illustrative Examples from My Teaching Practice

My reflections here are intended purely as an illustrative example of how intentionality concerning students' emotional labor in a course alongside their cognitive labor can augment thoughtful pedagogical design. I make no claim that my approach is problem-free, and I do not offer it as a template; rather, I am sharing a work-in-progress in order to invite my fellow teachers to contribute other strategies for structuring students' emotional labor that have been effective for student learning and development in their courses, so that we can then collectively identify best practices and craft orienting models.

I draw my examples from my introductory course in the critical study of Christianity, "What Is Christianity?" The course is a general education course that usually enrolls twenty to twenty-five students, around half of them first-years; enrollees are roughly split evenly by gender (along with occasional trans/non-binary students), between one-third and one-half students of color, and one-third to one-half from working-class backgrounds. The fundamental goal of the course is for students to be able to perceive and understand Christianity in a critical-comparative manner, as a culturally conditioned social phenomenon that has no single, univocal form or unified essence

We begin the semester reading Dennis Covington's hybrid spiritual memoir and profile of snake-handling Christians, *Salvation on Sand Mountain* (followed by a memoir different in almost every way, Sara Miles' *Take This Bread*).[16] *Salvation on Sand Mountain* presents a form of Christianity that only a few of my students have heard of and none so far has participated in. During our first class discussion, for which we have read Covington's description of his first encounter with snake-handling and glossolalia on Sand Mountain, I ask students what it felt like while they were reading those chapters: many of them report that it felt strange, bizarre, and, for a few, scary or disturbing.[17] I want to offer some time early on when students can openly voice emotions I know, or at least strongly suspect, they're experiencing.

By validating students' reported emotional reactions, we are able to acknowledge those feelings, rather than trying to stifle or bracket them, so that we can then spend some time examining what assumptions in our own thinking those reactions reveal. I ask them, in an inviting, non-judgmental tone: What about this makes you feel that way? What were you assuming about Christianity when you started this book? What is it like trying to imagine that this is just as legitimate a form of Christianity as the forms you are familiar with? Why or why not? Often some of the students will bring up how they realized, while reading or during the discussion, that this form of Christianity is not wrong, just different from what they're used to. Over the course of the book, we have a few more brief check-ins during class about what reading the book feels like and students' reactions to the various people profiled in the book. I do this because reading the book carefully requires getting to know more about real individuals from whom my students have at least some, if not vast, differences. In these moments,

I acknowledge the emotional effort involved in becoming open to a worldview and practices so different from their own. I aim to encourage students that the difficulty is worth it, which does not change the discomfort they may feel being mentally immersed in an unfamiliar world, but it can create a supportive environment for engaging that discomfort.

We do similar emotional temperature checks during our unit on Charles Marsh's book *God's Long Summer: Stories of Faith and Civil Rights*, which we read later, at the midpoint of the semester.[18] The book profiles five individuals active politically at the same time and place, Mississippi in the 1950s–1960s. We study four of these individuals, all of whom were active Christians: two pro-segregation White men, one anti-segregation White man, and Fannie Lou Hamer, an anti-segregation Black woman and legendary civil rights leader. Both of the pro-segregationists support a White supremacist social order, but one of them publicly celebrates and violently pursues it as a KKK leader while the other affirms it more implicitly, framing it as a desire not to change the segregated status quo. The book thus foregrounds racism, one of the most emotionally fraught topics to engage in the classroom, and it includes descriptions of several acts of racist violence, one of them in sufficient detail that I tell students ahead of time what pages it's in and that they may choose to skip it.[19]

Unsurprisingly, students express more intense emotional reactions to this book and on a deeper level than to *Salvation on Sand Mountain*. By far the most common emotions expressed are horror and anger at the injustices and violence described in the book, rendered in a palpable way that makes it impossible for racism to remain an abstract concept. Moreover, many students express anger specifically at the invocations of Christianity by the pro-segregation White figures, because it feels to them like a misuse of Christianity. It is difficult enough, in general, to read an account of someone committed to violence, but in this case, students must also confront my proposition that, from a religious studies standpoint, we cannot simply dismiss this person's religious beliefs and practices as a "distortion" of "true" Christianity. This allows us to detect normative assumptions about Christianity and its inherent goodness, which for many students evokes feelings of discomfort or disgust, that is, at the realization that Christianity *qua* Christianity can be used toward ends they consider evil.

How do I know students feel all these things? Because that is what they say they feel. And this points to one of the limitations of engaging the emotional dimension of learning: we cannot directly know the emotions our students are experiencing, but only what they convey by words, tone, and body language. At most, we can perceive a proxy indicator of students' emotional responses, which they can always adjust, intentionally or non-consciously, based on their perception of the social acceptability of the emotions they actually feel. This is an area where significant further research is needed. Despite this limitation, teachers can nonetheless make our best conscious efforts to foster a sense in students that they can be open about their emotional responses and to discern their reactions as carefully and accurately as possible. Often, just the practice of allocating some time to ask questions like "What does it feel like to read/think/talk about this?" and listening non-judgmentally creates credibility for the instructor; doing so repeatedly when studying more emotionally challenging material enhances it. And over time, as one works with successive groups of students on similar course material or issues, one develops both a prudential sense for the more common responses and a more precise gauge for subtleties and shifts. These skills of care-filled asking about, listening for, and discerning of emotional responses can be learned and practiced, yet most graduate training spends little if any time on them, especially compared to the time spent, for example, training future instructors how to discern good argumentation in writing.[20]

Thus far I have focused on the emotional labor students perform for specific units in the course, but another key consideration is the emotional arc of the course. For example, I intentionally schedule *Salvation on Sand Mountain* and *God's Long Summer* at different points in the semester for both cognitive and emotional reasons. Cognitively, *Mountain*, written for a popular audience, allows students to focus on one Christian's experiences in a community first, before moving to the comparative analysis of four highly differentiated forms of Christianity in the more academically written *Summer*. Emotionally, *Mountain* asks students to encounter something different from their experience, even though much of the other practices and discourses on Sand Mountain besides snake-handling are familiar to many students. *Summer* asks students to engage something that is not only different, but in some instances linked to extremist violence, raising the emotional stakes. Moreover, *Summer* centers on an emotionally fraught social-political issue in a way that *Mountain* does not.

Not only does our engagement with *Mountain* prepare the class for the more emotionally challenging engagement with *Summer*, but the time before we read *Summer* gives the class a chance to cultivate supportive group dynamics and allows me to shape my role in facilitating the learning process, including both cognitive and emotional tasks, for this particular class. Thus, the emotional arc of any course is contoured by, among other things, the different kinds and intensities of emotional responses typically evoked by course materials, the need to establish an environment that provides sufficient support for the emotional labor asked of students, and several other factors. Further scholarship of teaching and learning elaborating the various kinds of emotional arcs appropriate for different courses and learning outcomes would be highly practicable for enhancing pedagogy in religious studies.

God's Long Summer asks students to reckon with Christian support of White supremacy versus Christian resistance to it. Thus, it raises different emotional stakes for White students and for Black students and other students of color. This points to another crucial dimension of attending to the emotional tasks we expect students to perform in a course: recognizing that a given reading, exercise, or assignment might expect different things emotionally from different groups of students. For Black students and other students of color, this unit has the potential to evoke memories of racialized trauma in their own lives or communities as well as to draw to the surface frustrations with and anger at pervasive racial injustice that must, on a day-to-day basis in a White supremacist society, be dealt with internally. On the other hand, White students in the course at a minimum are aware of a social expectation not to express racist sentiments, and most of them have, in addition, at least a basic commitment to racial equality. Recognizing the realities of White supremacy, however, implicates their own racial identity in the injustices we read about in the book.

Given these high and group-differentiated emotional stakes, my overall approach is to validate the challenging emotional responses the book might raise while explicitly recognizing that different groups will have different reactions—and, more importantly, while being unambiguous that, consistent with our institution's stated commitments, racist attitudes and discourse are not acceptable in the course. In other words, I want students to feel allowed to feel whatever emotions the book raises, which will likely differ across racial lines, but at the same time I am clear that our shared cognitive task is to critically analyze the White supremacist mentality so as to more effectively disrupt and dismantle it in our present-day society.[21] I reserve a few minutes during each session in this unit to allow students to talk about what it feels like to read and discuss the racist attitudes and actions in the book. I briefly name some of my own reactions to the book, as a person of color; this ensures that White students hear at least one perspective of color, without putting the burden on students of color to bring this up, though it usually opens up space for at least some students of color to add their comments. I also spend time after we have begun the book explaining to students that we do not have to like the people we are reading about or agree with their stances to understand them better. I pay extra attention to how Black students and other students of color appear to be affected by the readings, assignments, and discussions, reaching out at the end of class if any seem distressed.[22]

It would be pedagogically unethical of me to expect students to engage with potentially emotionally distressing material without a worthwhile purpose that enhances their learning. This unit, in addition to the cognitive opportunity to understand and critique US White Christianity's tight enmeshment with White supremacy, allows students to experience what it feels like to hold a stance opposed to Christian White supremacy.[23] Based on student comments, both during class and in written reflections, I know that for many White students this is a chance to experience what it is like emotionally to explicitly name racism as such and acknowledge the suffering it causes; for some of my White students, this is a first, while for the rest it is still a rare occurrence. From comments by multiple students of color, I infer that the cognitive activity of being able to make White supremacy an object of critical analysis provides some validation for their own experiences of racism, so often ignored or minimized in White-dominated public discourses. Moreover, a number of students of all races find inspiration in accounts of Christian resistance to racism.

The examples I have discussed address emotional tasks that arise for students primarily due to the nature of the course material itself. But what about emotional tasks that arise because a given cognitive task stretches beyond a student's current abilities—for instance, when students feel frustration or self-doubt as they attempt to analyze or synthesize ideas more complexly than they have before? Attending to this kind of emotional labor is essential to good teaching. The reason I have not highlighted it here is because it is the component of the emotional labor of learning with which readers likely are already familiar, from their own formation as scholars. Each of us was a novice in the academic study of religion before, just as our students are novices, so we know what it is like to face cognitively challenging tasks as well as the emotional challenges they bring—a process that continues in research and writing projects over one's career. Even if the precise cognitive tasks (and concomitant emotional tasks) that challenge an instructor may be different from the tasks that challenge that instructor's students, they provide a basis for identifying potential challenges to students. In addition, this kind of emotional task may feel more comfortable for scholars to address, because we can draw upon our own firsthand experiences. Nevertheless, the emotional labor resulting from cognitive growth is a major topic for the deeper consideration of emotional labor this chapter is calling for in the discipline.

Cultivating an Ethos of Responsibility with Respect to Students' Emotional Labor

Every act of learning involves both cognitive and emotional efforts: every intended learning outcome is simultaneously an expectation of emotional output. Insofar as we, as instructors, decide the cognitive tasks students must perform in our courses, we are also, by implication, assigning a set of emotional tasks they must perform, which include any emotional tasks we intend as well as those that arise individually for each student based on their life-journey. We cannot pretend that the power to require a cognitive task does not simultaneously require students to work through whatever emotions they experience in that task. But we *can* repeatedly reflect on how we shape this dynamic in our courses and identify ethical norms that can protect students' emotional well-being and promote a greater degree of emotional agency in a course.

By way of conclusion, I articulate some of the guiding principles that have emerged thus far in my cultivation of an ethos of responsibility with respect to students' emotional labor in my courses. I offer these with the aim of sparking further consideration within the discipline, in the hope that we can regularly reflect together on how to ethically and effectively structure the emotional labor we assign students. I frame them as commitments I make to my students, which I strive to realize as best I can:

1. Actively avoid doing emotional harm.
2. Neither waste students' emotional energy nor demand more of it than is reasonable.
3. Recognize and factor in the emotional labor demanded of students in other parts of their lives.
4. Be especially attentive to and responsible toward possible additional or disparate emotional tasks expected of students who have marginalized or minoritized identities.
5. In designing assignments and activities and periodically reviewing existing ones, identify the emotional labor they are expecting of students and determine if they are appropriate and aligned with the learning outcomes of the course.
6. Set emotional tasks that develop students' emotional skills alongside their cognitive ones, especially emotional skills that encourage lifelong learning and social engagement.
7. Strive to create a classroom community in which we are emotionally supportive of one another.

8. Periodically check in with students about their emotional responses to the learning process and make adjustments if it becomes clear that students are being challenged in ways I did not anticipate.
9. Where possible, find ways for students to have input into the emotional tasks they are expected to perform.
10. When I intend or anticipate that an assignment or activity will be emotionally challenging or difficult, provide students with emotional tools to make the experience a constructive one and offer support and, if needed, the opportunity to process, within the limits of my professional qualifications and making appropriate referrals when needed.

In the spirit of ongoing dialogue, I invite readers to reflect with me on this list: *What ideas on this list resonate with you and why? What would you add, delete, or change? What would be the most important points on your list? And when you compose your own list, what feelings are evoked and what do you think they are responding to?*

5

Reorientation: Teaching Theory and Method to Future Faculty

Jill DeTemple

Introduction: The Problem of Time and Lessons for Orientation

Philosopher Robin Le Poidevin writes that there are two dominant theories of time. In the first, time moves as a river, in one direction, flowing inexorably such that we can know where it has been and make educated guesses about where it is going. In the second, time is allied to space such that where we are and what we can see and experience depend on the direction we face. It is all there, related, but relatively fixed. What changes is our perception as we turn and become able to see new things even as others fade into shadows or disappearance. What we understand as future is that which we haven't seen, areas into which we have not wandered or which have not yet wandered into us. The past is territory to which we have become distantly reoriented or which has reoriented to us.[1] How one understands time, Le Poidevin argues, has repercussions for human understandings of life and the possibility of life after death. These things make a difference in how we live. They may make a difference in how we teach.

Extrapolated broadly, Le Poidevin's framework sheds helpful light on several critical issues in religious studies pedagogy, especially as we consider how to teach religion as a field of inquiry to future faculty members. First, the framework invites questions of orientation to foundational works in the field. Are they simply further back along the banks of an intellectual river, or do we still see them if facing the right direction, familiar landmarks that mark lives and possibilities? If they are those things rushing at us from the past, are they deterministic? If they are points on the horizon, can we orient to them in ways that are less causal? Perhaps they mark a space which we can approach or from which we can flee. Le Poidevin's framework also raises questions about the ways we think about knowledge transmission and creation. When I share what I know about the way "religion" became an academic term, what do I invite graduate students to replicate, change, or discard as they then go on to be teachers and scholars in academic settings and in their communities? How do I want it to change or enhance the ways they can be in the world?

It isn't only the material we teach, in other words, but also how we invite orientation to that material. Whatever theory of time we embrace, we need to have some sense not only of what happened, but of what might happen next, of which ways people are able to face. This means we need to understand who we are and for what purpose we do what we do. Teaching religious studies as a field of inquiry thus means offering students not just opportunities for exposure to and mastery of foundational thought, but also opportunities for understanding their relationship to such thought as a key process of academic, personal, and communal self-authorship.

This chapter explores graduate core seminars that treat history and method in religious studies. Many graduate programs employ these seminars to ensure that their students have a common knowledge of the field such that they are able to teach religious studies courses in future endeavors. While there has been ample debate among religion scholars about what should be included in such courses,[2] there has been little discussion about how to teach them, especially with regard to the orientational dispositions discussed above. What happens if we reorient those courses to focus not only on the texts, intellectual traditions, and (colonial) histories from which they arose, but also, even primarily, on students' relationship to those texts, traditions, histories, and to each other as a community of scholars? How might this change those students, and our field, for the better?

A Story

I was hired to teach theory and method in a religious studies department at both the undergraduate and graduate levels. While I've thus long been interested in improving teaching and learning in classes dedicated to Tylor, Frazer, Durkheim, and their friends, the issue came to a head for me in a spring 2016 graduate core seminar in which we were considering those theorists as deep background to more contemporary cultural and critical approaches in the field. The class had often been tense, especially as many students who had come to our graduate program to study systematic theology were frustrated by the exclusion of theologically normative stances from the material. The historians in the class were frustrated by clumsy or invented historical details, even as they pushed back against the pleas for normative reasoning. The class started in January. Students were polarized by March, and so hostile by April that in the middle of a class session one student prefaced a comment by begging that there be "no weasels" working to undermine any replies. "No weasels!" became a sort of code for the group when someone just needed some space to speak, free of escalated discourse. The phrase was memorialized with a cookie cake complete with the international "no" sign drawn over the word "weasel" offered as a peace token on the last day we met. Though this is the only class I've taught requiring a cookie cake, it certainly isn't the only dysfunctional graduate seminar treating the history of the field that has ever existed.

Some of this has to do with the ways we associate graduate students with advisors, specializations, and commitments early in their academic careers. From the way we sort them in admissions processes to their first introductions at recruitment weekends and in seminars, students who may have had multiple undergraduate majors, careers outside of the academy, and talents and

Figure 5.1 "No Weasels" Cookie Cake, 2016. Photo by Jill DeTemple.

experiences unrelated to their course of study are quickly reduced to academic markers. A student who danced professionally quickly becomes John in biblical studies and another who double-majored in anthropology and economics and worked in finance before entering the program is Keisha in Hinduism. Political polarization works on the same axis of reduction. The neighbor who makes a great cup of coffee, who cleans the park every Saturday, and who brought over flowers when another neighbor fell ill simply becomes Dan the Republican in a divisive political conversation. Another who regularly runs PTA events, knows everything about birds, and plays the cello at her synagogue becomes Lia the Democrat. The flattening comes as the result of vigilance. If we experience opposing political views as threatening, we narrow our view, focusing only on the threat and our potential responses to that threat. Complexity, context, and connection are lost.[3]

That polarized seminar from 2016 had many of these same characteristics. Students were so alert for attacks against their particular commitments and worldviews that they often couldn't hear the complexities in another's answer, see them in each other, or think about them in the materials on the table for our consideration. This led to a profound, and palpable, guardedness in the class. No one felt they could take a risk. The weasels were everywhere. When it came time to teach in the core sequence again in 2019, and after a conversation with a colleague led me to the connection between graduate identities and political polarization,[4] I decided to wander into unknown territory, risking the possibilities of weasels I didn't know in the hopes of banishing those that I did.

Shifting the Landscape: What Reorientation Looks Like

My decision to shift the core seminar and the mechanisms by which I did so were profoundly influenced by Reflective Structured Dialogue [RSD], an approach to speaking and listening across difference and distance pioneered by Essential Partners, an award winning non-profit. Though initially developed as an approach to conflict transformation, RSD and its broader application as a pedagogy, something colleagues and I have developed as "dialogic classrooms," have proven effective for improving student sense of belonging, engagement, willingness to speak, and comprehension of course materials and concepts.[5]

Based on theory and practices from family systems therapy, RSD works to reorient participants from cycles of communication and cognition that favor quick, reactive, and vigilant stances to ones that favor reflection, listening, and constructive understanding. The goal of Reflective Structured Dialogue and of dialogic classrooms is not agreement. Neither is it an assumption that one idea or theory will prevail as the result of inquiry and debate. Rather, dialogic classrooms are designed to open spaces for deep listening, speaking that connects ideas with experiences, and the creation of trust that allows for personal and intellectual risk and subsequent growth in shared social spaces. Following Michael Roth, Nel Noddings, Carol Dweck, bell hooks, and other education scholars, dialogic classrooms cultivate what Roth calls "critical feeling" and connections to lived experiences as essential components of critical thinking and exploration.[6]

In the case of the core seminar, shifting toward a central question of student relationships to canonical materials in religious studies required providing ample space to consider those relationships and the values that informed them, as well as the social spaces in which those relationships exist. Some core teachings of RSD were especially helpful in this shift.

First, the course needed to be intentionally structured for this purpose. If the class was to focus on relationships and not just on mastery, we would need to highlight, reflect on, and practice relationships. This required creating space for all of those things, as well as transparency about their prominence as learning outcomes. The core readings for the course, what most readers would recognize as "canonical" thinkers in the history of Religious Studies, were still present, though intentionally placed alongside contemporary thinkers in the field and also in their context via some key contemporary works focused on colonial histories. Before digging into Tylor, for example, we began the course with David Chidester's *Empire of Religion* and an essay by Anna Tsing that explores the prevalence of entrenched patterns even in globalized societies.[7] Every "classic" author was paired with critical commentary, usually an essay from Mark C. Taylor's *Critical Terms* book, in order to create some context that expanded the positioning of the formative pieces. Such pairings invited reflection on students' positions in addition to their critical analysis of the texts. How should they think of *Purity and Danger* in light of transgression as a lens of analysis? Did Paul Stoller's essay on rationality make them think differently about Tylor or Frazer? The pairings of readings opened up space for broad conversations about how students understood the texts and where they may or may not be useful in their lives as scholars, teachers, and community members. We also read and reflected on Joshua Eyler's *How Humans Learn*, a work focused on some of the neuroscience behind teaching and learning, and Tomoko Masuzawa's *The Invention of World Religions*, in order to bring pedagogy to the table.⁸ This, along with weekly pedagogical demonstrations that asked students to teach core texts to their peers as if their peers were undergraduates, seminarians, graduate students, or community members, created a space for considering the ways in which teaching can be used to reify, resist, reform, or reject formative ideas in the field.

Indeed, much of the work of reorientation happened in spaces on the syllabus that invited continual reflection on vocation and in activities woven into every class meeting designed to give room for the relationships in question. Again, these spaces were influenced by practices commonly used in dialogic classrooms. Following dialogic models and teaching and learning literature that encourages connection before content/people before process,⁹ we began every three-hour seminar session with a quick improv game called "Five Things," and came back from our mid-session breaks with another improv exercise, "The Clapping Game" [see the appendix for detailed descriptions of the games]. These quickly became ritualized in the class. Then, students co-created communication agreements that guided speaking and listening norms. These included confidentiality, speaking to be understood and listening to understand, that we needed everyone's opinions, and that class was "not a competition," among others (Figure 5.2). The agreements were crafted using an Essential Partners exercise, "Moments of Dissent," that asks students to imagine what intentions they would need to hold for themselves, what conditions would need to be in place, and what agreements the class would need for them to say something contrary to opinions voiced by several other students in the group.¹⁰ We used the agreements throughout the semester, recalling them before dialogues or in

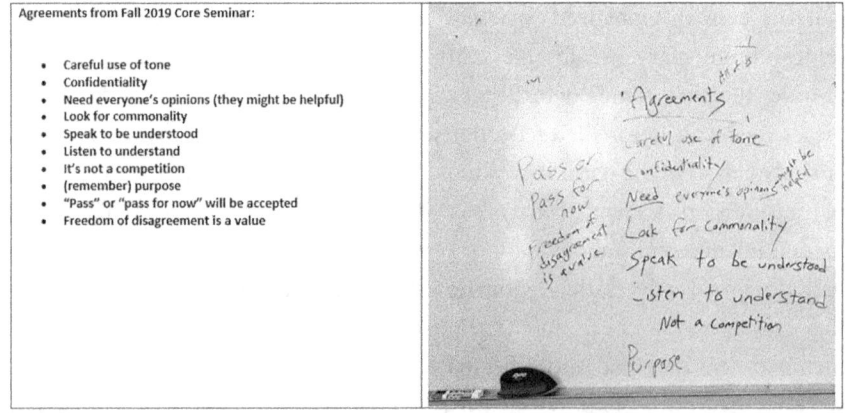

Figure 5.2 Communication Agreements, 2019. Photo by Jill DeTemple.

moments that seemed especially ripe for tension. Had someone slipped, having the agreements would have allowed me, as facilitator, to pause the conversation and reset before weasels were set loose in the room.

The agreements from Fall 2020 Core Seminar were:

- Careful use of tone
- Confidentiality
- Need everyone's opinions (they might be helpful)
- Look for commonality
- Speak to be understood
- Listen to understand
- It's not a competition
- (remember) purpose
- "Pass" or "pass for now" will be accepted
- Freedom of disagreement is a value

In addition to these activities, we did several improv games aimed at play and connection to content (e.g., "Hitchhiker" and "Playlist"), and three Reflective Structured Dialogues as in-class assignments. The first dialogue asked students to reflect on an experience that led them to their views on the relationship between rationality and religion, the second asked them to reflect on a time when an important part of their identity had been misrepresented, and a third asked them to think about what they do and do not disclose of their identity/commitments in classroom settings. The dialogues were followed by a brief piece of reflective writing that connected class readings with the dialogue. As a final exercise, students created and performed a brief spoken-word play, in groups, that connected their life stories to their deepest hopes as teachers and academics in the style of Ping Chong's *Beyond Sacred*.[11] When not engaged in one of these activities, the class resembled a classic seminar, with students presenting on and discussing shared readings.

Analysis: What Reorientation Invited

Shifting the course from one focused on mastery of classic texts to one that considered students' positions relative to those texts felt risky. How would graduate students, steeped in a climate of mastery in everything from core courses to qualifying exams, respond to such a repositioning? Would they feel free to take some risks speaking personally in dialogue circles? Would they engage in play during the improv games? Would they consider these things valuable, or perceive them as a distracting waste of time, diverting them from the "real," content-based work of the class? Would I lose all credibility as a faculty member and teacher, as an "expert" in the field?

The short answer is that, while the class certainly felt different than other seminars, students adapted quickly. Within a few weeks they were using Five Things to recognize and appreciate diversity in the room, asking a student from a place distant from Dallas to name five foods they missed from home, and another who had returned after missing a class for the birth of his first child about the five best things about being a father. On another memorable day, a student specializing in Luther was asked to name five reasons their home football team had lost the weekend before. The student immediately replied, "Because we live in a fallen world!" In one sentence, the student's geographic, intellectual, and theological inclinations were given a place to sit. During dialogues, students grappled with professional and personal identities, with what it means to be a scholar, and with values that often bumped up against each other as they imagined teaching, writing, and life after graduate school. In discussions related to course readings, they were able to lean into those connections and complexities as they wrestled with their positioning to core texts. They still worried about reductionism, colonial histories, ahistoricism, varying stances on normativity, and the usual spate of problems with early works in the field, but they were more open to imagining those texts as relevant, in whatever small way, to their work as scholars and future teachers. They were able to recognize differing commitments in the room, often asking curious questions about how a text might be useful or troubling for people exhibiting such differences. They did not agree. Systematicians did not cede a preference for normative work; historians did not start looking through confessional lenses. They did work collegially, collaboratively, and openly. Coming at the same piece of landscape from different locations, they focused on the landscape rather than feeling threatened by their varying positions around it.

Perhaps most strikingly, students in this version of the seminar were able to describe those positions with unusual acuity. Final papers for the course invited students to use the ideas of one of the theorists we had considered in application to a problem/text/or idea in their subfield. Students wrote intriguing and well-crafted papers on everything from economic theory (ethics) to secularisms (systematic theology). Students who opted to craft syllabi for future theory and method courses did so with remarkable clarity, purpose, and creativity. As they had been asked to do during the semester, many of them invited future students to think about how they related to formative texts in the field. Evaluations of the course were above average for a graduate seminar. Some students wished for more time for in-depth discussion of the texts under consideration, something I will take into account the next time I am scheduled to teach the course, and one found the focus on pedagogy irrelevant to the topic. Most, however, expressed appreciation for the space to think about positioning to core materials and to ways they may teach those materials going forward. One student, in private correspondence after the play exercise, wrote to say that the class "forever changed my views of what is possible in academia."

While as of yet untested in any systematic way, student work on reflection and research papers, syllabi, and work on in-class activities such as dialogues and improv games embraces a pedagogical goal often described as "self-authorship." Originally defined by Robert Kegan, self-authorship is the ability to make meaning within oneself as opposed to outside of it as a person takes external conviction, beliefs, values, ideas, and other stances

> as objects or elements of its system, rather than the system itself; it does not identify with them but views them as parts of a new whole. This new whole is an ideology, an internal identity, a *self-authorship* that can coordinate, integrate, act upon, or invent values, beliefs, convictions, generalizations, ideals, abstractions, interpersonal loyalties, and interpersonal states. It is no longer *authored by* them, it *authors them* and thereby achieves a personal authority.[12]

In a longitudinal study, Magdola finds that achieving self-authorship among young adults requires cultivating a strong internal voice that guides people in decision-making, identity, and relationships.[13] Her informants who had found they could rely on that internal voice were better able to narrate life events, felt more secure in decision-making, and were more able to meet challenges than those who didn't. Put another way, self-authoring people do not define themselves in opposition, as often happens in polarized and dysfunctional relationships, but are comfortable defining themselves relationally in various contexts as they can consistently call upon their core identities, values, and commitments to guide such relationships.

These findings relate in significant ways to other values and dispositions highlighted as beneficial or essential to students in teaching and learning research. First, naming open-mindedness and curiosity as shared intellectual values, reading about them as beneficial to student learning, and practicing them through activities such as the dialogues and "Five Questions" game appears to have created a classroom culture that encouraged and supported those values and attendant dispositions. Carol Dweck, Jason Baehr, Ken Bain, and others cite research showing that students who are curious about what they are studying are "intrinsically motivated" by that curiosity as opposed to external factors such as grades.[14] Intrinsically motivated students not only do better on immediate educational tasks such as tests, but are more likely to retain and be able to use what they learn after the class has ended. Baehr's work, which focuses on intellectual virtues, makes the case that virtues intentionally cultivated and practiced in classrooms also lead to better learning outcomes, especially when students are invited to think about the application of those virtues, along with course content, to their lives beyond classroom boundaries.[15] Especially for graduate students, who come to class intrinsically interested in course materials, creating spaces in which they can practice curiosity about those materials in relationship to their imagined careers, values, and each other provides an optimal space for learning and growth.

Second, the structure of the course and activities focused on improvisation and play allowed for the kind of self-expression and connection to previous experiences that education research has long upheld as optimal for students. Asking students to consider how they related to canonical materials along with more typical analysis of those materials opens up what Lev Vytgotsky dubbed the "zone of proximal development," a sort of sweet spot for learning something new that is created when students can connect new information onto extant experiences and information.[16] Reflection exercises, including in-class "dialogic moments" that invited students to think about a question related to an activity or reading for a minute or two before responding and papers that linked course materials to what students learned during dialogues, supported such connections. Indeed, reflection on readings and students' positioning to them was a regular feature of class sessions, something that opened space for thoughtful and considered interactions and discouraged the kinds of reactive and closed behaviors that can make learning and connection difficult.

Finally, as students became accustomed to approaching texts and each other with curiosity, the class often became multilaterally focused, with students asking each other questions about interpretation, evaluation, or potential applications. They learned, through these practices, to take control of the intellectual spaces created in the seminar and make them their own. As instructor, I was not the de facto engine or chauffeur, propelling and channeling conversational direction or outcomes.

Conclusion: Reorientation as a Paradigm for Religious Studies

There is a long and perhaps troubled history in the academy of understanding religions as "orientations," as specific and predictable ways of viewing the world.[17] My thesis in this essay is not that these approaches to understanding religion or the field of religious studies should be reinvented, replicated, or revived (if indeed they are dead). Rather, what I call for here is a reorientation to, or at the least, a reconsideration of, the assumptions we make about the goals of graduate training focused on religious studies as a field of inquiry within the academy. The catalogue language from the institution where I teach, Southern Methodist University, is typical in the way it describes our core theory and method seminar: "This course will introduce several of the principal approaches to the study of religion in the post-Enlightenment West, focusing on canonical thinkers from various disciplines, especially anthropology, sociology, and psychology."[18] In this case, the word "introduce" carries weight far beyond its surface meaning. As understood in the totality of our program, to be introduced to these principal approaches comes with the tacit assumption that one will understand and even embrace them as interlocutors, ancestors, models, and traditions that must be passed on to the next generation. To know them is to commit to them.

This mastery model of education, one famously critiqued by scholars ranging from Freire to Dweck and Bain, is one that does not invite the kind of thoughtful, reflective, curious, connected, and purposeful pedagogies teaching and learning research recommends. It also runs squarely into the problems of normativity, orientalism, colonialism, and ahistorcism for which "classical" approaches to religious studies are often critiqued.[19] Classrooms based on mastery, be they at the undergraduate or graduate levels, are not designed for the kind of self-authorship that Magdola explores. The focus is so narrowed to the (preselected) material at hand that student interpretation of it becomes secondary or irrelevant. Personal growth becomes a side effect.

Reorienting religious studies courses focused on theory and method such that students' relationships to those theories and methods are at the center opens spaces and possibilities that may have far-reaching implications for the field and its future. Asking students to think about where they may feel connected or represented in Durkheim's collective effervescence or alienated by Freud's neuroses keeps the reality that religious studies is in the representation business alive and active in the room. By inviting careful reflection on students' relationship to those representations and their roles in perpetuating, challenging, or changing them, such an approach shifts the ground of possibility in significant ways. Certainly, students have to understand something, thoroughly, to know how they want to relate to it. Understanding the material is not lost in this iteration of the seminar. But learning for a purpose—that one is actively considering what to do with what they know—invites the kinds of connections, curiosity, and knowledge that make for a meaningful (professional) life.

As we often teach in undergraduate settings, religion isn't destiny. There are many ways to be Jewish or Christian or Atheist or Baha'i.[20] If Le Poidevin is correct, history may similarly not be destiny. There is no reason, then, for Tylor or Frazer or the rest of our usual interlocutors to be destiny. But it is our responsibility to ask the right questions and provide ample room such that students can thoughtfully, meaningfully orient themselves to the spaces and ideas those thinkers helped create so that they may then, in informed and purposeful ways, invite others to do the same.

Appendix: Tools for Reorientation

Beyond Sacred Play

This is a structured, spoken word play in three acts modeled on Ping Chong's *Beyond Sacred*, produced and performed at LaGuardia Community College.[21] Students interview each other in pairs about their life stories and their deepest hopes as scholars who will teach about religion. Students then introduce their partners to a performance group of about six students, and a scribe notes convergences and divergences in stories and aspirations. The group then writes and performs a five-to-seven-minute play using a format given to them that includes speaking alone and in groups with clapping, stomps, and snaps to mark transitions. The play asks students to reflect on what they want to do with what they're learning in class, and how it fits into their identities and commitments. These are necessary skills for self-authorship, and the collective aspect of the play invites reflection on commonalities and divergences that support curiosity, sociality, and vulnerability.

Clapping Game

This game starts with everyone standing up in a circle. In the first round, everyone says their name, followed by a clap. The next round, everyone says the name of the person on their left and then claps. During the third round, a person looks at and names someone across the circle, or possibly next to them, and both the namer and the person being named clap together. The person who was named finds the next person, etc. For the final round, the namer does not speak, but instead makes eye contact with one person and both clap together. The person identified becomes the identifier. Go until things are running smoothly. The clapping game is focused on attention, direct and lateral, in a room. Giving attention, shifting attention, and receiving attention are vital skills for teachers and colleagues as they work together. I found the game allowed students to become more aware of how they were projecting presence and interest toward one another, and also skills in collaboration. This, in turn, created a better environment for intellectual exchange and growth; one where people felt connected and supported enough to take intellectual risk.

"Five Things"

This game begins with the instructor or a designated student turning to another student and asking that they name five things: "[name of student], what are five things in your refrigerator?" After being asked, the student must name five things declaratively, without making hesitation sounds. The group counts after each one until the student reaches five. If the student ums or ahs, they go back one number in the counting. Once they have completed naming five things, they ask another student to list a different five things, and the game continues until everyone has gone. Played at the beginning of class the game did several things that place it squarely in pedagogies that focus on engagement, comfort/belonging, the ability to take risk, and self-authorship as key components to learning. To do well in the game, students must speak declaratively, even when uncertain, and they must voice an idea even if it isn't fully formed. These are vital skills for advanced writing projects in their early stages, as well as for self-presentation in interviews and on public stages of all kinds. What the use of Five Things demonstrated in the graduate seminar, however, was that it opened up a rich place for connections, play, and recognition of personal elements well beyond the academic, especially as students used the game to recognize complex identities in the room.

Hitchhiker

This game starts by creating a "car": two rows of two chairs each. Four students sit in the chairs as if they are in a car, with one student driving. The remaining students form a circle around the "car." The student in the front passenger seat starts talking in the mode of a theorist without announcing who they are (Marx was very interested in how much money the driver made, Douglas wanted to know if the fictional seat covers were clean or dirty and why, etc.). The rear passengers and driver engage the conversation as like-minded interlocutors until the person seated behind the driver taps the driver on the shoulder. At that point, everyone shifts one seat clockwise, leaving the passenger seat open (the driver exits). The new driver then picks someone from the circle to be the new "hitchhiker" who sits in the passenger seat and begins talking in the mode of a new theorist. By inviting students to think about theory playfully and out of usual context, the game opened up new and intriguing possibilities for the use of classical theories in contemporary situations, as well as challenged students to recognize those theories out of their usual place. Eyler cites extensive literature showing that play is good for learning as it is intrinsically motivating.[22] Used in a graduate seminar, the game was ridiculous, allowing for new approaches to classical literature and lateral, personal engagement with that literature.

Playlist

Like "Hitchhiker," this game uses a ridiculous premise to invite creativity and cooperative thinking, and in this case, the beginning of summative critical thinking. As we were finishing up early classical literature I wanted students to pause and reflect on the themes that were emerging for them, both helpful and problematic, from that literature. Each student was invited to think about what a religious studies classical greatest hits playlist would look like. After thinking individually, students worked in groups and then together as a class to create the list, pictured below. Once again, play allowed new perspectives, new evaluations, and new connections—interpersonal and material—to emerge.

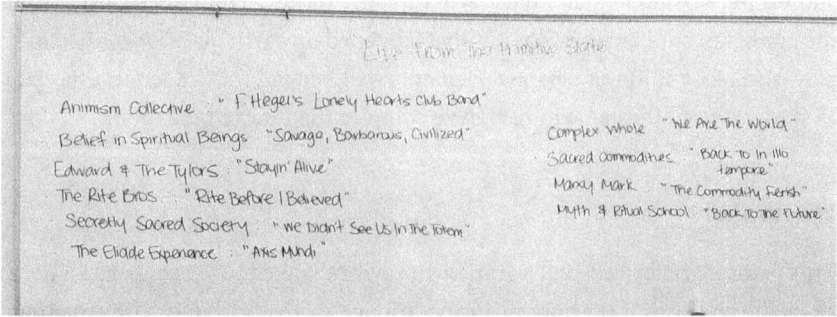

Figure 5.3 Playlist Capture, 2019. Photo by Jill DeTemple.

Reflective Structured Dialogue

This mode of speaking and listening across difference and distance was pioneered and continues to be used by Essential Partners, Inc., a nonprofit dedicated to conflict transformation. The dialogues use reflection and timed listening and speaking to invite listening to understand and speaking to be understood. Participants are asked to reflect on a carefully crafted question, for example, "please share a personal experience that would help us understand what you share of your personal identity or commitments in classrooms." Then, everyone has the same amount of time to respond and listen. Further questions, also done in timed go-arounds, dig into the values, commitments, and complexities that inform people's stories.[23] Open, curious conversation is then invited among participants. The process is beneficial for self-authorship as participants are asked how they came to hold a belief about something, and about the values underneath that belief. Preliminary research focused on the use of RSD in classrooms also points to benefits such as student sense of belonging in class, greater willingness to speak, and increased engagement with and comprehension of course topics and materials.[24]

Part Two

What are Religious Traditions?

6

Mustafa: Teaching Beyond the Five Pillars

Hussein Rashid

Introduction

In my introduction to Islam class, the first in-class activity I assign them is to write the first thing that comes to mind when I say "Muslim." I make it clear that the students do not have to share what they have written, it is simply for their record, and to help them keep track of their learning. During the course of the semester, I will ask them to return to those few sentences, and think about how their perceptions may have changed because of the course. I invite them to ask questions based on their reflections, and what it is they think we still need to cover.

We begin the course with a methodological framing. I explain that our approach will build on Diane Moore's explanation of religious literacy.[1] We go through the idea that you need to know some basic tenets of a religion, that all religions are internally diverse, and that religion and culture are not neatly separable. We think about what it means to approach religions in a context, so that we understand how text is interpreted and lived, and how that contributes to internal diversity. At no point in our early weeks do I talk about the "Five Pillars of Islam." To teach the Five Pillars of Islam would be a normative position, and antithetical to the method we are investing ourselves in as a class.

Despite my avoidance of the use of the Five Pillars, invariably at some point when I ask students to share their reflections on how their perceptions may have changed, at least one student will ask about them. Usually, the types of questions come from one of two broad perspectives.

The first perspective is from students of Muslim heritage, who have been brought up with an exposure to the Five Pillars since childhood. Their positionality does emphasize that the Five Pillars are important to some Muslims. It also invites us to think about whether the Five Pillars have become more popularly normative because of expectations of what it means to be Muslim.[2] It also opens discussions about how the Five Pillars are normative for a group of Muslims, and are not universally defining. For example, some Muslims have Seven Pillars.[3]

The second perspective comes from students, both Muslim and non-Muslim, who have been socialized to expect a discussion of the Five Pillars as a way to understand what it means to be Muslim. Part of this expectation comes from high-school textbooks, which often frame their introduction to Islam through this lens. In addition, they may have been exposed to other courses that mention Islam in college that default to the Five Pillars approach, because that is the training and the comfort level of the faculty. It is this group of students that is the focus of this chapter, those who have been socialized to accept the limits of the Five Pillars as defining what it means to be Muslim.

Identify the Problem

The problem is that many students come out of school systems that use textbooks that define Islam through the Five Pillars, or through Prof. Google when something happens in the news. Many teachers at the secondary level are comfortable with this approach, because many have not been trained in religious literacy or religious studies.[4] At the college level, some of our colleagues are comfortable entering the conversation in that way because of their own training and understandings of what Islam is. This approach is less prevalent among specialists, although it does exist there, and is more noticeable among those doing survey courses, where textbooks still use the Five Pillar approach.[5]

There are three distinct aspects to the problem of teaching with and around the Five Pillars. The first aspect is related to content. The concept of the Five Pillars is important to some Muslims, but they are not universally recognized by all Muslims. Therefore, while the material is not wrong, it is not complete. Unfortunately, unlike other simplified presentations of information, this approach does not lend itself to further deepening. For example, in biology, a student may be introduced to human organs as a way to understand how the body works. That does not preclude later learning about cells or genetics. In the case of the Five Pillars, it usually presented as the totality of Muslim experience, making it more difficult to add details, nuance, or complexity. The Pillars are often also presented in the context of Orientalist depictions of Muslims, denying Muslims any sense of agency in their own religion.[6]

The second aspect is pedagogical. Students enter the classroom with a certain amount of pre-existing knowledge. While that information may not be wrong, it is incomplete. Unlike other topics though, their previous knowledge on Islam has been transmitted to them as the totality of core knowledge; they are not expecting to have this knowledge challenged or disrupted. The limits of their formal exposure to Islam are compounded by larger cultural representations of Muslims, which tend to present Muslims negatively, and through the lens of national security.[7] Therefore, as educators we have to contend with their pre-existing knowledge in a cultural matrix that requires an additional type of pedagogical intervention.

The third aspect involves the dissonance with what we know from scholars like Tomoko Masuzawa about the construction of the World Religions paradigm.[8] Emerging from the discipline of Comparative Theology, non-Christian traditions were constructed into Christian molds, including the conflict between Catholic and Protestant Christianities. As a result, Islam is put into a Christian mold, with Sunnis who mirror Protestants, and Shi'ah who mirror Catholics.[9] Sunnis are thus the good Muslims, and constructed as the normative Islam that should be taught.

Ideally, of course, the teaching of Islam would have moved beyond this construction, but we know that it has not fully incorporated the critiques from the Study of Religion. Although this chapter focuses on the Five Pillars in the teaching of Islam, the Pillars is simply the most explicit expression of teaching Sunni normativity as Islam. Perhaps one of the most clear studies noting the Orientalist mode of framing Islam in higher education comes from Ilyse Morgenstein Fuerst, who notes that many job postings for positions related to Islam conflate religion with geography, language, and text.[10] It is this same framing which privileges Sunni understandings as normative. While this larger question of normativity is beyond the scope of this chapter, it is important to note the persistence of the Five Pillars approach is embedded in that context.

In the context of the classroom, it is possible for me to address the first two problematic aspects of the Five Pillars framing: content and assumed knowledge. The third aspect, the critique of the world religions paradigm, is implicit in my classroom work, but is much more difficult to explicitly address in an introductory Islam course. In order to fully address the framing issues, I cannot teach against the current system, as it risks reifying the problematic framing and does not actually offer students a constructive way to think about the religion.[11]

The primary task in rethinking the problem was revisiting what I wanted students to know about Islam and Muslims. Within fourteen weeks, the average length of the semesters I teach, I could not be comprehensive. To cover approximately 1,400 years of history and approximately a quarter of the world's population in a detailed way is impossible. Therefore, I think about material thematically, rather than chronologically. The themes I want students to understand are the devotional lives of Muslims, the history of Muslims, and the variety of cultures where Muslims are found.

It is the devotional lives of Muslims that are the focus of rethinking how to introduce students to what Muslims do. Devotional life is also intertwined with the other thematic points, as what Muslims do is tied to history and culture. My guiding proposition is that Muslims have religious lives, that these lives are broadly connected under the religion of Islam, and that connectivity does not dictate homogeneity.

Literature

With the framing concerns clearly outlined, my next task is trying to construct the course in a cohesive way that creates a new frame. The two groups of literature that inform my intervention are religious literacy, as outlined by Diane Moore, and cultural studies, through the Birmingham School. They offer theoretical interventions about how to think about religion, and particularly religious expression, which inform the ways in which my course is taught. Ultimately, it is about looking at how Muslims live their lives, and building a description from there, rather than deciding on how Muslims should live their lives and only finding the Muslims that fit that mold.

Through my engagement with the work of Diane Moore, I create a set of principles of religious literacy that I explicitly want students to think with during the course of the semester.[12] These principles are:

Knowing the basic tenets of a religious tradition. This point allows me to address the idea that there is something called "Islam," which bounds a religious community. It also allows us, as a class, to discuss how parameters of belonging are set and by whom. Generally, there is a deeper question that we return to over the course of the semester of how to get to a minimal set of descriptions of what it means to belong to "Islam," without essentializing the religion.

Accepting that no religion is a monolith. While discussing how to define the parameters of "Islam," I introduce students to the variety of different ways of being Muslim, such as Shi'i, Sunni, or Sufi. While superficial during the early part of the course, students begin to understand that they cannot speak of

"Islam" as an undifferentiated whole. Thus, they comprehend that commonality is not the same as homogeneity.

These are the two most relevant principles for this chapter. Between the two of them, they speak directly to notions of a defined tradition that is not uniform. With those concepts in mind, it is easier to approach the other principles of religious literacy that we discuss:

- Acknowledging diversity of expression;
- Understanding the way texts function in societies, and the interpretation of texts;
- Connecting the understanding of texts to the way the religion is lived;
- Recognizing that culture and religion interact and define one another.

Collectively, these principles allow us as learners in the classroom to constantly ask questions as to why people are doing what they are doing. It is that interrogation that makes visible the lived realities of people, rather than ascribing their actions in ill-defined ways to "religion," or "culture." As Moore says in her work, "all knowledge claims are 'situated' claims in that they arise out of certain social/historical/cultural/personal contexts and therefore represent particular and necessarily partial perspectives."[13] Therefore, with these principles, we can understand the situated knowledge of the people we are studying, as well as our own situated knowledge as interrogators of other people's tradition.

Moore's consideration of context, what she describes as "situated knowledge," moves us in the direction of Cultural Studies. As Stuart Hall describes the work of what would become the Birmingham School, he sees the work of Cultural Studies as a political project to analyze capitalist culture.[14] While Moore's considerations do not engage as explicitly with Marxism as Hall's do, it is worth considering how both are critiquing the World Religions Paradigm in different ways.[15] Religious literacy provides a way to contend with how adherents live their understandings of the religion, rather than the ascriptive modality of the WRP. Hall, by coming at Cultural Studies as a political analysis of capitalist culture, provides tools for the analysis of WRP as part of a colonial, and thus capitalist, project.

As Hall continues to define what Cultural Studies is, there are stronger resonances with Moore's work. He argues that Cultural Studies is an interdisciplinary endeavor that breaks the tyranny of the literary as the dominant discourse in defining a society. Rather, the way people live is equally as important as the text.[16] This point of decentralizing the text as a way to define a people is both a key component of religious literacy, which emphasizes a dialogic relationship between text and the way people live their lives, and a critique of the WRP premise that scripture is sufficient to determine how people will live their lives.[17]

For Hall, culture is "threaded through all social practices, and is the sum of their inter-relationship."[18] Therefore, we understand religion as being part of culture, and culture as being part of religion. This dialogic relationship, like the one between text and interpretation, emphasizes that practice, interpretation, text, and context are linked, and to discuss religion in its complexity is to incorporate all of these elements into a comprehensive discussion. This total way of engaging with religion, considering time and place with interpretation, provides the vehicle for constructing my introductory Islam course in a way that presents what I think is important, without risking affirming problematic portrayals of Islam. While the work I do in class is deeply informed by the discipline of Cultural Studies, what I engage with students is a much less structured form of cultural studies, allowing students to generate their own theories and approaches to the material, based on their experiences.

Teaching Tactic

Each module of my course attempts to demonstrate cultural studies, adopting the "show, don't tell" method of narrative, rather than simply discussing it. My goal in each unit is to show how context changes textual interpretation and practice. This goal also allows me to present students with a modified truth sandwich. The truth sandwich is a method of addressing lies and misconceptions without reinforcing them. You start with the truth, debunk the lie, reaffirm the truth. Since the Five Pillars are used by many Muslims, it is not a lie, but it is not the sole definition of what it means to be Muslim, nor is it necessarily the way most Muslims define themselves. So the modification of the truth sandwich rests in affirming that there are variety of ways of being Muslim. I frame this discussion through contestations of authority, resulting in different practices of the religion. In this system, I do not debunk the Five Pillars, but try to complicate the simplicity of looking only at one practice as a defining element of what it means to be Muslim. For example, in talking about the Hajj we discuss different interpretations and meanings that Muslims assign to that ritual, and end with the practical concerns of the limited number of people who can go Hajj. This limitation leads to the last part of the sandwich, which is an exploration of pilgrimage more broadly, rather than just focusing on the Hajj.

However, the first exposure we have to cultural studies and religious literacy in practice in the class comes when discussing Prophet Muhammad. The *shahada*, bearing witness that there is no deity but God, and Muhammad is the messenger of God, is considered a Pillar. However, it tells very little of who Muhammad is to Muslims, and that is part of the inquiry that informs my course structure. Generally, when I present material on Muhammad, I have two sessions of between seventy-five and ninety minutes. I conceive of the sessions as looking at Muhammad in history and Muhammad through history. I do not make this division explicit to the students, so they can experience a comprehensive engagement with the figure of Muhammad, in similar ways to Muslims themselves. As with all my units, I assign readings that are relatively short and are targeted at providing common vocabulary for us to use in class. Once we cover questions about the readings in class, we use the class discussion time to elevate the material in the reading.

In the case of the unit on Muhammad, the readings include a brief historical sketch, the impact of Muhammad on ritual, and the influence of Muhammad in the arts.[19] The unit is deeply informed by several books that engage with meanings made of Muhammad, so while students may not read those books, they are exposed to the ideas within them.[20] Each of the books that I use focuses on the meanings made of Muhammad through time, either artistically or in various communities of interpretation. In particular, the work of Kecia Ali demonstrates what is at stake for various communities in their constructions of Muhammad, and how they read history and texts.

Looking at Muhammad in history, Ali's work is particularly useful in discussing Muhammad's marriage to Aisha. I structure the course to focus on Khadija, Muhammad's first wife, when he married no one else, and his longest marriage. If a student knows something about Muhammad's personal life, it often involves Aisha, and her supposed age of 9 or 10 at the time of the marriage. The course is structured to pre-empt this line of questioning, so that students begin to question why they know what they know and what purpose it serves. Ali provides further details why some Muslim communities are focused on pre-pubescent marriage and a delayed consummation. Therefore, if a student is persistent to know the "truth," it becomes a teaching opportunity to talk about interpretation, not just of scripture, but of history overall.

This session does not simply cover the history of Muhammad's life, but also introduces the role Muhammad plays in interpretative and ritual life. In this first unit, we talk about Muhammad as the head of community, and the role he had to play in conflict mediation and group cohesion. We also discuss

Muhammad's role as intercessor, as mentioned in the Qur'an (4:64), and whether that role as intercessor survives for Muhammad after his death. The Qur'an also describes Muhammad as a "beautiful role-model" (33:21), so we explore what that may mean in practice, looking at the formation of the *hadith* corpus and its implications for the ways Muslims live their lives. Finally, because the Qur'an says God and the angels send their blessings on Muhammad, believers should also do the same (33:56). This verse is the origin of saying "peace be upon him" after mentioning Muhammad's name, a practice with which some students are already familiar. This verse opens larger conversations about Muhammad as a figure of devotion, and sets up the next session on Muhammad through history.

The class begins with me displaying an image of Muhammad, usually a Persianate piece from the thirteenth century. Usually unprompted, a student will ask very quickly about the permissibility of images in "Islam." This question allows us to revisit the principles of religious literacy the class was introduced to two weeks earlier. This review segues into what is at stake for various interpretations over the permissibility of images, and what texts are being interpreted, including the *hadith*.

As we talk about the collection of *hadith* and the impact of the record of Muhammad's sayings and actions on Muslims, students are introduced to the idea of emulation as an act of devotion. Like the interpretation of the Qur'an, they understand that Muslims are constantly interpreting this corpus and acting upon that interpretation, and as the practice is formed, it impacts how the corpus is read. We then turn back to the Qur'anic injunction to praise Muhammad, and explore how the praise tradition develops. After going through some poetry, I have them listen to songs in praise of Muhammad. We quickly cross the world, covering Yusuf Islam (né Cat Stevens, an English singer), Raihan (a Malaysian Muslim devotional group), and Pakistani *qawwali*, a South Asian Muslim devotional musical genre. For the later, I use two pieces by the group the Sabri Brothers. One *qawwali* is about Halima, Muhammad's wet nurse, to demonstrate that Muhammad's status in Muslim traditions extends beyond himself to his family, and those who acted as his family. The song praises Halima for her proximity to Muhammad. The other *qawwali* is *Ya Mustafa*, literally meaning "O Chosen One," with Mustafa being one of the epithets of Muhammad.

From *Ya Mustafa*, it is an easy bridge to Queen's *Mustapha*, which has the contours of a praise song to Muhammad. By repeating certain phrases it is similar to a *dhikr*, or repetition of devotional phrases, that many Muslims include in their extra-liturgical practices. However, in content, it is not coherent, and references the soundscapes of devotion to Muhammad, rather than actual devotion to Muhammad. The Queen song is an opportunity to talk about how Freddie Mercury's personal history is way to talk about Muslim cultures as a participatory space for everyone in that society, not just Muslims. Mercury was embedded in Muslims soundscapes that he absorbed and transformed in the work he did with Queen. Staying on the theme of modern music, we turn to songs by hip-hop artists like *Prayer Song* by Mos Def/Yasiin Bey and K'naan, and *Muhammad Walks* by Lupe Fiasco. The material allows students to witness that devotion to Muhammad is very much a living tradition, and one that is located closer to them than they may have realized.

Solution

The approach of the truth sandwich allows me to emphasize what it is that Muslims do. In the example of the Muhammad unit, it affirms that Muhammad is central to the lives of Muslims, it challenges categorical notions of the "correct way" to demonstrate devotion to Muhammad, and it demonstrates a variety of devotional approaches to Muhammad.

From that discussion, it becomes easy to link it to cultural studies, and the idea that culture permeates all aspects of people's lives, and that culture is determined by their material realities. The connection brings me back to a discussion of religious literacy and the relationship between expressions of religion and culture, and that no religion is a monolith.

In the unit on Muhammad, the history of Muhammad is the basic information about a religious figure that students should know. Looking at Muhammad through history is the diversity of interpretation and what shapes the practice of that interpretation. The sessions are structured to make students think beyond the basic information and to question what tenets look like in practice. After they ask what a belief looks like in practice, they are also thinking about how time and place affect that practice. If the *shahada*, the Muslim declaration of faith, states that "Muhammad is the messenger of God," and that phrase helps to bound the Muslim community, than in class we can see what that boundary looks like to different Muslims.

The arts are an instrumental part of moving students away from only considering scripture as the determining factor for how Muslims think and act. Scripture becomes a common touchstone for Muslims, who then incorporate a variety of other considerations in their embodied practice. I encourage students to experience a variety of these arts so they have visceral exposure and reactions to these practices, instead of reading about them and imagining what they may be about. Cultural studies emphasizes that culture is a social *experience*, and so while I do not explicitly introduce my students to cultural studies theory, they live it in class.

The use of the arts also has them thinking beyond text, as the unit prior to Muhammad is about the Qur'an. In that unit, we go over the ways in which literacy is privileged in modernity, but that the Qur'an sees itself as both a written text, a reading, and an oral/aural text, a recitation. With knowledge about the rise of mass literacy as a relatively recent phenomenon, they recognize how some of the lyrical material serves as a didactic source of information about the religion for believers. If Muhammad's family is important, than believers should act in a manner that honors Muhammad's family. The idea of lyrics and poetry serving as both commentary and didactic text is a concept the class returns to in the unit of Sufism, especially when the work of Rumi is introduced as the "Qur'an in Persian."

Songs are also something that the students are familiar with, even if they are not familiar with the particular songs that we are listening to in class. From earlier conversations in the semester, when we first go over religious literacy, I use songs that can be understood as having a religious meaning to them, as a way to talk about how embedded religious language and imagery are in the United States. For students to hear devotionals, and then go to Queen's *Mustapha*, they can easily be disoriented without that prior grounding to how religion and culture interact. By having students listen to Queen or Yasiin Bey, as artists with whom they may already be familiar, those students who have not interacted with Muslims before also understand that the religion is not fossilized and distant. Muslims are near, and their understanding and expression of their religion are dynamic.

The use of images is useful in having students think about their preconceptions of Muslim beliefs and practices, without telling them they are wrong. While it is true that some Muslims do consider depicting Muhammad to be forbidden, it is not a categorical belief. Students are then able to interrogate their situated knowledge, without being told they are wrong. Rather, they have a partial truth, and they are being invited to deepen their knowledge. The class also looks at images of Muhammad in which his face is obscured, affirming student knowledge as a starting point, not an ending point.

By starting with text, then centrality of the Qur'an for Muslims is confirmed for students. However, by showing how the text is lived demonstrates for the students that there is not one way the text is experienced or understood by

Muslims. Devotion to Muhammad is the first vehicle through which students are exposed to this diversity of interpretation and practice. The approach I outline for the unit on Muhammad also exemplifies the implicit critique of the World Religions Paradigm, which, like Orientalism, seeks an Islam without Muslims, privileging text over practice. In addition, the linkage between colonialism and the WRP means that the privileging of text involves interpretations and interpretative methods from outside Muslim traditions, as meaning is ascribed to Islam by scholars embedded in WRP. Focusing on religious literacy and cultural studies is a way to return agency back to Muslims and cultivate a mindset among students that people are experts on their own lives, and do not need the imposition of meaning by other people.

I maintain this structure of units in a spiraling way, so that we keep coming back to these ideas of interpretation and diverse practices over the course of the semester, students are hopefully internalizing that Islam cannot be defined by Five Pillars, and we are better served by talking about Muslims than Islam.

Conclusion

In teaching my Introduction to Islam course, I have to contend with the knowledge of Islam that my students bring into the course. Sometimes this knowledge comes from prior study, sometimes from lived experience, and sometimes from media framings. In each of these instances, the students come into the class with partial and situated knowledge. Rather than treating them as *tabula rasa*, or telling them that what they know is wrong, especially if it comes from the perspective of an adherent, I invite them to question their own positionality.[21] That invitation comes through combining content on Muslim traditions and methods of religious literacy and cultural studies.

Religious literacy provides students with the analytic framework with which to understand the material I introduce in class, emphasizing interpretation and lived experience. Since interpretation is framed by that lived experience, I am teaching them to think about time and place when making statements about religious practices, rather than seeking categorical statements about what Muslims do and believe. This approach allows us to think about defining a religious tradition, without essentializing it.

The focus on lived experiences allows me to bring in aspects of Muslim life, predominantly through the arts, which illustrate the diversity of practices that emerge from different interpretations. The use of the arts allows students to join in that experience, even at a distance, that makes the learning less theoretical and more visceral. Students are embodied and can learn through that embodiment. In this course, I will assign students artistic projects, such as writing a praise to someone or something important to them, and have them reflect on how their life experiences shaped that poem. This approach provides students an introduction to cultural studies.

Over the course of many years of teaching at a variety of institutions, including R1s, large and mid-sized private universities, large public universities, small liberal arts colleges, and seminaries, I have found the basic approach consistently improves students' understandings of the variety of ways of being Muslim. The constant iteration of the key themes and constant exposure to diversity of thought and location make sure that students are given ample opportunity to internalize the ideas that we establish early in the semester.

The example of Muhammad that I use in this chapter outlines the basic structure of all the units I teach. While each varies in the details of the historical component, there is consistently a session on basic information that students need to know about the topic, such as Shi'ism, and then at least one other session on diversity of ways that material is lived. And whenever students get stuck in a narrow understanding of what it means to be Muslim, I can always point back to Queen's *Mustapha*, and tell them if Freddie can think big, they can too.

7

Pedagogical Strategies for Critically Examining the Consumption of Asian Religions

Beverley McGuire

Introduction

"There's an app for that!"[1] This phrase sometimes erupts from students' lips when we discuss Buddhist meditation techniques, and they proceed to recount their experiences using Calm or Headspace. They come to my introductory Asian religions class having downloaded a meditation app or taken a yoga class, but they have rarely reflected on the ethical and cultural aspects of such consumption of Asian religious practices.[2] Although I previously incorporated Orientalist critiques[3] into the class so that students might interrogate their assumptions about Asian culture—indeed, the category of Asia altogether—the ensuing discussions about cultural essentialism and commodification always seemed to shift responsibility to others rather than acknowledge their own participation in the commercialization and consumption of religions.

In response I developed a critical, constructivist approach that surfaces students' prior knowledge about Asian religions and brings it into conversation with disciplinary critiques of consumption and commercialization.[4] Research shows that prior knowledge can help learning if it is activated, sufficient, appropriate, and accurate, but it can hinder learning when inactive, insufficient, inappropriate, or inaccurate.[5] Assessing students' prior knowledge allows instructors to redress misconceptions or inaccuracies that would otherwise impede their learning.

The Problem

How do we surface such knowledge when it makes up such a large part of our social reality? As Kate Lofton notes, all of us have some relationship to consumer culture: "Consumerism, the theory that a progressively greater consumption of goods is economically beneficial, has become the organizing value of social life."[6] Michael Storper remarks, "Consumerism, however it begins, ultimately sustains itself by becoming an intimate part of the action frameworks of individuals, how they see themselves and define their interests, how they approach the world, and how they present themselves to others."[7] Consumerism undergirds our sense of identity, our relationships, and our worldviews. How might instructors assess students' knowledge of such an integral part of their personal and social lives?

One way is to make the familiar unfamiliar. Specifically, we begin with the familiar (students' prior experience), introduce and explore the unfamiliar (theories of consumerism, commodification, Orientalism, etc.), and then apply the unfamiliar to the familiar (students analyzing a magazine and reevaluating their previous experience). The activity involves students in an everyday act of consumption—flipping through a magazine[8]—but asks them to adopt a more critical lens to the media consumed. It facilitates critical thinking by progressively moving up Bloom's taxonomy from defining theoretical terms, to identifying examples and instances in a magazine, to finally applying it to their own lives and habits of consumption.

Relevant Literature

Critical, constructivist, and participatory pedagogies emphasize the importance of tapping into students' curiosity, developing their capacity to examine their learning, their experience, and societal conditions, and encouraging them to question knowledge, society, and experience so that they can engage in critical thought and action. They seek to empower students to develop into citizens who think critically and act democratically.[9] As Peter McLaren writes, the learning process is one "through which students learn to critically appropriate knowledge existing outside their immediate experience in order to broaden their understanding of themselves, the world, and the possibilities for transforming the taken-for-granted assumptions about the way we live."[10]

Constructivism offers strategies for surfacing such prior knowledge. Constructivists view knowledge as personally and socially constructed. Jean Piaget argues that students learn by interpreting the results of their interactions with the environment, modifying existing knowledge structures as necessary. Lev Vygotsky says that learners personally construct their knowledge within a social context: we make personal meaning for ourselves, share that meaning with others, and develop collective understandings as a group. Constructivist Learning Design encourages instructors to frame the situation (the goals, tasks, and form of learning), group students, use bridges to surface students' prior knowledge, incorporate guiding and clarifying questions to challenge misconceptions and extend thinking, have students exhibit what they have learned, and finally engage in reflection about their personal and collective learning.[11]

Critical pedagogy encourages the unsettling of commonsense assumptions and the questioning of texts, institutions, and social relations.[12] As Paolo Friere writes, "In problem-posing education, people develop their power to perceive critically *the way they exist* in the world *with which* and *in which* they find themselves; they come to see the world not as a static reality, but as a reality in process, in transformation."[13] Learning involves the transformation, rather than the consumption, of knowledge. As Henry Giroux states, "Critical pedagogy asserts that students can engage their own learning from a position of agency and in so doing can actively participate in narrating their identities through a culture of questioning that opens up a space of translation between the private and the public while changing the forms of self- and social recognition."[14] Engaged pedagogy expects students to be critically aware and active participants in the learning process, and it also calls for instructors to be vulnerable themselves.[15]

Teaching Tactic

This teaching tactic was used within a midsize public university in the southeastern United States where students are predominantly white (84 percent), female (63 percent), and in-state (86 percent). It was taught within an introductory class on "Asian Religions" in the fifth week of the course. The teaching tactic filled the seventy-five minutes of class, though it could be adapted to a shorter class.

My strategy has five steps in which students (1) reflect on prior knowledge; (2) define theoretical terms of neoliberalism, consumerism, capitalism, spiritual capitalism, Orientalism, and Virtual Orientalism; (3) find and discuss examples in the popular magazine *Yoga Journal*; (4) reflect on ways they participate in neoliberalism, consumerism, spiritual capitalism, and Orientalism; and (5) discuss and reflect as a group on our responsibilities and participation in neoliberalism, consumerism, and spiritual capitalism.

To activate and surface prior knowledge, I begin by asking students to journal about their personal experience with Asian religions, asking: What do you think you know about Hinduism? What do you think you know about Buddhism? Where did you learn this information? Was it through: Talking with a friend or relative? Reading a book? Watching a movie? Visiting a religious site? (If you remember, list the names of the books, films, apps, etc. that you used to gain this knowledge.)

I share selections from scholarship on religion and consumption as well as Orientalism, and I provide a list of definitions of the following terms:

> **Neoliberalism**: an ideology that promotes individual competition for and the purchasing of all of one's needs through the market—which replaces the structures and even the concepts of social institutions and the public good. It redefines citizens as consumers, whose democratic choices are best exercised by buying and selling, a process that rewards merit and punishes inefficiency. (Liberalism being a theory in economics emphasizing individual freedom from restraint and usually based on free competition and the self-regulating market)
> **Consumerism**: the theory that a progressively greater consumption of goods is economically beneficial. Some argue it has become the organizing value of social life.
> **Capitalism:** an economic system characterized by private or corporate ownership of capital goods, by investments that are determined by private decisions, and by prices, production, and the distribution of goods that are determined mainly by competition in a free market.
> **Spiritual capitalism:** spirituality co-opted and reduced to being another commodity for sale
> **Orientalism**: a way of seeing that imagines, emphasizes, exaggerates, and distorts differences of Eastern vs. Western culture, viewing the former as exotic, backward, uncivilized, and at times dangerous.
> **Virtual Orientalism**: prevalent cultural stereotyping by visual forms of media.

We discuss each term to ensure that they have a decent grasp on their meaning.

I give each student a copy of *Yoga Journal* and ask them to find examples that could be critiqued as neoliberal, consumerist, capitalist, and Orientalist. As a class, we then discuss and debate the examples identified by students. I then ask them to identify the target audience, which they argue is white females, noting how people of color rarely appear, and if they do, it is often to authenticate certain practices or products. After agreeing with their assessment, I point out that I fit this target demographic: I am a white woman who practices, teaches, and consumes yoga, paying $15 for each class at my local yoga studio. I draw their attention to my name and address on the *Yoga Journal* subscription label and tell them it was gift purchased by a relative. In this way, I highlight my own participation in the consumption of religion.

I then have them reflect on their participation in spiritual capitalism and Orientalism by responding to a series of self-reflective questions: Reflecting on your prior knowledge about Hindu and Buddhist traditions, do you think they could be criticized as Orientalist? Reflecting on the ways you previously learned about Asian religions, or previously experienced yoga or meditation, do you think they were examples of consuming spirituality? Do you agree that consumerism has become the organizing value of social life? Why or why not? Can you think of examples of Orientalism (or Virtual Orientalism) that you have come across? In what ways have you found spirituality co-opted or reduced to being a commodity for sale?

We conclude the class by discussing and reflecting as a group about our responsibilities and participation in neoliberalism, consumerism, and spiritual capitalism. They debate and discuss the line between cultural appreciation and cultural appropriation, and we reflect as a group on what we learned individually and collectively about religious consumption and commercialization.

Findings

In the fall 2019 semester I incorporated this activity into two sections of my Asian Religions survey course, where we spent two weeks each studying Confucian, Daoist, Hindu, Sikh, Buddhist, Jain, and Japanese religious traditions. They did the activity at the beginning of the fifth week, when we began our study of Hinduism after studying Confucianism and Daoism. One section consisted of twenty first-year students (all of whom were female), who were participating in a residential Learning Community about Yoga and Mindfulness that includes a physical education course in yoga, a First Year Seminar, and Asian Religions. The other section had twenty-one students from all years, who were taking the course largely to fulfill a general education requirement for Historical and Philosophical Approaches and Living in a Global Society requirements.

In their survey about their prior learning about Hindu and Buddhist traditions, as well as prior exposure to yoga and meditation, students said they knew that Hindus worshipped multiple gods (thirty of forty-one students), the tradition originated in India (thirteen of forty-one students), they believed in reincarnation (eight of forty-one students) and were vegetarian or had food restrictions (six of forty-one students). They said that Buddhists followed the Buddha (twenty-five of forty-one), their goal was *nirvana* or enlightenment (eighteen of forty-one), they engaged in meditation (seven of forty-one), and they emphasize peace or non-violence (seven of forty-one). They largely learned this information from classes that they took in middle or high school (twenty of forty-one), though they also learned it from friends and family members (eleven of forty-one), especially Hindu friends. In both sections, about half of the students had done yoga previously (twenty-two of forty-one), with several mentioning that it was incorporated as a form of exercise or stretching in various sports. Comparatively few students had engaged in meditation (eight of forty-one students), but the vast majority mentioned that they did it to reduce anxiety or stress, in therapy, and two mentioned using the Headspace app.

In class, students identified many examples of cultural appropriation and religious consumption, including advertisements for products that "uplift the soul," marketing about the "chakra power of beer" or how a product draws three cultures into one, and smoothies that include the "healing powers of the Amazon." They pointed out images depicting people of color as exotic gurus, suggestions for how to cleanse karma, and the incorporation of Sanskrit and other languages in the magazine's graphics. They identified the target audience of *Yoga Journal* as white females, and they noted how people of color only appeared in order to "authenticate" certain practices or products. They noted how products—certain clothes, earrings, yoga mats, accessories—are portrayed as imparting a yoga lifestyle to the consumer. They also identified instances of Orientalism, such as the marketing of Acro-yoga, which emphasized how its founder is an "Iranian-born" guru.

The students had a lively group discussion about where one might draw the line between cultural appreciation and cultural appropriation. One student suggested that if you knew the underlying significance behind things, and you avoided purchasing $50 yoga pants because they are a particular brand, you would not cross into cultural appropriation. Others were less sure. Many students said you could do yoga and learn from people—either from India, or elsewhere—who have studied yoga. When it came to purchasing religious statues and objects, most students insisted that if one knew their significance and treated them with respect, it was okay to purchase statues of Siva or the Buddha. They said it would be no different from someone purchasing Gucci so that others perceive them as having a certain status. That particular analogy resonated with others in the class.

In their post-class reflection, half of the students said that their prior knowledge about Hindu and Buddhist traditions could be criticized as Orientalist (twenty-one of forty-one). They observed that those who taught them often had Orientalist perceptions, or that they considered Hindu practitioners exotic because they believed in many gods. Several remarked that unless one lived in Asian countries, it would be difficult to avoid such misperceptions. Among those who said their prior knowledge could not be criticized as Orientalist (seven of forty-one), they said that they derived their knowledge from classes or research, or that they learned from friends who practiced the religion. Reflecting on whether they had previously consumed spirituality, almost half said they had (seventeen of forty-one). They noted how they paid for yoga classes, how their classes were hot or cardio yoga workouts, and two specifically identified the brand Lululemon as promoting the idea that you need the best leggings or mat to have a good practice. Those that said they had not previously consumed spirituality said they had not paid for yoga, or it was focused on breathing and spiritual connection rather than toning one's muscles, or that they had learned about it in an educational context. One student who grew up in South Korea noted that the religious "things" she had were not bought.

Overwhelmingly students agreed that consumerism has become the organizing value of social life (thirty-nine of forty-one). Some students pointed out that societies depend on consumption to keep their economies running, and how any changes to purchasing goods would have detrimental effects on the economy and subsequently affect society. Most students wrote about the social pressure placed on having the newest or most expensive items in order to be seen as valuable or worthy, how every purchase "defines" them, and how they are constantly exposed to commercial advertising that tells them that they need certain items to fit in or have a better life. As one remarked, "Yes, most people believe the more 'stuff' you own the better you are and the cooler you'll be. Living in a materialistic society, consumerism strongly prevails." Another wrote, "In America, it's seen as a status symbol to wear or own designer products or have the newest tech. This starts conversations and can be seen as socially valuable." Another wrote, "I do not think that it is necessary to be social, but in today's society, it definitely advances your sociability." Several remarked that social media platforms contribute to this pressure, as they try to get you hooked on the next trend, or YouTubers flaunt their wealth to young fans. The two students that disagreed wrote that only some people view their consumption as a symbol of social status, and that most people did not think this way.

Students said they encountered many examples of Orientalism in American movies, television shows, cartoons, and video games. Several students (seven of forty-one) described seeing features of Jane Iwamura's "Oriental monk" in movies and shows: an old, wise, bald, robed man who, as one student remarked, "only speak when the sentence is considered 'deep' or 'philosophical.'" They described how such media portray the East as more spiritual and exotic than the West; as one wrote, "Growing up, I was under the impression that China was just farmland and traditional temples. This is because of cartoons." They identified particular films with Orientalist views, such as "Kungfu Panda," "Mulan," "The Great Wall," and "Big Trouble in Little China"—the last one, one student wrote, has "the hyper exaggerated version of Eastern/Chinese culture that leans heavily on the spiritual and mythological aspects of the culture." A few students (four of forty-one) described the stereotypical Asian martial arts expert in films (four of forty-one) and how often Asians were portrayed as speaking broken English. One student listed a series of tropes from popular media, including

> The Asian (mostly East Asian) equivalent of the manic pixie dream girl, but this time she's got cool blue/pink hair and can fight off a bunch of guards with her *katana*. The 'passive wife/girlfriend' trope with female Asian characters. The 'broken English' trope with *all* Asian characters. The 'stoic and quiet badass' trope that kind of plays off the monk trope for men.

For some, the question about Orientalism allowed them the opportunity to consider how Americans were portrayed in Asian popular media, as one wrote, "I also watch a decent amount of Asian media, mostly Japanese anime, and it is always fun to occasionally see their stereotypes of Americans being loud, rude, usually blonde, and sometimes just dumb."

Finally, when asked what ways they have found spirituality co-opted and reduced to being a commodity for sale, many students (eighteen of forty-one) noted how Buddha statues were often bought from stores like Hobby Lobby, World Market and Urban Outfitters and used to decorate homes and gardens. Many students (twelve of forty-one) also observed how crosses and *mala* beads were often worn as jewelry for stylistic rather than spiritual purposes. Some noted (eight of forty-one) how clothing and accessory often feature spiritual symbols or tribal prints to give it a "bohemian look" without acknowledging its religious meaning, and how many yoga products are geared toward fashion. As one student wrote, "For example, there are high-brand, expensive yoga pants geared towards those who want to show off their buying power. The same can be said of yoga mats: more expensive yoga mats have intricate patterns or specialized designs to show others how much money the owner can spend." Students identified a variety of things that exemplify spiritual capitalism: the selling of incense, essential oils, *henna*, tattoos, crystals, chakra bracelets, etc. One student shared how their yoga studios sold essential oils at the front desk claiming it would improve their yoga practice, and another wrote, "The Sanskrit OM is literally everywhere (like one of my bracelets made by Alex and Ani), and there are shirts that say 'Namaste in Bed.'" Two students identified spiritual retreats (yoga vacations, silent retreats, etc.) as an example of spiritual commodification; as one wrote, "Spiritual retreats that cost a lot of money is the example that sticks out most to me because they feel so insincere and like a fake spiritual experience that has no real meaning in the end because you paid for it." Such comments about the inauthenticity of purchased retreats create an opportunity to further distinguish between commodification—packaging an object or experience for sale outside of its original cultural context—and the fact that it takes money to sustain religious life and institutions. Instructors might point out that the cost of such retreats can be comparable to church tithing or synagogue membership, and they might draw into question why students discredit the former but defend the latter.[16] They can invite students to consider at which point such retreats become commodities or status symbols rather than religious or spiritual experiences.

Why It Works

Although some instructors may be reticent to tackle such a complex topic in an introductory course, the tactic works for several reasons. First, it surfaces misconceptions that would otherwise hinder learning. Students' prior knowledge can help learning if it is activated, sufficient, appropriate, and accurate, but it can hinder learning when inactive, insufficient, inappropriate, or inaccurate.[17] Assessing students' prior knowledge allows instructors to redress misconceptions or inaccuracies from the outset.

Second, it engages students in active learning as they find concrete examples of religious consumption in popular culture and reflect on their learning.[18] After defining and discussing theoretical terms, they apply their knowledge to the particular case of a popular magazine that they themselves might read in their daily lives. It mimics the act of consumption as they flip through their issue looking for examples of commercialization and commodification.

Finally, it draws attention to students' own participation in consumer culture, as they examine ways that they may have consumed spirituality and whether consumerism has become the organizing value of their social lives. It also encourages reflection on responsibilities that they have as consumers and citizens within neoliberal, capital society.

It could be adapted to other courses that similarly want to examine spiritual capitalism or the consumption of religion, and it could use other popular media including digital media. The underlying principle is that it surfaces prior learning, equips students with basic theoretical definitions that they apply to particular examples, and engages them in broader reflection about their own participation in the consumption of religion.

Conclusion

Although some instructors might be reticent to tackle such a complex topic in an introductory course, there are pedagogical payoffs when one addresses misconceptions that might arise from students' prior experience, such as the mistaken assumption that all Hindus practice yoga or all Buddhists meditate, at the outset. First and foremost, it redresses mistaken ideas that would otherwise remain unchecked and hinder learning through the semester. Secondly, it builds on aspects of prior experience that *were* appropriate or accurate, which can facilitate deeper learning for students. Finally, since instructors share their own misunderstandings with their students and work alongside students to generate collective understanding, they make space for everyone to acknowledge their responsibilities as members of consumer society.

8

Telling the Story of American Religions: Responding to Protestant and Pluralist Paradigms

Martha Smith Roberts

Introduction: Teaching American Religions

Telling the story of American religious history is an exercise in mythmaking. As instructors, we know that we are picking and choosing moments from the countless possibilities that history offers us. We craft a syllabus that attempts to be at once chronologically comprehensive and historically rich. This tension between breadth and depth is constant in survey courses. Our students, however, are often blissfully unaware of our struggle. They come to learn the unchanging facts of an unchanging history. Because I have been unable to resolve the tensions between breadth and depth, the tensions of narrative choice and normativity, I have tried to at least become more transparent about them in order to help dissolve what I see as the more problematic issue: the notion that there is one history of American religion at all. My introductory course in "American religions" is thus an exercise in laying bare the negotiations of power at work in narratives of American religion. Making the myth-making work of history clear to my students in a way that does not completely deconstruct and relativize human meaning-making is the new tension that I have decided to navigate in my course.

In terms of American religion, I am walking on well-trodden ground. How we tell this story has been the focus, and in some cases the life's work, of many scholars. Catherine Albanese, whose work on metaphysical religions serves as an example of shifting dominant narratives, has written extensively about the ways in which historians have consistently reshaped this story. Consensus histories centered Protestant traditions, conflict histories attempted to remedy this by centering minority traditions, and her own work, a combinative approach, looked at religion that defied traditional boundaries and existed alongside and fluidly intertwined with rigid institutional structures. In her widely used textbook *America: Religions and Religion*, she attempted to change the dominant narrative of the American religions introductory course as well, re-organizing the narrative to simultaneously decenter and interrogate Protestant dominance as a cultural force.[1]

Problem: Protestantism to Pluralism—Paradigms of Teaching American Religions

Even texts that problematize the optimism/idealism of these pluralist constructions can slip into an idealization of pluralism. For example, in *God is Not One*, Stephen Prothero condemns the "pretend pluralist" strategies that espouse an "all paths lead up the same mountain" notion of religious commonality. Instead of adopting the "all religions are one" mantra, he argues that difference is key to truly understanding religious traditions.[2] Similarly, in Prothero's new world religions textbook, *Religion Matters*, he argues against this pluralist perennialism, noting that "it just isn't true that the beliefs and practices of the world's religions are essentially the same, and it isn't helpful either."[3] A better form of pluralism is implied, one that recognizes difference, and not just similarity. The idea that we can teach an authentic form of American religion by acknowledging diversity is itself a product of pluralist idealism. Diana Eck's Pluralist Project at Harvard is one foundational example of the push for religious literacy that embraces diversity. These forms of pluralist education are seen as progress, a move away from a Protestant-centered narrative that erases minority groups and traditions. And, of course, they do offer nuance and complexity overlooked by those early accounts.

Often the discussion of diversity in the American religions classroom is rooted in this additive impulse in which, either through the lens of similarity or difference, talking about more religions is the most important determiner of both diversity and pluralism, and therefore, accuracy. However, this approach also creates a narrative that can be quite misleading to students who are learning the story of American religions for the first time. Texts like Diana Eck's *A New Religious America: How a "Christian Country" Has Become the World's Most Religiously Diverse Nation* can, despite their best efforts, create a sense of equity and inclusion for minority traditions that just is not real. Focusing on difference and struggle helps, but often the larger "lesson" is the triumph of religious freedom in the United States. Religions are added, they struggle, they assimilate to some degree, and then we have religious pluralism. To avoid this kind of essentializing, teaching students about pluralism must be separated from teaching students to be pluralist, the former offers space for critical thinking, the latter perpetuates a pluralist paradigm that is an extension of the Protestant-centered template it seeks to replace.

In a sense, we can think about this problem in American religions as a microcosm of the world religions paradigm, a hegemonic construction thoroughly examined by Tomoko Masuzawa in *The Invention of World Religions: Or, How European Universalism was Preserved in the Language of Pluralism*. Masuzawa's now classic work deconstructs the notion of "world religions" as neutral or equitable practice, and instead reveals its deep entanglements with Protestant theology and European universalism. In fact, she argues that the idea of diversity may be "the very thing that facilitates the transference and transmutation of a particular absolutism from one context to another—from the overtly exclusivist hegemonic version (Christian supremacist dogmatism) to the openly pluralistic universalist one (world religions pluralism)—and at the same time makes this process of transmutation very hard to identify and nearly impossible to understand."[4] When we apply this theorization to the concept of pluralism in the American religions classroom, we see the same machinations at work: the acknowledgment of diversity as an improvement over the blatant discrimination of past accounts, and the flawed notion that pluralism itself is somehow immune from the hegemonic ideological workings of diversity.

Lori Beaman's work on the legal inequalities carried out under the banner of diversity in North America reveals some of the dangers of accepting pluralism at face value. Her critique of scholarship on diversity can translate quite directly to the classroom. She notes that the focus

> on religious diversity or, perhaps more accurately, diverse religions, has a laudable background. It represents a shift in focus to the religiously marginalized ... However, the effect of this has been to sometimes give the false impression that these groups represent a majority of religious participants who are assumed to be legally protected and socially accepted, and thus [create] the illusion that they somehow hold an "equal" place in society.[5]

Here we see the conflation of religious diversity (the existence of diverse traditions) and religious pluralism (the ideal way in which diverse religions should coexist in society). Again, to quote Beaman:

> The very existence of religions outside the mainstream is sometimes taken as evidence of ... a flourishing margin that is eroding the hegemony of mainstream Protestantism and that represents the positive effects of a constitutional regime

that officially separates church and state. In fact, there has been little erosion of the hegemony of the religious mainstream. Diversity is diversity of "brands" or style, and represents a shift in religious form that remains true to Protestant substance.[6]

In the American religions classroom, we thus face a dilemma of not just who to include in the content of the class, but how to include them in a way that does not simply replicate a narrative of the triumph of public Protestant values as pluralism and religious freedom. To do this, especially in an introductory course, is a challenge. We want students to see the diversity of American religious life. However, we do not want them to stop there and assume that this diversity represents a point along an inevitable progression of a Protestant pluralist ideal that has succeeded in creating an inclusive and equitable environment for all minority traditions (i.e., the perfection of religious liberty). To counter this kind of easy American exceptionalism, I present the course thematically rather than chronologically, and power and cultural norms become the center of the narrative. In other words, this is not simply *the* history of religion in America, it is a history that is contested and constructed, and one whose telling depends on the narrator.

The project of teaching American religions as a history, a concept, and a process is quite daunting. The introductory course challenges me every semester. I try to balance content and form, and I rely on paradigms (of religion, religious literacy, tolerance, American identity, diversity, pluralism, and more) to guide the class, even as we seek to disrupt them. The class examines American religion from three perspectives, based on three different answers to the question "what is American religion?" The answers to that question, for the scope of this survey course, take "America" to mean the United States, and they build upon common conceptions of what counts as American religion. We begin with Protestants ("America is a Christian nation"), move to minority traditions ("America is home to every religion"), and then finish with American-made religions ("American religions are those that begin in America"). Each unit relies upon—and pushes back against—ways of thinking about "American religion."[7]

Solutions: Making Paradigms Visible

My own reorganization of the content of this narrative is of course, not the first attempt to do so. I draw upon several scholars who attempt to contextualize the story of American religion in terms of the influences of Protestant culture.

Catherine Albanese's widely used textbook not only provides a reconfiguration of the narrative, in it she also models how to deal with the "public Protestantism" central to religion in the United States.[8] Charles Long's work, especially on American Civil Religion, also directly deals with the "epic saga of mighty deeds" that is a part of the "American cultural language," a language of power that renders some groups visible, others invisible.[9] I introduce students to short texts from Albanese and Long, as well as Albert Raboteau, Khyati Joshi, Jane Iwamura, and others, all of whom challenge the dominant narrative.[10] All of these authors offer versions of American religious history that reveal the fissures, conflicts, and erasures that remain peripheral to the pluralist paradigm.

In addition to the content of the course reflecting religious studies scholarship that pushes back against the pluralist paradigm, the scholarship on teaching and learning also models the ways in which this can be done effectively. To recognize and reject a paradigm is to commit to radical rethinking of accepted ways of knowing. This is no small task for introductory students. Critical thinking is central to this endeavor, and critical thinking must be learned. Several recent works have focused on the process of building skills in the religious studies classroom.[11] Jenna Gray-Hildenbrand and Rebekka King use the competencies of description, analysis, and critique as the framework for Middle Tennessee State University's religious studies major.[12] Eugene Gallagher and Joanne Maguire recently published a student-centered text on religious studies skills that focuses on close reading, critical thinking, and comparison.[13] These competency-based frameworks support the fact that students gain knowledge and transferable skills not simply from mastering content but from practicing a variety of ways of knowing and interacting with that content.

In "The Necessary Lie: Duplicity in the Disciplines," Jonathan Z. Smith notes that "We are really lying, and lying in a relatively deep fashion, when we consistently disguise, in our introductory courses, what is problematic about our work."[14] But what if we can avoid these lies and make the problematic elements visible? In my American religions introductory course, I am attempting to increase transparency and to give students a chance to practice describing, analyzing, and critiquing the narrative of the course itself. While they cannot change the events of the nineteenth century, they can begin to see that the events we choose to include in the narrative can be changed, and that these changes have consequences in the real world. Similarly, as we begin to think through the power structures that have organized the narrative of American religions in the past, we can begin to think of ways that we could tell the story differently. Perhaps the pluralist narrative of religious diversity as additive and indicative of religious liberty is not the best or most accurate telling. I ask them to come up with their own narrative structures and to imagine how their stories might change the real world as well. The truth-telling that Smith is interested in takes on another layer of meaning in this context. We are not simply trying to uncover the lies; we are trying to challenge the power structures that sanction them, albeit, in a very controlled setting.

In a broad sense, bell hooks's teaching trilogy offers insights into the ways in which educators can challenge hegemonic ways of knowing by teaching to transgress, teaching community, and teaching critical thinking. In one of her insightful chapters, she gives particular attention to the role of imagination in creating and sustaining an engaged classroom, and she reminds us that "what we cannot imagine cannot come into being."[15] For me, creativity and imagination, even as smaller moments woven into the fabric of a fundamentally rigid semester schedule, offer students the possibility to think critically about what problems and solutions might exist. When applying this to a pluralist paradigm, I ask students to imagine their own ideal way to navigate diversity and to tell the story of American religions.[16]

Teaching Tactic: Table of Contents: Creating Narratives of American Religion

In this exercise students are working on several important religious studies skills, and they are asked to utilize description, analysis, and critique.[17] Students first describe the narratives of American religion they observe in their assigned texts, next they analyze the power structures at work in those narratives, finally they offer a critique of those narratives in the form of a creative revision. To begin, students examine the tables of contents from several textbooks and classic histories of American religion. Students are divided into small groups and asked to examine one text in detail. As a group they answer descriptive questions together (see below). Each group then "presents" some of the details of their book to the class. And everyone has access to a file or handout with the title page, table of contents, and introductions of the books for reference.

We begin with descriptive work: What do these books contain? Which traditions? What order of appearance? What larger narrative is reflected? Chronological or thematic? There is also a handout (or online space) for the group to record this information and other basic observations on the work (authors, publishers, year published, number of pages/volumes, table of contents information, genre, intended audience, and more). After the group presentations, we work together as a class to answer comparative questions and analyze the narratives. This includes looking for patterns that reveal power structures and dominant traditions. Are some identities centered, while others are made peripheral to "American" religion? How does the story change in these different examples? What does shifting the narrative order of events do to change our conception of American religion?

I then ask students to compare these texts to our class textbooks (John Corrigan and Lynn Neal's *Religious Intolerance in America* and Bret Carroll's *Historical Atlas of Religion in America*)[18] and the course syllabus as examples of other ways of organizing the story of American religion. As a class, we discuss ways that we could write "good" narratives of American religion. What does this mean? Objectivity? Centering different groups for different reasons? New perspectives? We come up with examples of possible narratives. Finally, back in their small groups, students decide on their own choice of a narrative of American religion. The second major part of this assignment is producing that narrative.

In their small groups, students create a textbook for a class like ours without replicating any of the examples from class. They decide on a title, table of contents, and very short introduction or abstract. They also decide on their own perspective and use that as the organizing principle. Each group takes a different perspective, recognizing that this positionality is key to this project. We begin this process in class. However, the actual production of the groups' textbooks happens outside of the classroom as well. This means providing time for small group work in additional class sessions, often the last fifteen minutes of class, and outside of class as well. Students then return the next week and do a group presentation of their textbooks for the class. Students are encouraged to be creative and to use a variety of means to communicate their position: cover art, title, authors' names, acknowledgment/epigraph, publishers, table of contents, abstracts, introductions, and other genre-specific markers.

This activity is meant to tie explicitly to the course learning outcomes at my institution that require that students identify and explain important events that have shaped the American religious experience, compare and contrast religious movements that arose in response to American Protestantism, and analyze two effects that modernity had on American religious life. As students describe and analyze well-known textbooks and create their own, they are asked to consider these questions. The activity is a cumulative one, we work on it at the end of the semester, and it gives students the opportunity to review the course content and theory. It also demands critical thinking and writing skills, as they must explain why they are making particular content and structural choices in their projects. In a sense, there is no wrong way to organize the textbook as long as students have evidence and arguments to back up their choices.

Conclusions

While the ideal of pluralism can be quite appealing at first glance, it is not a neutral claim or narrative, but rather, an extension of previous narratives that continue to center Protestant experience and marginalize others. In American religious studies particularly, many scholars have written extensively about this dominant white Protestant national narrative. However, when teaching American religions it can be difficult to offer students a way to think outside of pluralism as the solution, or to see that a pluralist paradigm can be equally hegemonic.

This tactic investigates how American religion is constructed in relation to power, and it gives students a chance to "play" with that power by telling a different story. It also reinforces earlier lessons on positionality, shared American cultural knowledge, and the ideas of invisible and visible histories, religions, and identities. The assignment also allows for creative forms of writing and expression. Not only do students have to imagine a new narrative structure, they can also play with other forms of storytelling and narrative convention to make the retelling even more creative. Expanding the parameters for the audience or genre a bit can be one way to do this. For example, an American religions textbook for elementary school children that centers the Black American experience will create spaces for a very different form of storytelling than a college intro textbook but would be equally important exercise.[19]

The main lesson I want students to leave with is that there is no one way to tell the story. Every telling is a retelling. This does not equal meaningless relativism, however, quite the opposite. The way we tell the story is in fact extremely meaningful and just as powerful. In a recent chapter on innovative pedagogies that reconstruct religious studies after the world religions paradigm, David McConeghy discusses having students watch *God in America,* a 2010 PBS miniseries about American religious history, and then asking them about the possible changes that can be made to the narrative of American religions portrayed in the series. He suggests straightforward substitutions, like "What if Catholic New Spain is emphasized instead of Puritan New England?" or "How might the Civil Rights movement look if the focus is placed on Malcolm X instead of Martin Luther King, Jr.?"[20] McConeghy's pedagogical strategy here is quite similar to my own: find narratives that can captivate students, and then ask students to deconstruct and reconstruct them in ways that both maintain historical integrity and contain new possibilities. While his assignment is in some ways on the micro level, mine is on the macro level. Both levels have endless possibilities for creativity, critical thinking, and historical analysis. The important part of this lesson for me is that students begin to understand that telling the story of American religious history is an exercise in mythmaking, an exercise that they are participating in whether they accept a narrative or challenge it. The practice of challenging narratives of power is a transferable skill of its own, one that I hope my students will continue to practice outside of the classroom as well.

Appendix: Narratives of American Religions: Textbook Tables of Contents

Each group will examine their assigned text and record information to share with the class. Start with the basic descriptive information then, start thinking about the Table of Contents specifically and what it tells you about this narrative. There are three parts to this assignment sheet, we will work through them together in class.

PART ONE: Descriptive Information
Authors or editors (list names):
Publisher and year published:
Number of pages, volumes, and/or editions:
Genre (is this a textbook or something else?)
Who is the intended audience?

PART TWO: Contents as Mythmaking
What do these books contain? Which traditions?
How is the book organized? (What comes first, last?)
What larger narrative is reflected? Chronological or thematic?
How many pages are allotted to different traditions?
Are some traditions missing or overlooked?
Which traditions are central to the narrative?
Where is Protestantism?
How is diversity represented?

In the introduction, does the author/editor give any information about why they organized the book this way?

In the introduction, how does the author/editor describe or define "American religion"?

PART THREE: Creating Narratives of American Religion

(Answer each question as you design your TOC and textbooks. Don't forget to explain why.)

What important events in American religious history must be included if we are to accurately describe the American religious experience? Why?

Which religious traditions should be central to the narrative? Why?

Which are peripheral? Why?

Which will you leave out? Why?

How does Protestantism fit in? Which religious traditions are responses to Protestant dominance? How do we tell this story?

How did major historical periods (colonialism, modernity) shape the story of American religion?

Who is your intended audience?

How will your textbook define "American religion"?

How do you explain the organization of the book? What is the organizing principle of your work?

What power relations are reflected in your organization of the material?

9

Teaching Critical Religious Studies in the World Religions Public Sphere

Henry Goldschmidt

Introduction

This essay will explore a fundamental tension in my work at the Interfaith Center of New York (ICNY), where I develop religious diversity education programs for a range of audiences, including K-12 teachers, social workers, police officers, and the general public.[1] On the one hand, ICNY's education programs work to subvert and exceed the limitations of "world religions" pedagogy—a pedagogic model that reduces the vibrant diversity of religious life to a fixed set of relatively static traditions, each of which is defined by a fixed set of ostensibly common characteristics, including its doctrines or beliefs, sacred texts, and major holidays. On the other hand, however, ICNY's education programs need to meet the needs of partner organizations and professional audiences who tend to think about religion in just such terms.

This tension is at once conceptual, political, and pedagogical. Like a growing number of religious studies scholars, I am convinced that world religions pedagogy constitutes a form of cultural imperialism—reimagining the practices and beliefs of diverse communities in conceptual terms dictated by European Christian, and largely Protestant, thought. While it sets out to celebrate religious diversity, it ends up (in Tomoko Masuzawa's memorable phrase), "[preserving] European universalism in the language of pluralism."[2] Even more importantly, to me at least, world religions pedagogy simply does not do justice to the depth and complexity of religious life. It misses all of the subtle details, and thus promotes a superficial form of religious literacy—substituting a decontextualized knowledge of dates and doctrines for an empathic understanding of one's neighbors' lives. Let's just say I'm not a fan.[3]

And yet, like a growing number of civically engaged scholars, I am convinced that academic knowledge production must be shaped by the needs and concerns of the communities it serves.[4] Public educators in academia and the nonprofit sector cannot simply impart expert knowledge to passive audiences. We are not Moses, coming down from the mountain. We must meet our partners where they are, engaging together with a shared social world, even if they see that world in terms we do not entirely share. In my case, this commitment to community-based education means teaching in ways that help professionals work effectively in social contexts structured in terms of "world religions"—in what I will describe as the world religions public sphere.

Let me offer an introductory example, to flesh out this dilemma in practical terms. In 2016, ICNY collaborated with the filmmakers Lea Sheloush and Sean McGinn to create a twenty-minute religious diversity training video for the New York City Police Department, which came to be called *Policing in Today's Multifaith New York*.[5] The video offers extremely brief introductions to the city's seven largest religious communities (Christians, Jews, Muslims, Hindus, Buddhists, Sikhs, and members of African diaspora faith traditions), while highlighting the diversity within these communities, and resisting generalizations about them. It is built around interviews with local religious leaders, and images of local religious life. By exploring themes that cut across communal boundaries—like religious dress and sacred space—it places the city's faith traditions in conversation, rather than setting them apart with artificial clarity. In other words, we tried to meet the needs of NYPD officers while avoiding world religions pedagogy.

In 2020, however, our partners in the NYPD approached us to ask if ICNY could create a new series of training videos. They liked *Policing in Today's Multifaith New York*, and were using it for training in the Police Academy and other contexts, but they were concerned that a twenty-minute video was not accessible to officers while they are "on the job." They asked if we could create a series of seven separate three-minute videos, each introducing a single religious tradition. Ideally, they said, all seven videos should follow a uniform structure or template, so officers can easily find the same information about each tradition, including key beliefs, major holidays, and advice for respectful interactions. In other words, they really want world religions pedagogy.

As the project moves ahead, we will likely find a middle ground between our differing approaches to religious diversity, but let me be clear about one thing: the NYPD's insistence on world religions pedagogy will not stand in the way of our collaborative work. We at ICNY may feel that a series of brief videos following a uniform—arguably cookie-cutter—template does not do justice to the rich religious diversity of the city, but we trust our NYPD colleagues' judgment that this is what police officers need. We might be the experts on religious diversity, but we are surely not experts on community policing. We have never sat in a patrol car in front of a gurudwara, for example, trying to learn something about Sikhism in the five minutes before our appointment with a community leader. ICNY is working to build a more inclusive city for all New Yorkers—in this case, by helping NYPD officers understand the religious lives of the people they serve—and this sometimes means sacrificing theoretical principles in order to work collaboratively with partner organizations, in a way that respects our partners' understandings of their own needs.

In the body of this essay, I will explore some of the pedagogic principles and teaching tactics that have helped me navigate the tensions sketched here—exceeding the limitations of world religions pedagogy, while helping professionals work effectively in the world religions public sphere. I will stress the importance of teaching about the diversity within all faith traditions, as well as the personal stories and political projects that connect those traditions to people's lives. I will argue that one way to do so is by facilitating panel discussions with diverse religious leaders, and suggest guidelines for structuring such conversations.

First, however, I will connect the tensions shaping my work at ICNY to broader questions of teaching, learning, and knowledge production by discussing Michel Foucault's distinction between "universal" and "specific" intellectuals, as well as his underlying arguments about the relationship between power and knowledge. This theoretical detour will raise—and hopefully clarify—far-reaching issues about the role of academic knowledge in social life.

"Compatriot of Power": Working within World Religions

There is a second-order, analytical tension running through my description of the pedagogic tensions that shape my work at ICNY. On the one hand, I have argued that world religions pedagogy is inadequate, in part, because it does not do justice to the complex realities of religious diversity. On the other hand, however, I have argued that world religions pedagogy is appropriate, even necessary, at times, because it reflects widely shared perceptions of religious diversity—perceptions that are themselves realities, as they are linked to social practices and institutions. World religions pedagogy, in my account, seems to both betray and reflect our everyday experiences of religious diversity.

This is an important tension, but not a contradiction. The world religions framework is undoubtedly a historical product of European colonialism, Christian hegemony, and other social forces—a "social construction," in the overused but still valuable slogan of contemporary critical theory. But that does *not* mean it is not real. It is a poor description of religious diversity, yet it has shaped the contours of that diversity, including the self-described religious identities of many New Yorkers, as well as the ways that authoritative institutions—like K-12 schools, the police, and social service agencies—engage with the city's religious communities. I may not be a fan of the world religions framework, but I still work within its constructed-but-real constraints. I cannot simply wish it away, and I cannot teach effectively if I pretend to do so.

According to the historian and social theorist Michel Foucault, this is the predicament—and power—of the "specific intellectual." In a written response to a 1977 interview question, later published in English as "Truth and Power," Foucault distinguishes between two ways academics have sought to contribute to civic life and social justice struggles.[6] For Foucault, the "universal intellectual" claims to speak as a kind of secular prophet, from an ethically or epistemically privileged position outside of the systems and institutions they critique. They render judgment "as the spokesman of the universal,"[7] giving voice to timeless truths and principles. Think Jean-Paul Sartre in the mid-twentieth century, or ironically Foucault himself as he is often read in the twenty-first. The "specific intellectual," by contrast, makes more limited assertions and targeted interventions, "within specific sectors, at the precise points where their own conditions of life or work situate them."[8] Far from occupying an ethically privileged position, they are often compromised by their morally ambiguous role within the systems or institutions they critique—they are "technicians," working "in the service of the State or Capital."[9] Foucault's example is the dissident atomic scientist Robert Oppenheimer, whose peace activism rested, in part, on his uncomfortable relationship with the military-industrial complex. Somewhat similarly, though on a much smaller scale, my efforts to build a more just and inclusive society rest, in part, on my ambivalent relationships with institutions like the NYPD—hardly a consistent champion of social justice or inclusion.[10]

As a "specific intellectual" working at a small nonprofit organization, I draw whatever power I may have from this network of relationships, and this network situates me—like it or not—within the world religions public sphere. My modest ability to advance truth claims with an impact on the world is entirely dependent on my personal and professional ties with religious and civic leaders, teachers, social workers, police, and countless others, as well as ICNY's institutional ties with peer organizations, civic institutions, government agencies, foundation funders, and others. My work must meet their needs and expectations, as a threshold of its viability—even if those needs and expectations are shaped by flawed assumptions about "world religions."

Of course, this is equally true of university-based scholars, whose research and teaching must meet the needs and expectations of their students, colleagues, administrators, publishers, and many others. Indeed, for Foucault, *all* truth claims are produced within such power-laden social networks. There is no truth without power, and therefore no innocent or unfettered position from which to make assertions about the world. As Foucault puts it:

> The important thing here, I believe, is that truth isn't outside power, or lacking in power: contrary to a myth whose history and functions would repay further study, truth isn't the reward of free spirits, the child of protracted solitude, nor the privilege of those who have succeeded in liberating themselves. Truth is a thing of this world: it is produced only by virtue of multiple forms of constraint.[11]

This is as much the case in a graduate seminar as in a police training video, but these constraints are made particularly clear in education programs for professional audiences, as these audiences—unlike many academics—are primarily concerned with truth as "a thing of this world."

The people who participate in ICNY's education programs are not generally interested in learning about religious diversity for its own sake. Most are curious about the topic personally, but they attend (and sometimes pay registration fees) to gain knowledge they can *use* in their work. In Foucauldian terms, they are concerned with the power effects of knowledge—the practices and relationships made possible by an understanding of religious diversity. As Foucault argues: "'Truth' is linked in a circular relation with systems of power which produce and sustain it, and to effects of power which it induces and which extend it."[12] ICNY's education programs "[induce] effects of power" for the audiences we serve, helping them reshape the everyday social world through the application of expert knowledge—for example, by helping teachers, social workers, and police officers build relationships with religiously diverse students, clients, and community leaders, or by helping them design what we hope will be more inclusive lesson plans, treatment plans, and public safety plans.[13] This "circular relation" between power, knowledge, and practice is what Foucault famously describes as a "regime of truth."[14]

This regime depends upon the conceptual fit among its constituent discourses, practices, and institutions—never a perfect fit, but at least a working alignment of ICNY's education programs, New York's religious communities, and the professional lives of teachers, social workers, and police. Which brings us back, in what I hope are more precise or subtle terms, to the familiar dilemma of "world religions." If ICNY's education programs were entirely defined by world religions pedagogy they would fail to "[induce] effects of power" for professional audiences, because they would not reflect the realities of religious diversity. But if they entirely disregarded it they would fail just the same, because they would not reflect the institutional structures within which our students work. Our programs might still be interesting—perhaps *more* interesting—without world religions, but they would not provide knowledge people can use.

This does not mean, however, that we have no freedom of movement within constraint—no space for critique or creativity in the ways we teach. We can and do find ways to exceed the limitations of world religions pedagogy, while still meeting the needs of the audiences we serve. Again Foucault, in a written answer to another 1977 interview, later published in English as "Power and Strategies":

> It seems to me that power *is* "always already there," that one is never "outside" it, that there are no "margins" for those who break with the system to gambol in. But this does not entail the necessity of accepting an inescapable form of domination … To say that one can never be "outside" power does not mean that one is trapped and condemned to defeat no matter what. …[R]esistance to power does not have to come from elsewhere to be real, nor is it inexorably frustrated through being the compatriot of power.[15]

I can now restate the fundamental question of this essay, in what I hope are helpful Foucauldian terms: How do ICNY's education programs offer meaningful resistance to the world religions "regime of truth," while working as a "compatriot of [its] power"? The next two sections will answer this question by describing some of the pedagogic principles that guide our work, and one of the teaching tactics that brings those principles to life.

Pedagogic Principles: Internal Diversity, the Personal and Political

In this section I will sketch two broad principles that help ICNY's education programs complicate—and occasionally subvert—world religions pedagogy from within. In each case, I will introduce a scholarly critique of the world religions framework, point out some of the challenges in applying this critique to education programs for professional audiences, then show how ICNY's pedagogy nevertheless addresses key elements of the critique.

Highlight the Internal Diversity of Faith Traditions and Communities

Scholarly critiques of the world religions framework often highlight the colonial histories and artificially clear boundaries of the phenomena typically described as "religions." A growing number of scholars have argued, in short, that the "ism" in terms like Judaism or Buddhism—the process of reification that makes these fluid traditions appear to be static objects—is a product of Christian hegemony and cultural imperialism. Of course, this does *not* mean that the world's diverse faith traditions were simply fabricated by colonial powers. But it does suggest that their contemporary forms emerged through power-laden encounters with dominant Christian societies—they are, in David Chidester's phrase, "European and indigenous cocreations."[16] For example, in *Religion and the Specter of the West*, Arvind-Pal S. Mandair shows how European Christian assumptions about the exclusive nature of religious identity led nineteenth- and early twentieth-century Sikh reformers to highlight, or perhaps invent, a clear distinction between Sikhism and Hinduism—a distinction that betrayed the multiplicity and fluidity of South Asian traditions.[17] "In this view," writes Mandair, "every time an Indian responds to the word 'religion' s/he is obliged to speak … in another's language, breaking with her own and in so doing giving herself up to the other."[18]

In time, I hope critical analyses like Mandair's will help scholars and others understand the heterogenous languages of identity, community, and cosmology that are simultaneously translated and obscured by the category of religion. But in the short run, unfortunately, this deconstructive or genealogical approach is not so helpful for K-12 teachers, who are often required—by both state standards and community expectations—to use curricula structured in terms of distinct and equivalent "religions." It is difficult to interrogate the distinction between Sikhism and Hinduism, for example, when each is found in its own textbook chapter—and when Sikh and Hindu students, parents, and community leaders insist, for understandable reasons, on separate and equal curricular representation. Similarly, questioning the boundaries of familiar faith traditions will not help social workers or police work effectively with self-described Sikhs and Hindus, or Christians and Jews, regardless of the fraught histories of such terms.[19] As I have argued, these categories are constructed but real. The professional audiences ICNY serves cannot simply step outside of them.

Rather than interrogating the external boundaries of religious traditions, ICNY's education programs highlight their complex, shifting contents—stressing the racial, ethnic, gendered, generational, and doctrinal diversity within all faith traditions and communities. This emphasis on intra-faith diversity takes different forms in different contexts. For example, the panel discussions I will discuss below often place diverse faith leaders from a single tradition in conversation. A panel of Christian community leaders at ICNY's summer institute for teachers might include the White, female, purple-haired pastor of a theologically progressive mainline Protestant church, a theologically conservative but politically radical Latino Pentecostal pastor and seasoned community organizer, the young volunteer bishop of a local ward of the Church of Jesus Christ of Latter-Day Saints, and an Irish-American social justice educator from Catholic Charities—and their conversation would soon be followed by a visit to an African-American Baptist church. Similarly, our 2016 NYPD training video includes, among other examples of internal diversity, a visual montage of Muslim New Yorkers—Arab, South Asian, African-American, African immigrant, Albanian, and others; young and old; men, women, and children; with and without hijab and niqab. By highlighting such forms of intra-faith diversity, we emphasize the fact that faith traditions and communities are never static or monolithic.

This approach splits the difference, so to speak, between the homogenous "religions" of conventional world religions pedagogy and the fluid heterogeneity revealed by critical religious studies scholarship. We remind our students that religious identities are never as simple as they are sometimes made to seem, while leaving in place the fundamental categories that structure the world religions public sphere.

Highlight Faith-Based Personal Stories and Political Projects

While the world religions framework focuses almost exclusively on canonical doctrine, ritual, and text, scholars of what is often called "lived religion" tend to explore quirky forms of religious practice and belief that flout formal doctrines or cut across the boundaries of established faiths. This emphasis on religious creativity stands in contrast to stereotypic images of hidebound, rule-following religious life. One influential example of this approach is Robert Orsi's analysis of the "Bronx Lourdes" grotto—a replica of the Grotto of the Apparitions in Lourdes, France, built in 1939 in what was, at the time, a working-class Italian-

American neighborhood in the Bronx.[20] Orsi shows how a wide range of New Yorkers (not all Catholic) put the grotto's "holy water" (which comes straight from the tap, as nearly all visitors are well aware) to creative uses such as filling their car radiators "for protection on the road."[21] Orsi argues that such practices:

> invite a redirection of religious scholarship away from traditions—the great hypostatized constructs of "Protestantism," "Catholicism," and so on—and likewise away from the denominational focus that has preoccupied scholars of American religions, toward a study of how particular people, in particular places and times, live in, with, through, and against the religious idioms available to them in culture—*all* the idioms, including (often enough) those not explicitly their "own."[22]

Orsi thus finds a transgressive fluidity in contemporary American religious life much like that which Mandair locates in precolonial South Asian traditions.

ICNY's education programs have been deeply shaped by scholarship on lived religion. In fact, we regularly bring K-12 teachers to visit the Bronx Lourdes grotto, and encourage them to teach about such practices and beliefs. Our

Figure 9.1 K-12 teachers Lavie Raven (left) and Aaron Bible explore the Bronx Lourdes grotto at the 2017 Religious Worlds of New York summer institute for teachers. Courtesy of Kevin Childress.

conferences for social workers, religious leaders, and others are committed to showing how diverse New Yorkers "live in, with, through, and against … religious idioms." But Orsi's call to look beyond the "hypostatized constructs" of traditions and denominations is not especially useful in programs for social workers and police. These professional audiences tend to seek clear, more-or-less causal ties between faith traditions and the actions or perceptions of community members, so it would undercut their impetus to study religion if ICNY programs highlighted the ways New Yorkers draw on "religious idioms … not explicitly their 'own.'" Why, our program participants would justifiably ask, should I learn about Buddhism or Islam, for example, if the Buddhists and Muslims do not follow their own traditions in patterned, consistent ways?

To convey the vibrant creativity of lived religion, while (usually) remaining within the boundaries of established faiths, ICNY's education programs stress the role of religious values and beliefs in people's everyday lives and political projects. Rather than asking speakers to discuss their faith in abstract, theological terms, we ask them to tell stories that illustrate the role of their faith in their personal life, professional work, or social activism. For example, at a 2019 conference for social workers exploring "Faith-Based Perspectives on Trauma and Healing," faith-based mental health professionals shared the scriptural passages, ritual practices, and other spiritual resources that helped them heal from their own personal traumas, or treat religiously diverse trauma survivors. At a 2020 conference for religious and civic leaders exploring "The Climate Crisis and New York Faith Communities," faith-based activists and community leaders discussed the religious values that inspire them to work for environmental sustainability.

Every once in a while, a Jewish or Muslim leader, for example, will share how they have been influenced by Thich Nhat Hanh or the *Bhagavad Gita*—or by the moral wisdom of their grandma. But most of our speakers reflect on authoritative sources from their "own" faith traditions. ICNY's focus on personal stories and political projects thus blunts the transgressive edge of lived religion scholarship, while nevertheless complicating the static view of doctrine at the heart of the world religions framework. By eliciting stories from religious leaders, we offer human portraits of what Orsi describes as religion "taken up in [people's] hands."[23]

Teaching Tactic: Panel Discussions with Religious Leaders

There are any number of ways for classroom teachers and public educators to highlight the internal diversity of religious traditions, and the personal stories and political projects that connect those traditions to people's lives. These pedagogic principles may be adapted to serve a wide range of students, in different curricula and classroom settings. For example, students can explore the diversity within religious communities by reading classic novels like Chaim Potok's *The Chosen* or James Baldwin's *Go Tell it on the Mountain*—each of which portrays interpersonal conflicts linked to deep tensions within American Jewish and African-American Christian communities, respectively.[24] And the Pluralism Project's Case Initiative offers a remarkable collection of case studies for use in classroom teaching—decision-based cases that place students in the shoes of diverse Americans, as they take their religions "up in their hands."[25] Given such resources, I do not mean to suggest a one-size-fits-all approach to subverting world religions pedagogy from within.

However, in most ICNY education programs we realize the pedagogic principles sketched above by facilitating conversations between program participants and groups of diverse religious leaders. These panel discussions sometimes explore multifaith perspectives on a topic or theme, and sometimes explore the diversity with a single tradition. Despite the reservations expressed by the American Academy of Religion,[26] such conversations with religious leaders seem to be increasingly common in religious studies

Figure 9.2 Brooklyn rabbis Avi Lesches (left) and Heidi Hoover speak on a panel discussion at the 2012 Religious Worlds of New York summer institute for teachers. Courtesy of The Interfaith Center of New York.

classrooms, as a growing number of college and university faculty members incorporate community-based, experiential education into traditional academic curricula.[27] In this section, I will therefore suggest a few guidelines for structuring panel discussions with religious leaders, based on my teaching experience at ICNY.[28]

For panel discussions exploring intra-faith diversity, I would encourage faculty members and other facilitators to *choose speakers who reflect social, political, or ideological differences within local faith communities*, as much or more than doctrinal or denominational differences within the faith tradition writ large. For example, in panel discussions with New York Muslim leaders I always try to include both Sunni and Shia community leaders, but frankly it is more important to include racially diverse speakers (given the mistaken popular equation of Muslim with Arab, and the historic significance of New York's African-American Muslim community), and to include women who both wear and do not wear hijab (given the extensive public discourse about Muslim women's religious dress). If the Sunni–Shia divide were a "hot issue" in local community life it would be essential to include both doctrinal perspectives, but in today's New York the racial, ethnic, and gendered diversity within Muslim communities is far more pressing.

For multifaith panel discussions, which usually have just one speaker from each tradition represented, I would encourage facilitators to *state clearly at the outset that the panelists are not speaking on behalf of their faith traditions or communities*—they represent *a* Jewish or Buddhist perspective, for example, but not *the* Jewish or Buddhist perspective. It is essential to flag the diversity within all faith traditions, even (or especially) if it is not represented in the conversation. Nearly all speakers welcome this clarification, which invites them to speak for themselves rather than their faith.

For all panel discussions, I would encourage facilitators to *choose speakers who exemplify different forms of community leadership*—a mix of clergy members, lay leaders, faith-based social activists, educators, or social service providers. If you limit the conversation to clergy members you are more likely to exclude women's voices, as well as faith communities that do not have ordained clergy. And *choose a mix of conventional and quirky or surprising speakers*—some who fit comfortably in the "mainstream" of their faith community, and some who defy assumptions about it. For example, in panel discussions with New York Christian leaders, I have often invited a speaker from a small, progressive "dinner church" in Brooklyn, where the worship service consists of a sacramental meal, rather than speakers from more typical "tall steeple" Protestant churches.[29] The dinner church is hardly the largest or most influential congregation in the city, but it stands against the stereotypic stodginess of mainline Protestant denominations, and highlights emerging forms of Christian liturgy and community.

I have pointed out a number of different forms of diversity one should ideally include in a panel discussion, but facilitators must *be prepared to make difficult, imperfect decisions in choosing speakers, because you can never include everyone*. It is almost always a bad idea to have more than three or four speakers on a panel, so facilitators need to set priorities and make tough calls. Inviting six or eight speakers may be more inclusive, but it can also be restrictive or even dehumanizing. If your speakers do not have enough time to tell stories and engage in conversation, they will turn into cardboard cutouts of themselves. And if too many speakers go on for too long, your students will almost inevitably lose interest.

As you are reaching out to speakers and confirming their participation, it is important to *communicate clearly about the format and learning goals of the panel discussion*. Tell speakers a little about your course and your students, and share the syllabus if they are interested. Suggest topics or guidelines for their presentations (which they may or may not follow), as well as clear time limits (which they may or may not respect). Establish ground rules for the conversation if necessary. At public universities—and most private ones, for that matter—it is essential for speakers to understand that the panel discussion is not an opportunity to promote their religious practices or beliefs.

In suggesting topics for presentations, facilitators should *never ask speakers to summarize their faith traditions' "main ideas" or canonical doctrines*. I generally hesitate to declare hard-and-fast rules for panel discussions, but in this case I really mean *never*. It is a wasted opportunity to ask a religious leader doing important community work—or, for that matter, to ask anyone with a fascinating personal story—to serve as a walking world religions textbook. Students do not usually need to know the Five Pillars of Islam, for example, in order to learn a great deal from their Muslim neighbors,[30] but if you feel your students need a basic introduction to a faith tradition before speaking with a community leader, it is your job to provide it.

At the same time, however, facilitators should *discourage panelists from speaking entirely personally about their beliefs or experiences*—try to keep their faith traditions in the mix. I have sometimes been frustrated by speakers telling lengthy stories that make no reference to their faith, and have tried (with mixed success) to redirect them toward the topic at hand. Panel discussions should explore the ties and tensions between received traditions and personal creativity, and it is sometimes the facilitator's job to ask follow-up questions that connect speakers' stories to their traditions.

In order to strike this balance between tradition and creativity, facilitators should generally *ask speakers to discuss practical applications or implications of their religious values or beliefs*—faith-based personal stories and political projects, as I argued above. The framing question for a panel discussion should almost always be some variation on "How does your faith tradition shape your life?" Speakers' answers might touch on their everyday experiences, personal faith journeys, family lives, community leadership, social activism, professional work, or what have you—but always religion "taken up in their hands."

As these suggestions make clear, it can be a complex, time-consuming process to organize and facilitate panel discussions with religious leaders. It is anything but a day off from your classroom teaching. But it is well worth the time and energy spent, as a rich conversation with diverse faith leaders will inevitably exceed the limitations of world religions pedagogy—or any other conceptual framework you might apply to it.

Conclusion: We Are All Specific Intellectuals

This essay has touched on a range of topics, from theoretical issues in religious studies and other fields, to the social and intellectual contours of the world religions public sphere, to practical advice for civically engaged classroom teaching. Each section speaks in a different register, but they all revolve around a few basic facts. Whether in academia or the nonprofit sector, educators are rarely, if ever, free to teach precisely as they would like. We are all constrained by the needs and expectations of our students and colleagues, as well as the conceptual systems and institutions we inhabit together. But these constraints are never absolute. More often than not, we can find creative ways to accomplish our pedagogic goals—workable compromises with the "regime[s] of truth" that bind us.

Given my position at the Interfaith Center of New York, I have highlighted the distinctive constraints placed on religious diversity education programs for professional audiences—teachers, social workers, and police who expect, and arguably *need*, to learn about "world religions" because they work in contexts and communities that are often defined in such terms. This is my predicament as a critical scholar of religion working at a community-based nonprofit organization. This is, in Foucault's phrase, "the precise [point] where

[my] own conditions of life [and] work situate [me]." But honestly, I do not think my predicament is dramatically different from that of most university-based academics. We are all "specific intellectuals," ethically and epistemically compromised by our role within systems we are working to critique. There is no space outside of power for us to "gambol in," but that does not mean we are "trapped and condemned to defeat." To the contrary, our work gains whatever power it may have by successfully navigating the limitations that shape it.

Part Three

Is There Religion Outside of Religion?

10

Who and What's Included?: Teaching Religion and Science

Benjamin E. Zeller

Introduction

When I was a child there was a highway interchange nearby nicknamed "the spaghetti bowl." Roads criss-crossed across each other, leading traffic this way and that, sending motorists in different directions. Locals navigated with ease, even efficiently. Newcomers often ended up lost, or worse, in wrecks caused by indecision or confusion. Teaching religion and science, I see the same pattern. Scholars come to the field with a multitude of approaches, methodologies, and driven by diverse sets of research questions. Professional academics generally get where they are going, navigating away from wrong turns along the way. However, students often enter the religion and science classroom from totally different directions, frequently unsure of their desired outcomes. The instructor must provide a map and guidance, and with careful navigation, direct students toward the learning goals. But it is far too easy to end up in a wreck.

I teach religion and science yearly, and it has become one of my most popular courses, drawing students primarily majoring in STEM fields. My institutional location is that of a small liberal arts college, and I benefit from a population of students interested in the broad liberal arts as well as their STEM majors. Yet in an average religion and science class of twenty-five students, twenty of them will identify as majoring or potentially majoring in STEM or health-related fields. If I am lucky, I'll have one or two majors in history, religion, or anthropology. Importantly, the class also tends to attract first- and second-year students, many of whom are first-generation college students, often unsure of what to expect and what they should be learning in my class. For most, my course provides their first exposure to religious studies and the norms of the academic study of religion.

The first day of class I ask what relationship, if any, students envision between religion and science. The vast majority describe the relationship as one of conflict. They then provide examples of this conflict, often erroneous ones: that the Catholic Church burnt Galileo at the stake (did not happen), that Darwin was an anti-Christian secularist or even Marxist (he was not), that the courageous young evolutionist John Scopes stood up on behalf of progressive science against anti-scientific American Christian Fundamentalists (mostly wrong). It is worth noting the centrality of Western Christianity, white men, and individualist hero narratives within this model of the conflict of religion and science. Suffice it to say, neither I nor most religion and science scholars wish to reinforce those approaches.

Simultaneously, most students in my religion and science class enter with very little knowledge of religion as an academic concept or specific religious traditions, nor do many have strong religious commitments of their own. Unlike the students in Barbara Walvoord's groundbreaking study on students' expectations of religious studies courses, few of my students take my religion and science class for personal religious edification.[1] However, many are curious about what they refer to as "the world religions," and want to know how different religions engage the topic of science. Because most of my students are secularly minded and scientifically focused, they generally also want to know how religious people might respond to their areas of study, typically biology, psychology, neuroscience, environmental science, or the health fields.

As an instructor, I seek to challenge underlying assumptions about what constitutes science and religion as overlapping social and cultural constructs, rather than reinforce the idea of these two as monolithic categories. I also seek to avoid reinforcing the "world religions" paradigm, which religious studies scholars recognize as deeply problematic (see other chapters in this volume for further critique).[2] Extending the freeway metaphor, I come from the direction of epistemological and definitional questions, and travel in the direction of social constructivism and the sociology of scientific knowledge (SSK), a field within science studies that emphasizes science as a social phenomenon. My destination—the learning goals in my course—is also different: in addition to wanting to challenge students to think more critically about the concepts of religion and science, I also seek to challenge the narrative of religion and science as centered on a series of righteous elite white males representing the ascent of Western science against the regressive forces of religion.

So the question is, given where I am coming from and where I want to go, and where my students are coming from and where they want to go, how can we navigate and travel together rather than end up in a crashed wreck? This chapter answers that question, suggesting how instructors in similar courses might do the same.

The Problem: A Christian-Centric Conflict Narrative

The fundamental pedagogical problem with teaching religion and science is that popular conceptions, paralleling traditional but outdated scholarship, have tended to center white male Christian elites in the narrative of religion and science, to emphasize a model of conflict between rationalist scientists and backwards religionists (often echoing latent Protestant anti-Catholicism), and reified science and religion as universal and cross-cultural categories that replicate Western Protestant norms. Scholars of religion and science have argued for decades that the "conflict narrative," that is, the model of a chronic and consistent battle between religion and science, fails to accurately portray the complex relationship between religion and science. Ian G. Barbour, whose voluminous works cemented the subfield of science and religion in the latter years of the twentieth century, and whose books still serve as the most common textbooks in religion and science courses, explained over two decades ago, "in recent decades this *conflict thesis* has been extensively criticized as a selective and oversimplified historical account. Science and religion were not unified forces opposing each other like armies on the battlefield. Often ... scientific and religious ideas interacted in complex ways within the life of the same person."[3] This criticism, in other words, is hardly new or cutting-edge. It is nearly fifty years old. Scholars have insisted that we move beyond the conflict model for decades. Yet students often assume it when they enter the religion and science classroom.

Ronald L. Numbers, another luminary of the subfield, roots the myth of conflict in the historiography of the field. Academics, he argues, formed and foisted this narrative upon the public in the nineteenth century. Amplified by both secularist critics of religion as well as Christian—primarily Protestant—reactionaries against science, the conflict model becomes a self-fulfilling and self-amplifying paradigm that can be extended by proponents for their own reasons.

> Historians of science have known for years that [conflict] accounts are more propaganda than history ... Yet the message has rarely escaped the ivory tower. The secular public, if it thinks about such issues at all, *knows* that organized religion has always opposed scientific progress (witness the attacks on Galileo, Darwin, and Scopes). The religious public *knows* that science has taken a leading

role in corroding faith (through naturalism and antibiblicalism). As a first step towards correcting these misperceptions we must dispel the hoary myths that continue to pass as historical truth.[4]

For Numbers, who points in his parenthetical to the problematic narratives surrounding the same elite white male Christian champions of science who are so often centered within the historiography, the myth of conflict represents the primary challenge in addressing the study of religion and science. Instructors must move beyond the conflict model in order to help students understand the topic in a more accurate and nuanced manner.

Scholars of religion and science have produced numerous publications seeking to disrupt this conflict myth, rooted in historical, philosophical, ethnographic, and theological methodologies, much of which is accessible and digestible for undergraduate students. Sociologist Elaine Howard Ecklund, whose study of elite American scientists challenges the conflict model, writes that "the 'insurmountable hostility' between science and religion is a caricature … hardly representative of reality."[5] Ecklund's study complicates the conflict narrative, showing that a significant percentage of elite American scientists do in fact perceive religion as problematic, but noting that their reasons for doing so are seldom rooted in their scientific vocation. But many scientists integrate religious practices, beliefs, and identities, and conflict does not define their perspectives. While some scientists seek to suppress any connection between their vocation and religion, Ecklund identifies numerous manners in which scientists constructively engage religion, ranging from addressing religion as an important public issue, to spiritual entrepreneurship wherein scientists develop religious or spiritual approaches to science, to synthesizing contemporary scientific developments with traditional religiosity. I teach Ecklund's book in my religion and science class, and students are often surprised to learn how diverse the scientific community is in its engagement with religion.

All too often, scholars, students, and the general public tend to equate the "religion" in religion and science with Western Christianity, often a Biblically centered Protestantism, and rather Anglo-Saxon and male at that. This not only risks projecting a Western norm of what counts as religion and what merits being called a science, but also prevents students from glimpsing the complicated ways that individuals in non-Western and non-Christian societies have grappled with cultural, social, and intellectual currents that in English we call religion and science. A growing number of scholars have simultaneously sought to expand the understanding of religion and science outside of the realm of Western Christianity. For example, Samer Akkach and his contributors have centered the concept of 'ilm, generally translated as "knowledge," as the key theoretical concept to understand the relationship between Islam and what English speakers would call science.[6] Doing so brings cultural practices often considered science, such as astronomy and anatomy, together with those not often considered science, such as calligraphy, architecture, and fashion, and of course with religion as well. This not only disrupts the narrative of Western science as supplanting premodern forms of knowledge, it challenges specific claims about what constitutes the category and concept of science.

Challenge the Reification of Religions and Religions

If religion and science scholarship has begun to decenter elite male Christianity, it has further to go to challenge reified models of religion and science themselves. Here, the contributions of the critical study of religion (what is sometimes called "theories of religion") and the sociology of scientific knowledge each offer a disciplinary critique of the manner in which instructors and students sometimes fall into uncritical assumptions about what constitutes the categories of religion and science.

To be clear, students do not enter my classroom with any interest in this topic. In fact, few have ever considered that their ideas of what constitutes religion, let alone science, are cultural constructions. Generally, they assume that religions exist as reified externalized entities, generally predicated on hierarchical, institutional, textual, and dogmatic norms. Religion, in other words, looks like Christianity, and even more so like Protestantism. To the extent that most of my students are aware of non-Christian religions—most are culturally Christian in background, though I will typically have a few Muslim and Jewish identifying students as well—they tend to see other religions through the lens of Protestantism, reducing Islam, for example, to the Five Pillars (see Chapter 6 of this book).

My first duty—and in fact, one of the first readings of the semester!—is to challenge those assumptions. Scholars of religion will likely immediately jump to a variety of approaches that deconstruct this Protestantized reification of religion, and individual instructors will presumably know what works best in their classroom, with their students, and in keeping with their pedagogical approaches. I use J. Z. Smith's excellent "Religion, Religions, Religious" essay that, although older than all of my students, still captures the heart of the critique of how religion has been constructed as a category in Western society.

Smith uses several examples from the era of Spanish colonization, which works particularly well in my classes, since I tend to have a lot of Latinx students. When Smith unpacks how Hernán Cortés deployed the concepts of *personas religiosas*, *secta*, *religiosos*, and *mezquitas* to understand the Mesoamerican cultural world, thereby constructing the category of religion as predicated on Iberian norms, such students immediately grasp the way that the rhetoric of religion claims to operate transculturally but actually emerges from a specific colonial context.[7] (It helps in terms of comparative linguistic analysis to have numerous Spanish speaking students in the class, as I typically do.)

This is doubly true for science, since while students have an implicit awareness that there are different religions and that not everyone's religion looks the same, they tend to assume there is only one science, that it transcends culture, and that it is both universal and inherently correct. Such claims about science have long historical roots. Science is predictive, empirical, rational, and universal, according to such a position. Yet from Thomas S. Kuhn forward, historians and philosophers have challenged those claims. Kuhn famously argued that science operates not through smooth progressive development of a single science but through crises and wrong turns of competing scientific paradigms.[8] Kuhn's model helped lay the groundwork for the development of the field of the history of science, positioning science as a cultural activity rather than a universal constant. The development of the field of the sociology of scientific knowledge (SSK) likewise has demonstrated that science must be understood within specific social contexts. Scholars of religion likely are familiar with some of the foundational theorists in SSK, such as Bruno Latour and Donna Haraway. Michel Foucault's *Birth of a Clinic* represents another example.[9] SSK has developed into both the "hard programme" that positions science purely as a social construction and devoid of any special claim to privileged knowledge, and the "soft programme" more willing to grant that science possesses special epistemological status owing to empiricism and rationalism.[10] Neither instructors nor students need to delve too deeply into SSK to recognize its power in disrupting the claims that science is somehow both universal and culturally dependent.

In deconstructing reified notions of religion and science, along with decentering the elite white male Protestant story, one lays the groundwork for further decolonizing the syllabus. As historian Su Lin Lewis explains, "[t]he process of 'decolonizing history' is broadly about making historians aware of and committed to addressing the disproportionate focus on Eurocentric history in the profession, and attuned to the structures of power underlying this."[11] In the broadest sense, decolonizing the religion and science classroom means not only expanding the sort of topics considered—moving beyond Galileo, Darwin, and Scopes—but also challenging the way that religion and science have been configured as supposedly universal concepts, yet predicated on Western norms. This fundamental structure of power, as Lewis labels it, undergirds not only the academy but broader society and the vocations and fields into which my students seek to enter. By challenging the notions of universalist, reified science and religion, one pushes oneself and one's students into the sort of (re)attunement to structures of power to which Lewis points.

Mallory Nye makes a similar argument, that religious studies scholars must confront and challenge the colonial nature of religious studies in our research and classrooms. This involves not only tweaking the readings—though, to be clear, inclusive readings are a good start and absolutely necessary—but a revisioning of the theoretical and methodological basis of how we do religious studies. "Despite the fairly recent take up of the term in mainstream academia, decolonization is not the same as 'inclusion' or 'diversification': it is not about a paternalistic offering of inclusion to outsiders. … Decolonizing is not about a reluctant addition of an extra reading; it requires a wholesale change."[12] Nye calls for rethinking the religious studies canon. Students in my religious studies class are not religion majors, and the nature of the canon does not concern them. But the way we configure religion and science does. By pushing students to rethink these categories in our classrooms we accomplish the same goal as Nye calls for in the academy.

Providing Alternative Narrations to Common Myths

In her guide to teaching about race and racism in higher education, educational psychologist and teaching faculty member Cydni Kernahan explains that confronting myths—a term she uses in its pejorative sense of inaccurate but persistent social narratives—represents the first challenge when teaching controversial topics.[13] In her case, Kernahan confronts myths of color blindness and individualism rather than systemic understandings of racism. Kernahan argues that instructors must confront such myths in such a way that we avoid repeating and therefore amplifying the myth itself. "According to research, engaging with misinformation directly inadvertently strengthens peoples' belief in that misinformation."[14] This notion, derived from the psychology of learning, makes intuitive sense in the classroom. In order to address a myth such as the prevalence of the conflict narrative, or the rootedness of religion and science within Christian norms, or the centrality of white male individuals within narratives of religion and science, one ought not begin with those very same points. If one imagines such concepts as lurking behind one's teaching, and constantly refers to them even as negative reference points, one amplifies their presence and power.

Kernahan instead argues for offering substitute models. "Most relevant for us as instructors is the technique of providing an alternative narrative while avoiding repetition of the misinformation."[15] If one can get through a class period without referring to conflict, Christianity, or elite white male actors, this provides a new model for how to study religion and science that decenters the problematic assumptions that many students and faculty bring into the classroom. Akkach's centering of *'ilm*, and teaching a class session using this model, represents one such example. In this case, I asked students to return to the idea of *'ilm* and apply it to different non-Islamic contexts, rather than framing our analysis using the term "science." We found that when we framed cultural activities in this way, we avoided reifying a Protestant Christian understanding of science and a set of related assumptions about conflicts between religion and science. Importantly, this opens up new avenues for analysis. Students sometimes think it is weird or even inappropriate to talk about *'ilm* when discussing non-Islamic traditions. This affords an opening to discuss how ideas like "religion" and "science" are invisibly normalized and universalized, and how Christian norms are applied (often in colonial contexts).

One clear tension in this approach emerges from the fact that students do by and large continue to judge new material against these persistent myths. As part of my religion and science class students maintain and contribute to a course blog that connects our readings to each other, to contemporary events, and to their areas of interest. On their own, students often return to questions of conflict and the elite figures of whom they already know. Since most of my students either identify with or were raised within Christian households, they also tend to assume Christian norms. Curtailing these assumptions by ignoring them completely may be good philosophy, but it is bad pedagogy. Students need a chance to bring their own interests to the class, and instructors need to meet them halfway in doing so. While one must avoid repetition of incorrect myths, noting the presence of powerful cultural narratives and that students and faculty have internalized them represents a manner to engage students where they are and to push them forward. Unlike Kernahan, who confronts racist myths that pose existential and real dangers to individuals and societies, one has a bit more leeway in a religion and science classroom to minimize the presence of these myths without needing to excise them altogether. Hence one might assign Ian Barbour's four-part model (conflict, independence, dialogue, integration) on the relation of religion to science, recognizing that Barbour neither champions nor reinforces the conflict narrative but simply asserts that it exists and can be found in specific locations (he notes Biblical fundamentalists, for example, but outspoken scientist and critic Richard Dawkins is another good example).[16]

Guided by Kernahan's suggestion that we must provide alternative narratives, instructors of religion and science can address the pernicious myths of the subfield by helping students to directly analyze primary sources and create new narratives. Directly addressing the most problematic cases avoids the "elephant in the room" problem. Since the popular narratives around Galileo, Darwin, or Scopes center so many problematic positions, instructors may wish to address one or two of these cases directly. To take an example that reveals how to tangle with several problematic assumptions, one can teach the case of Galileo in a way that decenters Galileo himself as a heroic white male elite Western Christian championing science in a deadly fight with backward religion— the myth—and instead situates him in a competing flow of ideas about religion and science as conveyed by a more diverse set of individuals. Since this particular episode has been so well documented, instructors can make use of Finocchiaro's translations of the documentary history so as to guide students through this exploration.[17] While many of the surviving documents themselves were written by white male Christian elites—a perennial problem for historians!—they contain glimpses of other social actors, such as Benedetto Castelli's attestation to the theological and scientific acumen of Dowager Duchess Christina of Lorraine and Archduchess Maria Maddalena.[18] One can supplement this with Islamic sources that show the way in which heliocentrism and the Copernican model emerged from analogous discussions among Muslim religious and scientific thinkers whose work had been recently translated and made accessible at the time of Galileo, such as the works of Al-Biruni and Alpetragius. Students are often surprised to learn that many of Galileo's defenders were in fact leaders within the Church, and that contestations over heliocentrism and Galileo's writings had as much to do with politics and social wrangling as they did over theology.

Certainly one might assign secondary sources as well that provide a counter-narration of Galileo's life and what came to be called the "Galileo Affair." Such secondary sources are valuable, but they tend to do exactly what Kernahan calls for us to avoid, assuming the myth and arguing against it. For example, Richard Blackwell's short treatment included in Ferngren's popular religion and science textbook begins with the claim that "the classic case of conflict between Western science and religion is the confrontation between Galileo and the Roman Catholic Church in the early decades of the seventeenth century."[19] While Blackwell himself historicizes and complicates this claim, it nevertheless brackets his analysis, since he ends his essay with a similar statement about the "long and disturbing shadow over the relations between science and religion."[20] A student cannot help but enter and leave Blackwell's consideration of the topic thinking about conflict. Not only are these and similar secondary source treatments problematic, but in providing ready-made narratives they alleviate the need for students to construct the narratives themselves. Active learning strategies call for students to wrestle with primary sources and their competing, confusing, and contradictory nature in order to develop their own narratives. The act of doing so encourages students to challenge the received mythology through the construction of their own interpretations.

An Example from the Classroom

To demonstrate how the pedagogical and disciplinary critiques explored above actually come into play in the classroom, it is helpful to consider a single topic that most religion and science courses explore: religion and ecology. While a minority of students in my religion and science class intend to major in environmental studies, and my biology students tend to have pre-health focuses, the vast majority of my students do bring an ecological consciousness into the classroom, which includes an acute sense of environmental crisis. While only a very small number of my students are explicitly anti-Christian, many of them generally believe that there is a latent tension between Christianity and environmentalism, and that Christianity is in the wrong in that way. Recent history of Evangelical hostility to climate change science, an association of Christianity with politically conservative pro-industry and anti-environmental activism, and an overall coalescing of ecology with liberalism and secularism seem to explain these assumptions.

Scholars, of course, would object to all these positions. Not even all conservative Evangelicals oppose environmentalism, and certainly not progressive Evangelicals. Even more problematically, many students (and the broader public) seem to equate Evangelicalism with all of Christianity, and Christianity with all religion(s). This is another of those myths, like the conflict narrative, that overshadows the classroom and which Kernahan warns us must be challenged without being reinforced.

Importantly, students' own assumptions about the conflict between religion and environmentalism are reproduced in the scholarship. Many religion and science textbooks, syllabi, and courses include treatment of the subject relying on the work of Lynn White, Jr. The "White thesis," as it has come to be known, which positions Christianity as the root of the environmental crisis.[21] White argued that Christian theology, particularly its emphasis on humankind holding dominion over nature and existing apart from the natural world, combined with the technological advances of the industrial revolution to lead to massive environmental devastation. Scholar of religion and science Noah J. Efron explains that "White's thesis has been debated endlessly and with fervor for forty years, and scholars now agree ... that whatever damage modern science and technology have caused cannot blithely be chalked up to Christianity."[22] Scholars may agree on this point, but it has not reached the popular audience, as evidenced in everything from new religious movements' critiques of Christianity as anti-environmentalist[23] to public sentiment that Christians do not care about ecology.[24]

Problematically, the White thesis also centers Christianity, explicitly indicating that Christianity has had the greatest impact on the environment, and implicitly positioning it as a stand-in for all other religions. White's model relies upon a Christian-centric gaze, looking at the topic through the perspective that religion and science (in this case ecology) should be interpreted in terms of the categories of Christianity and not-Christianity.

The classroom solution is to recognize that students assume something like the White model, not repeat it so as to avoid reinforcing the myth, and provide materials to help students develop a more nuanced perspective. I do not assign the White article itself, not only because it is over fifty years old but also because students have already internalized the basic ideas. Rather, I provide primary source material from non-Christian religions that show the diverse manners in which religious institutions and individuals engage questions about ecology and environmentalism. Because I want to avoid reinforcing Orientalist assumptions that Asian religions are somehow more "in harmony" with nature—which likely would reinforce the distinction with the Occidental religions, as Edward Said so clearly argued—I instead start with Islam and Judaism, since students do not tend to think much about those traditions and ecology. I assign students accessible primary sources that do not assume any specialized background knowledge beyond the material on those traditions we have already studied in class. In recent years I have used a set of legal opinions (*fatwa*) from the Indonesian Council of Ulama on the protection of endangered species and ecosystems, and several statements and opinions (responsa) from the Central Conference of American Rabbis in the United States, but I change these every few years. After students have worked through these sources and feel empowered to create their own analyses of how religions relate to environmentalism, I provide several more from Buddhism and Western Christian traditions that both challenge as well as reinforce the stereotypes, aware that students will be more intentional and nuanced in how they read these sources. Ideally, students leave the exercise having disrupted the internalized assumption that conservative Evangelical anti-environmentalism represents all religion.

Conclusion: What Students Want, What Instructors Want, What Students Need

This chapter has used several cases to show how instructors can navigate the challenge of responding to what students want to learn about and what scholars of religion and science point to as important. Yet there is a third overlapping category, one that is specific to each institution, classroom, and instructor: what students actually need to learn but don't know they need to, which can also be described as what they would have wanted to learn at the beginning of the course if they knew then what they knew at the end. Successful courses in religion and science, but more broadly in religious studies generally, find a

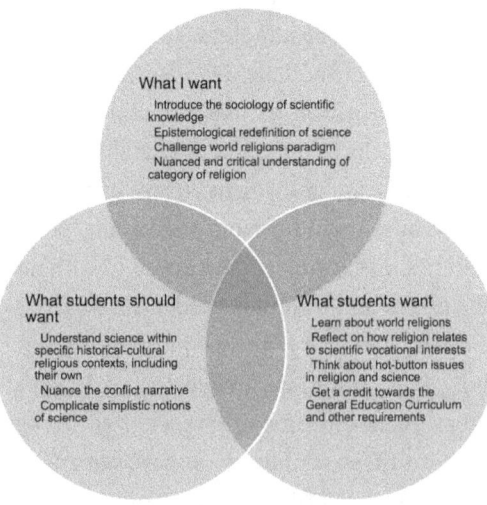

Figure 10.1 Goals of Religious Studies Venn Diagram. Created by Benjamin Zeller.

balance between these sets of goals. It is helpful to visualize these goals with the commonly utilized aid of the Venn diagram.

My own goals for the class follow the scholarship of religious studies, science studies, and the specific subfield of religion and science. None of them diverges from the mainstream disciplinary trajectories of the past decades. I want students to think more critically about the categories of religion and science and their connections, to complicate simplistic definitions and models of these concepts, and to move beyond the Western Protestant normative assumptions that drove much of the development of the academic conversation about religion and about science until recently. Scholars in both religious studies and science studies can readily point to these disciplinary conversations and developments. We really don't want to spend our time discussing Galileo or Scopes, or defending Darwin from his critics. We want to show how religion and science are messy concepts that need to be deconstructed and resituated in new ways. I want students to think critically about the multiplicity of sciences and religions, the way that these emerge from specific historical-cultural contexts, and how the categories themselves must be deployed more critically, with attention to its roots in the colonial European context.

Students, on the other hand, enter my religion and science classroom wanting to learn about a reified thing they identify as "science" and how it relates to a set of reified things they call "religion" that one finds in examples called "world religions." I know this because I ask them the first day of class, and the most common answer I get for why students take the class is that they are going into scientific fields and want to know what "members of the world religions believe about science." This approach builds upon both the world religions paradigm as well as a specific philosophical model of science that identifies it as transcultural and universal, but nevertheless defined along the lines of the Western scientific establishment.[25] Since so many of my students identify as students in STEM fields, they naturally also seek to understand how religion (however they understand it) relates to their chosen areas of study. Finally, it should be noted that most students in the class ultimately are driven by the need also to complete the humanities requirement in the college's general education curriculum or the medical humanities requirement of the pre-health program. They selected my course from a menu of options satisfying these requirements, but their initial entrance into the course generally comes from such pragmatic concerns.

My course seeks to address both what I want to teach as well as what students want to learn. But there is a third category too: what I think students really should or would want if they knew at the beginning of the course what they learn by the end. This counterintuitive category emerges from conversations with students who have taken the course as well as qualitative course evaluations. To offer an analogy to explain the concept: my elementary-school age daughter enjoys crème brulee. When I offered her a flan she was not interested. But once I explained what a flan was, she realized that she liked that too. Now she knows that she enjoys flan as well as crème brulee.

Students in my religion and science class show the same pattern. The course is extremely diverse, with students coming from a variety of cultural backgrounds. As the course develops, they often share experiences about grandparents or great-grandparents and their religious-spiritual healing practices. One memorable year, this included a Namibian student descendent from a *sangoma* (spirit-healer), a Latino grandchild of a *curandera*, and a Polish student whose grandparents kept alive the old healing ways of Eastern Europe. As students learn about the complex relationship between religion, science, and health they often want to contextualize and understand these experiences and compare them across cultures. They find that learning about the various forms of science as practiced across different historical-cultural locations helps them to not dismiss such familial legacies as "superstition," but to understand them as emergent from specific contexts. I must admit that I prefer deeper dives into the material than the more surface-level consideration of religion and science across numerous historical-cultural locations, but students often report that this "world religions" style tour of science across different religious traditions is their favorite part of the class, often the most personally impactful, and useful to them as they consider their futures.

Where the three circles in the Venn diagram intersect is where one should find one's course objectives and assessable learning outcomes. What is it that I want, what my students want, and what I know they will want by the end of the class? This is less a negotiation than a recognition that these intentions are complicated, and as an instructor I must be thoughtful when designing my course. Over the years I have designed it and adjusted these course objectives and learning outcomes in recognition of what my students bring to the course. My initial set of course objectives (excluding those related to general education and other institutional requirements) focused on what I wanted:

Students enrolled in this class will learn to:

- think about science from the perspective of the humanities and social sciences
- think about religion from the perspective of human culture
- understand the historical and contemporary issues in religion and science

Today, the enumerated list has changed:

- understand religion and science in a diverse range of cultural-historical locations
- think about religion and science from the perspective of human culture
- understand the historical and contemporary issues in religion and science

The changes are actually relatively minor, but they get at the heart of good course design: finding what I want, what my students want, and what I know my students would want if they knew at the beginning of the course what they know at the end.

Navigating the religion and science class offers the same challenges as navigating confusing roadways, but just as drivers can do so with the proper tools, so can instructions and students in religion and science classrooms. Recognizing course learning objectives is the first step, but it extends into syllabus design and ensuring a decolonized curriculum, guiding principles of how to teach in the classroom so as to avoid reinforcing myths, and judicious choices of course materials, such as readings and assignments, in keeping with those principles, curriculum, and objectives. With the right guidance, students reach the right destination, and the course doesn't crash along the way.

11

Using Sports to Tackle the Problem of Defining Religion

Annie Blazer

Courses on religion and sports have been highly effective at bringing non-religious studies majors into the religious studies classroom. Students drawn to this kind of course are often athletes or sports fans. I teach a course called "Religion and Sports in the US" at William & Mary in Williamsburg, Virginia, and every semester I offer it, I am inundated with override requests. Students tell me that they enroll for the course because they love sports, and they want to have an opportunity to think about sports in an academic way. William & Mary is a public four-year college, and most students are from Virginia; it is also a highly competitive liberal arts college that draws out-of-state and international students. The undergraduate population is around 6,000; most are aged eighteen to twenty-two and enter W&M with better than average writing and critical thinking skills.[1] I share this context to frame my approach to the departmental challenge of the one-and-done student: the student who takes one religious studies course during their college career, and that one course is our opportunity to show what we do in religious studies.

In this chapter, I'll describe how I use one piece of my Religion and Sports in the US course to address a foundational challenge in religious studies: the problem of defining religion. Some disciplines like anthropology or history are defined by their *method* of study, but religious studies is defined by its *object* of study. This has made defining religion a central and ongoing problem in the field. While those of us in the discipline know that scholars have long debated (and will continue to debate) what belongs in the category of religion, for students first encountering the study of religion, the myriad definitions of religion can be confusing and frustrating. Allowing students to investigate the question, "Is sport a religion?" invites them into a scholarly conversation that has the potential to move beyond simple comparison of different kinds of definitions.

What Is "Religion"?

Introductory classes in religious studies often open by offering students multiple definitions of religion. These definitions may differ by discipline (anthropology vs. philosophy, for example) and may emphasize different aspects of what students would already recognize as "religious." One challenge students encounter with a range of definitions is that they can struggle to identify the "right" definition of religion or come to see religious studies as an ambiguous and confusing discipline. Introductory textbooks in religious studies address this long-standing problem in a variety of ways.[2] Offering students a range of approaches to defining religion can feel overwhelming, so I suggest using sports to practice applying different perspectives. I will lay out the range of approaches that scholars have developed and then describe how using sports can provide a path for students to navigate these.

How You Define Religion Will Influence How You Study It

Gary Kessler's *Studying Religion: An Introduction Through Cases* contains a chapter titled "On Defining and Studying Religion." He opens the chapter by noting that most people use the word "religion" thinking that they and others know what it means. However, he argues that the academic study of religion needs a more rigorous definition of religion. He lists three characteristics of a good definition: "useful for the purposes at hand, as precise as possible without being too narrow, and as free from bias as possible."[3] Kessler notes that definitions can be too broad or too narrow and finding the correct degree of precision is a challenge. He draws a comparison between a functional definition of religion (what religion does) and a substantive definition of religion (what religion is). "Substantive types often turn out to be too narrow because of the vast diversity of religious beliefs and practices, and functional types often turn out to be too broad because different things can often function in the same way."[4] Kessler notes that some scholars have attempted to solve this problem by offering a family resemblance definition of religion—a list of traits that describe religions, and while a religion might not have all of them, if it has enough of them it belongs in the category of religion. His critique of this sort of definition is that it solves the problem of being too narrow or too broad but tends to lack precision.

Kessler frames the topic by saying, "Definitions are not necessarily true or false, but more or less useful."[5] He points out that scholars study religion using a range of methods like history, sociology, psychology, anthropology, literature, and philosophy, and for each of these methods, different definitions of religion will be more or less useful. For Kessler, definitions are starting points that help us investigate.

Paul Myhre takes a similar approach in his *Introduction to Religious Studies* chapter, "What is Religion?" For Myhre, humans have a tendency to demonstrate something that we would call religion regardless of their historical time period or cultural context. He writes, "Consider the history of any people and you will find numerous examples of religious beliefs and practices playing a part in wars, leadership succession, human relationships, purity codes, legal documents, social and environmental ethics, and so on."[6] Because of religion's ubiquity, Myhre points out that it's not surprising that scholars disagree on what religion is and how to study it. Like Kessler, he emphasizes disciplinary lenses noting that "how you define religion will directly influence how you study it."[7] For both Myhre and Kessler, disciplinary approaches are starting points for developing questions about religion. They do not attempt to identify a "correct" definition of religion but note that definitions are ways of seeing—a definition will reveal some things and obscure others.

Religion Is Something Humans Do

In his opening chapter, "Religion: Some Basics," in *Religion: The Basics,* Malory Nye addresses the problem of how to define religion. Before presenting and assessing definitions, Nye emphasizes that we should think of religion as something humans do. The study of religion is the study of humans acting in the world. Using this basic foundation for religion, he argues that religion is "nearly always *both* a set of ideas and beliefs that people engage with (to some extent or other), *and* also the framework of their lived experiences and daily practices."[8] Nye uses the example of Sigmund Freud. He points out that Freud defined religion as a misguided and unhealthy impulse arising from failed attempts to work through one's relationship with their father. Nye points out that Freud assumed that all religions were similar to Christianity and Judaism in their inclusion of a father-figure deity. For Nye, this example is useful because it shows that Freud's impressions of religion were constrained by his cultural context that made him more familiar with some religious traditions than others. Nye hopes to emphasize the interrelatedness of religion and culture and asks students to think about how their own familiarity/unfamiliarity might inform their impressions of what makes a religion.[9]

Nye points out that Jonathan Z. Smith has famously posited that religion is the invention of the scholar and only exists as scholars have defined it within the bounds of the academy.[10] Nye agrees that scholars have often defined religion in ways that help their scholarship and might not resonate across all cultures, as in the example of Freud. Nye opts to use the term religion in a broad and blurry way to "refer to the vast array of different things encompassed by this everyday usage of the word."[11] By treating religion as something that humans do, Nye emphasizes discourse and practice over belief.

Religion Is a Word that Changes Meaning over Time

The previously discussed works were published in 2007–9. More recent introductory texts have opted to trace how the concept of religion has changed over time. Craig Martin's "Religion and the Problem of Definition" in *A Critical Introduction to the Study of Religion* takes this approach. He makes the case that "how the term is defined, as well as what's included or excluded in the definition, depends on the interests of those making up the definition."[12] To illustrate this, Martin turns to a case study questioning if yoga is religious.[13] He notes that yoga studios became tax-exempt in Missouri by claiming that yoga is religious, while in California, yoga teachers and enthusiasts argued that yoga was not religious and could be included in public-school physical education classes. He uses this juxtaposition to show that asking the question, "Is yoga religious?" is ultimately unhelpful. He writes, "Thus, rather than ask ourselves 'What is religion?,' it would be better to ask, 'Why does this group define religion this way rather than that way, what do they hope to accomplish, and how does the definition serve their interests?'"[14] In this way, Martin establishes that definitions are perspectival.

He then traces the history of the term "religion." Since there was no word for "religion" in premodern languages, Martin warns against using the concept to analyze premodern societies. "When we translate premodern terms as 'religion,' we are actually projecting our own, contemporary ideas back into the past."[15] The violence that emerged after the Protestant Reformation led to the first usage of "religion" that contains some components that we associate with religion today, namely that religion is a private choice beyond the bounds of politics and the state.

At the time of this shift in definition, Europeans were only concerned with the Christian religions of Catholicism and Protestantism, but in the seventeenth century, Europeans began to consider non-European cultural traditions as potential religions. In general, their concern in studying these other religions was to show that Christianity was the true religion and others such as Judaism or Islam were false religions. During the era of colonial expansion, Europeans continued to differentiate true and false religions, and they began to apply an evolutionary framework—primitive religions could eventually evolve into advanced religions like Christianity. This mindset succeeded in painting Christianity as the pinnacle of human development and justified colonial missionary work, settlement, exploitation of and war against non-Europeans. As Martin notes, "Presenting 'primitives' as evolutionarily backward was useful for justifying colonialism and slavery."[16] In this way, definitions can be tools of war and colonialism; definitions can have deadly consequences.

Another shift in understanding of religion occurred over the nineteenth and twentieth centuries as scholars began to describe religion as essentially irrational compared to other ways of knowing like science and reason. This approach maintained the evolutionary schema of the colonial past, but now posited "secularism" as the pinnacle of human development. This understanding of religion also has deadly consequences. Martin provides the example of the 9/11 attacks:

> Al Qaeda's attack killed almost 3,000 civilians and was publicly viewed as irrational and immoral. By contrast, the subsequent invasion of Afghanistan by the United States resulted in the deaths of 92,000 people, more than 26,000 of whom were civilians. Despite the fact that *this resulted in almost 9 times the number of civilian deaths* as Al Qaeda's attack, almost no one views the invasion of Afghanistan as 'irrational.'[17]

For Martin, this portrayal of religion as irrational has the consequence of excusing "rational" actions from critical inquiry.

Is Sport a Religion?

Inviting students to test these approaches using sports offers an opportunity for students to enter an ongoing scholarly debate with tools that they already understand. Testing definitions through application lets students see that definitions are arguments. This section offers sport as an application category and looks at ways that scholars have argued for and against including sport in the category of religion.

How You Define Religion Will Influence How You Study It

Emile Durkheim argued that religions function to orient persons in sacred time and sacred space, allowing believers to separate the sacred and the profane. Durkheim was a late nineteenth- and early twentieth-century social theorist who wrote a number of books including *Elementary Forms of the Religious Life*, first published in 1912. According to Durkheim, the separation of the world into the sacred and the profane allows people to experience "effervescence," an exciting sensation of power only accessible through the sacred. Durkheim says, "In one world [the religious person] languidly carries on his daily life; the other is one that he cannot enter without abruptly entering into relations with extraordinary powers that excite him to the point of frenzy. The first is the profane world and the second, the world of sacred things."[18]

According to Durkheim, effervescence is the overwhelming feeling of belonging to something greater than oneself. This feeling is only possible socially, not individually. Effervescence serves to give religion emotional meaning and therefore ensures the continuation of the institution.

Durkheim's emphasis on sacred space and its ability to inspire a feeling of effervescence might remind you of a crowd feeling in a winning stadium. Religious studies scholar David Chidester has applied this idea to baseball. He writes, "[Baseball] is a religious institution that maintains the continuity, uniformity, sacred time, and sacred space of American life. As the 'faith of fifty million people,' baseball does everything that we conventionally understand the institution of the church to do."[19] Chidester goes on to describe baseball in terms strikingly similar to Durkheim, emphasizing the function of baseball in the lives of baseball fans: the season serves to delineate sacred times and sacred spaces.

While Durkheim offered a functionalist definition of religion, other theorists use substantive definitions of religion to describe religion's essence or core. For example, Rudolf Otto, a German philosopher writing in the early twentieth century, argued that the concept of "the holy" contains an "overplus of meaning," which he named "the numinous." According to Otto, the numinous quality of religion can stir in people a feeling of absolute powerlessness and holy dread in the face of absolute power.[20] This was Otto's attempt to name an integral aspect of religion. For Otto, if something does not invoke this sensation, it is not religion.

A second example of a substantive definition of religion is theologian Paul Tillich's assertion that what makes a religion is the quality of "ultimate concern." For Tillich, religions provide a person with a sense of the holy that infuses their life and decision-making. An ultimate concern demands surrender from the believer and takes priority over all other concerns. For Tillich, then, everyone has a religion because everyone has an ultimate concern.[21]

While some have argued that sport can inspire holy dread or serve as an ultimate concern, other scholars have used substantive definitions of religion to challenge the idea that sport is a religion. For example, Joan Chandler's article, "Sport is Not a Religion," argues that religions raise questions of ultimate meaning and provide followers with answers based on the supernatural. She writes, "While sport may provide us with examples of belief, ritual, sacrifice, and transcendence, all of them take place in a context designed wittingly and specifically by human beings, for the delight of human beings."[22] For Chandler, sport is explicitly void of supernatural content and hence cannot be considered a religion.

Religion Is Something that Humans Do

In Catherine Albanese's introductory religious studies textbook, she states, "it may be more fruitful to think not of defining religion but, instead, of trying to describe it."[23] Her description points out four features of a religious system: creed ("explanations about the meaning of human life"), code ("rules that govern everyday behavior"), cultuses ("rituals to act out the insights and understandings that are expressed in creeds and codes"), and communities ("groups of people either formally or informally bound together by the creed, code, and cultus they share").[24] Using this understanding of religion, we might argue that sporting communities constitute religious communities and, indeed, Albanese makes this argument, noting that sport constitutes an "American code of living." She writes, "[Sports and deliberate religious rituals] both are examples of dramatic actions in which people take on assigned roles, often wearing special symbolic clothing to distinguish them from non-participants. ... Through their performances, [these activities] create an 'other' world of meaning, complete with its own rules and boundaries, dangers and successes."[25] Albanese draws attention to similarities between religious rituals and sports to show that both create meaning through specialized activity, and this meaning can impact life beyond the boundary of the activity.

Religion Is a Word That Changes Meaning over Time

When we look at the historical development of concepts, we often see how these concepts are connected to systems of power and oppression that continue to impact our lives and cultures today. The definitions of religion explored in this chapter are all inheritors of the history of the concept of "religion," and it is worthwhile to note that tendencies to position some practices as "religious" and others as "superstitious" or "magical" reflect colonial judgments that often positioned the worldviews of Native Americans, Africans, and other indigenous peoples as invalid or primitive.[26]

Does "sport" have a similar historical trajectory? Did Europeans use the concept of sport to evaluate the cultural sophistication of other groups of people? Sort of. For much of human history, physical activities not necessary for survival were predominantly ritual practices for acting out symbolic meanings. During the European enlightenment in the eighteenth century, sport activities began to look like modern sports today, but rather than serving a ritual function, Europeans tended to treat these activities as diversions, as secular forms of entertainment and fun. Some Europeans, like the Puritans who came to North America, frowned on all forms of diversion and saw games and physical contests as not only frivolous but dangerous to the human soul. Because of the European affiliation of games and physical contests with either fun or danger, Europeans tended to judge other cultures that used games or physical contests as forms of symbolic expression as inferior or barbaric.

For example, the modern sport of lacrosse originated as a Native American athletic contest in northeastern North America. Multiple tribes in the region played variations of a game of moving a ball to a goal using sticks. Historian Donald Fisher has noted that the game served multiple purposes: physical fitness prepared men for war; intertribal competitions served as diplomacy to avoid violent conflict; tribal religious leaders called for games to heal the sick, alter the weather, or honor the dead; and gambling on the game's outcome allowed for wealth redistribution.[27] The carving of sticks for play was a specialized activity in a tribe, and tribes treated the sticks as sacred objects. Jesuit missionaries were the first to refer to the game as "crosse" and, while the missionaries worried that playing distracted Indians from learning about Christianity, they tolerated the sport.

In the mid-nineteenth century, Canadians organized lacrosse games between white men and Native Americans. George Beers was an enthusiast of the game and thought that with standardization, the sport would grow in popularity and could become Canada's national sport. (One change that he advocated was the shortening of the field. Native Americans would play on fields as long as one mile, and white men could not compete with the running style of play that the Indians used.) Beers saw the Native American game as a savage holdover and saw his role as modernizing the game to make it "civilized."

Beers' project was largely successful; the sport grew in popularity, and Canada organized a tour to England to showcase whites and Indians playing lacrosse. The exposition organizers intended to showcase the differences between "gentlemen" and "savage" players to cultivate an image of Canada that would inspire immigration from England.[28]

In this example, we can see how the trajectories of the concepts of "religion" and "sport" are intertwined with colonial and imperial understandings of civilization and savagery. When we consider religion as a word that changes meaning over time, we might shift the question we ask from "Is sport a religion?" to "What can we see that's new and interesting if we consider, for the purpose of study, sport a religion?"[29] Using the variety of definitions of religion offered here, students can consider what aspects of sport come into relief when we compare sport to religion (emotional intensity, rituals, complicity with colonial ideas of power).

Teaching Tactic

In the book and the film *Friday Night Lights*, football appears as a sacred event surrounded by powerful rituals.[30] The lives of high-school players, former players, coaches, and community members revolve around football season, and they deeply respond to the joy of winning and the grief of defeat. The film does a good job of showcasing the ritualization of high-school football like the pristine layout of uniforms pregame, the sacred objects of football like championship rings, and the community fervor in the stands at games. It also shows the disadvantages of treating football this way—the disposability of injured athletes, the lack of enduring benefit from winning, and the ways sport maintains systemic racism.

I assign students to watch *Friday Night Lights* and discuss it in groups of five or six. Instead of meeting as a full class, the small groups meet without the instructor present to have an hour-long conversation about the film. I assign one student per group to act as moderator. All the students in the group watch the film independently and develop discussion questions that they submit to the moderator the night before the discussion. I also provide a few discussion questions like, "What arguments could someone make that Permian high school football is a religion? What arguments could someone make against this claim?" I suggest that the moderator organize the questions thematically to assist with the flow of conversation.

After the students meet, they submit a report about their conversation. I use the following prompts:

1. What was the most interesting thing you learned from your group discussion? Why was this interesting to you?
2. What was confusing or remains unclear after your discussion?
3. What contributions did you make to the discussion that you thought were particularly strong? (These could be comments that led to further discussion, new ideas that you raised, or some other positive contribution to the group.)

Additionally, the moderator submits a separate report that includes each person's discussion questions and lets me know if each member of the group submitted questions on time, arrived at the discussion on time, and participated throughout. I include in the assignment this information on how I will grade it:

- Your **discussion questions** should reflect engagement with the material and your group should be able to discuss them without outside research.
- You should submit your questions on time and **be punctual and prepared** for your meeting.
- Your **reflection assignment** should be fully completed and should convey your active participation in the meeting.

In general, students appreciate the opportunity to talk without instructor presence and work through ideas and arguments together. One feature of these conversations is that students are willing to bring their personal experiences into the conversation and since many students that enroll for a course titled "Religion and Sports in the US" are athletes or sports fans, their personal experiences often resonate with the material from *Friday Night Lights*. This makes the assignment rewarding in two ways: it validates students' personal experiences as useful for comparison, and it allows students to explore the themes of the course in a way that makes sense and matters to them.

Meeting Students Where They Are

Friday Night Lights is set in high school, and students having recently experienced high school resonate with the film. Though the actors playing the high-school students are not teenagers, students still get the sense that, in the words of one exploration of Texas high-school football, "The prospective heroes are mostly fifteen and sixteen years old, unused to being depended upon for anything at all, justifiably haunted by the fear that they're really still just children."[31] Using something that is likely familiar (high-school football) and an accessible dramatization of the way high-school football can be central to a community (*Friday Night Lights*) allows students to develop discussion questions and dig into these ideas with each other. Through this assignment, students are able to practice critical thinking regarding both defining religion and sacralizing sport.

It may be useful for me to share students' own words on what they gained from this assignment. Since *Friday Night Lights* also showcases Christian rituals like the Lord's Prayer before games, students hesitated to call football the religion of Odessa, but focusing on the social and cultural role of high-school football in Odessa allowed them to engage in comparison with religion. One student shared:

> We were all definitely hesitant to call [high-school football] *the* central religion of Odessa football fans, players, and coaches. However, *Friday Night Lights* showed really well that football brought together a whole town (or state, looking at the prominence of football in Texan culture) as a sort of religious community that shared certain rituals and values.

Students were able to use this comparison to raise critiques of religion, like this student who considered the downsides to religious devotion:

> When comparing religion to football in Mojo [nickname for Permian High School football], it is clear that those who worship football are entirely consumed by it. Their everyday lives are centered around the game in such a way that prevents them from believing there is something more to amount to. Football is the end all be all for the people of Mojo. When looking at religion through this lens, it is evident that this type of relationship is wildly unhealthy. Does this mean that if one puts too much of their faith in religion, that they too, will venture into a toxic, co-dependent relationship?

Similarly, students raised critiques and questions about devotion to sports. Like this student who was struck by the racial discrimination connected to football in Odessa.

> I think the most unclear aspect after the discussion is if football acted as a dividing or unifying force in the Odessa community. My group made strong arguments for both sides, such as the whole community coming together to cheer on the team at Friday night games, versus the clear socioeconomic tensions and stigmas that were perpetuated from the community. I do not think either answer

retracts from a religious categorization argument (as religions have been both forces throughout history), but I would like to get a better grasp on if the living legacy of Permian football helped, harmed, or did not change group feeling in the town. I think the answer to this question is important because it can be applied to how we value the effects of sports in our own community. Should we treat William & Mary Athletics as a potentially social problem-solving force, or just competitive games that can sometimes increase divisions?

Considering these three responses, we can see that *Friday Night Lights* provided a fruitful discussion topic to engage with similarities between religion and sports. Priming students to consider multiple definitions of religions allows for reflection between the two categories and moves beyond assumptions that religion (or sport) is inherently good.

Conclusion

Jay Coakley, a foundational scholar in sociology of sport, has identified a pervasive and unshakable American belief in what he calls the "great sport myth." Coakley describes this as three interrelated, unsubstantiated claims: (1) sport is inherently good and pure, (2) the purity and goodness of sport is transmitted to those who play or consume it, and (3) sport inevitably leads to individual and community development. Coakley argues that for those under the spell of the great sport myth, "They already know the truth about sport and their faith in that truth is much like religious faith—isolated from empirical reality and regularly expressed through unquestioned support of policies and programs in which sport is the focus."[32] Coakley notes that the great sport myth blinds people to the idea that sport may have systemic flaws that can lead to dubious moral actions. Instead, when unethical conduct occurs, media and institutions tend to blame individuals for tainting the purity of sport with their own greed. Introducing students to this idea adds another layer to their discussion. As one student put it:

> The GSM (great sports myth) declares anything sport related to be holy and pure which allows strange and sometimes terrible aspects of Odessa to be observed within *Friday Night Lights*. The GSM is responsible for more of Odessa's social and political structure than I initially thought.

In *Friday Night Lights*, students observed not just the community's commitment to high-school football, but the immense pressure on young men to represent their community, the casual racism in fans' treatment of black players, and the disappointing reality that winning a high-school football championship does not translate into success or satisfaction later in life.

Religious studies scholars have long debated and will continue to debate the boundaries of our discipline. Students new to the study of religion might be surprised to find that the concept of religion is often amorphous and perspectival. When we invite students into our scholarly conversation about the basis of our study, it can help to give them some mooring in something they feel familiar with. Using sports is one method to meet students where they are and offer an avenue into complexity that feels accessible. Since the comparison of religion and sports can resonate with multiple definitions of religion, students can engage in a thought experiment of considering what the similarities between religion and sports might tell us about our culture, our history, and ourselves.

Appendix: Class Discussion Exercise

Discussion 1: *Friday Night Lights*

During this course, you will participate in three small discussion groups. Each meeting will have a clear set of preparatory work and discussion questions. As a member of a discussion group, it is your responsibility to come prepared and on time to your meeting and to actively participate in the discussion. I expect conversations to last about an hour.

You will be graded on this assignment based on three criteria:

- Your **discussion questions** should reflect engagement with the material and your group should be able to discuss them without outside research.
- You should submit your questions on time and **be punctual and prepared** for your meeting.
- Your **reflection assignment** should be fully completed and should convey your active participation in the meeting.

One member of the group will have a special role: the moderator. The moderator's job is to lead the discussion using the discussion questions. The moderator role is worth five points extra credit. This role will rotate every meeting. Moderators are also responsible for writing two or three discussion questions. **All reflections and the moderator's report must be submitted via Blackboard and will not be accepted late. Detail is encouraged.**

Preparation:

- To prepare for this discussion, all members of the group should **read** Jay Coakley, "Assessing the Sociology of Sport: On Cultural Sensibilities and the Great Sport Myth" and **watch** the 2004 film *Friday Night Lights* (not the TV series). Optionally, you can read the Prologue from H.G. Bissinger's book on which the film is based. Links to these are provided on Blackboard.
- Come up with two or three discussion questions based on the themes of our class/unit and the assigned material. Email these discussion questions to your moderator by **midnight the night before your conversation.**

Meeting Agenda:

Introductions: The moderator should lead the group through short introductions. Tell your group members something interesting about yourself. Get to know each other a little bit.

Discussion Questions: The moderator should lead a discussion using some or all of the following questions as well as the questions submitted by group members:

1. What arguments could someone make that Odessa high-school football is a religion? What arguments could someone make against this claim?
2. Do you see evidence of the Great Sport Myth in action? What examples support Coakley's argument and what examples contradict it?

Reflections. It will be helpful for you to **take notes** during your discussion to help you write your reflection.

Moderator's Report. The moderator should collate all submitted discussion questions into one document that includes the names of the students and their submitted questions. The moderator should also include the following regarding each participant:

1. Did the student submit discussion questions on time?
2. Did the student arrive on time and prepared for discussion?

"I Want to Break Free": Abolition and Full Participation in the Religious Studies Classroom

Joseph L. Tucker Edmonds

Introduction

"This feels like a prison." This was not a description of the many prisons that we visited over the course of the semester, but rather it was a comment about the university in general and our classroom space in particular. Needless to say that I was shocked that my imaginative and well-constructed pedagogical space was being compared to a prison by one of my students of color. It stung because this comment came before we had read about carcerality as an organizing framework for the United States and many of its associated institutions. It came before we visited any of our sites or even read about the religious character of American prisons. This off-the-hand comment was uttered as we worked through the syllabus. The class, the assignments, and the creative activities were experienced as constraining rather than creative, as rigid rather than enriching, and as abstract rather than attentive to their needs, concerns, and communities. This class, despite its critical encounter with the scholarship and creative name, felt like many of the other classes that this student had experienced prior to the university and much like the other ones that he was experiencing during the semester. The class was predicated on and organized around the same models and interventions that structured the university, the discipline of religious studies, and my biases as it related to teaching and engagement. It was scaffolded by surveillance and control, and students felt that their full participation and engagement would be limited. This learning environment was clearly not experienced as a space of freedom, liberation, or fugitivity. "Religion Behind Bars: Religion and Mass Incarceration in US Society" was just another class.

At a public university embedded in an urban center in the midwest, I teach a course entitled "Religion Behind Bars." The goal of this course is to help students theorize the carceral state and to engage the relationship between the carceral state, its institutions of confinement, and American religion. Particularly, this course addresses the ways carceral institutions have been shaped by the logic and language of Christianity. In a number of ways similar to how carceral institutions and the carceral state discipline us, shape our behavior, and even inform the broader structure of our society, the discipline of religious studies and our deployment of it discipline and shape our understanding of religious experience and religious communities. In this class, my goal is to challenge the discipline of religious studies in both the texts that we read, our engagement with religious traditions, and the structure of the classroom exercises and assignments. In conversation with Tomoko Masuzawa's groundbreaking text, *The Invention of World Religions,* breaking free or the call to engage the relationship between the category of religion and coloniality needed to be foregrounded.[1]

Breaking free is a pedagogical imperative, or at least a pedagogical framing, for this particular classroom and its encounter with religion in the modern age. The carceral state in the United States is one that has been shaped by the logics of modernity. Modernity is constituted by the logics of racism, capitalism, and colonialism. These logics not only create the modern state but also the modern university. In Lewis Gordon's *Disciplinary Decadence,* Gordon argues that academic disciplines are decadent in the ways that narrow or reduce our understanding of religion to "reductive disciplinary rubrics."[2] Moreover, theories of religious studies have outlined the ways in which the field of Religious Studies has failed to move beyond colonial logics and continues to privilege methods that occlude the vibrancy and diversity of religious experience in the modern world. In this regard, the religious studies classroom and the discipline's peculiar and particular history with coloniality make it an ideal place to question carcerality, embedded categories, and variety and dissonance within lived experience. Just as religion and religious experience have at times been at the center of surveillance and control, they can also be engaged as a space where non-normativity and difference flourish. The study of religion, therefore, provides a compelling opportunity to study the limits and possibilities of the classroom.

In thinking through the process of "breaking free," this article will look at how the theorization of abolition provides a model/metaphor for organizing the class, challenging the hegemony of disciplinary practices, and rethinking the role and need of the carceral state in the current age. In this regard, students and I will use Vincent Lloyd and Joshua Dubler's *Break Every Yoke* and Fred Moten's

The Undercommons: Fugitive Planning and Black Study as texts to think through the process of abolition, full participation, and breaking free throughout the course. It is the argument of this intervention that "abolition" will not only enable students to disrupt long-held assumptions about religion and the carceral state, but also provide them tools to think critically about the university, the production of knowledge, the classroom, and their ability to develop and answer questions that are critical to their experiences and communities of belonging. The classroom, therefore, is transformed into a space where students are encouraged to imagine and inhabit new worlds, create alternative vocabularies, and be fully seen and engaged collaborators. This space is particularly important for students and communities, particularly working-class and first-generation students, who have been misrepresented or not fully included in the university experience.

This chapter will begin with an engagement of fugitivity and abolition. Particularly, it will address the ways in which fugitivity and abolition function in the structure of the classroom, the study of religion, and our encounters with state-sponsored carceral institutions (from the classroom that students inhabit to the prisons and rehabilitation centers/programs that we visit over the course of the semester). What might it mean to abolish the university, classroom, disciplines, or either carceral spaces that shape and inform their lives? Secondly, the chapter will address the ways in which full participation and democratically engaged pedagogy provide space for the process of abolition and the exploration of the discipline of religious studies and the content for this particular course. Finally, I will explore the ways that abolition functions as a pedagogical intervention (or methodological suspicion) within the course design and classroom experiences by exploring a set of tactics/practices that are engaged in this classroom. The hope is that this attention to abolition and full participation as pedagogical practices will be useful in a wide variety of religious studies classrooms and provide a model for rethinking the carceral logics that overdetermine our thinking and our classrooms.

Abolition and the University Classroom

Dubler et al. in *Break Every Yoke* begin with the claim, "The prison needs to be abolished, full stop."[3] "The prison, and the society that depends on the prison, is violent and cruel. Prisons break people. They ravage communities. They are brutal and unjust, and they should be abolished."[4] Abolition in their theoretical scaffolding is not just the end of a particular system, institution, or way of being in the world. Abolition is a real and a disruptive practice. Dubler argues that abolition is a practice that has been and can be deployed throughout democratic society, ranging from the end of enslavement to gun control to the end of prisons. In this regard, abolition can and should be thought of broadly. For the purpose of students at a public university sitting in a religious studies course, I argue that the category is useful for thinking about the classroom and the discipline of religious studies. I want to propose that the classroom as it is traditionally constructed is a carceral space and that students do their best work when they apply a theory like abolition to spaces that are proximate to them and their well-being. This means that rather than beginning with the content of the course, the relation of that problem to academic disciplines or even pressing popular issues, this intervention begins with abolition.

Furthermore, for Dubler et al., abolition "provides a horizon for struggle without which transformative change is impossible."[5] Abolitionism, they argue, "has the power to remake the world."[6] Abolition, like it has been argued by Angela Davis, is about seeing the world, and in this case the classroom, as new and as opening up possibilities or models that were heretofore unimaginable.[7] In *Break Every Yoke*, Dubler argues that radical imagination often requires something beyond what we currently see—this attention to ideas, projects, and models that have yet to be imagined or often forbidden within the classroom or to most who inhabit the university. While the university has traditionally been theorized as a space for academic freedom and radical imagination, academic freedom and the freedom that accompanies it are only available to a chosen few. The spirit of abolition is both a spirit of righteous protest and a concrete, grassroots organizing process. "It gathers those dissatisfied with the menu of options on offer."[8] The abolition spirit haunts the American spirit, Dubler argues, as he surveys its relationship to revolutionary change in the Americas. This history and haunting of abolition is what makes it fertile ground for first-generation students at urban-based research universities. This "haunting" was most clearly articulated by students who remarked that after this class they were not able to turn off their abolitionary spirit or their desire to remove colonial structures and practices.

Abolition is experienced as difficult when the system it is supposed to undo is experienced as indispensable. Abolition requires fundamental changes and recognizing that for many of our students that the university classroom nor any of the classroom spaces that have preceded it have been liberating spaces. Abolition, therefore, as a pedagogical practice is "collectively imagining what will follow after, and experimenting in the present with those possibilities."[9] Angela Davis reminds that this process of abolition and reimagining must not result in a new universal that dominates and denies freedom for the many, but she argues in *Are Prisons Obsolete* that "we imagine a constellation of alternative strategies and institutions."[10] Experimenting in the classroom does not mean that we resolve to create a new university, but rather abolition provides us a lens to resist carcerality in all its forms and to consider new and alternative forms of the university. If Dubler is correct, and the United States is a "prison nation," then this impulse to deny, enslave, and to break folks is present in more spaces than we could imagine. The classroom or our disciplines tend to be more carceral than we like to admit. It is especially a space of control and discipline for those who are new to the university and its patterns of socialization. What does it mean for an abolitionist spirit or a critique of carcerality and the practice of surveillance to be foregrounded in the university classroom? With what should it be paired? Where shall it happen? And with whose permission does it take place?

The Classroom as the Undercommons

If abolition is to be foregrounded in the university classroom, fugitivity must be engaged alongside it. The classroom must function as what Moten and Stefano call "undercommons" or it must at least make space for the student to challenge the very existence and primary disciplining function of the classroom.[11] The undercommons are maroon communities of people who are looking for community and connection in spaces that often deny or criminalize those acts. These communities tend to operate under and outside traditional systems and regimes. Therefore, the university needs an undercommons. The university is not the opposite of the prison as "they are both involved in their way with the reduction and the command of the social individual."[12] The university's business, they argue, "is nothing less than to convert the social individual … into state agents."[13] How do we then abolish this logic or break free of this practice in the religious studies classroom? Fugitivity in and by means of the undercommons is the way by which we create and maintain "maroon communities." It is the way in which students can begin to assess and address the limits of the university classroom. That, however, will not be a part of an evaluative regime, but rather we will begin with practices and pedagogies of abolition at the start of our classroom experience.

As Moten and Stefano argue, the goal is not simply the abolition of universities, classrooms or prisons, but the interrogation and "the abolition of a society that could have prisons, that could have slavery, that could have the wage, and therefore not abolition as the elimination of anything but abolition as the founding a new society."[14] We begin, therefore, by queering or questioning the very foundations of the religious studies classroom—the university, the discipline, the classroom, and its evaluative and formative regimes. Fugitivity requires that we resist the logics of reform politics or rehabilitation that both Moten and Dubler find contemptible and begin to imagine spaces and techniques that free the student. Both marronage and fugitivity articulate a process or pedagogy that suggests that there is a movement toward these new realities. The undercommons or the fugitive student must live "with brokenness, to neglect our debts, and to refuse to repair (or reform) ourselves."[15] There is a community for the fugitive scholar and student, and these places are precisely unmoored from these normative spaces, assignments, and surveillances. And in this new or broken space, our goal is that students would find something new and compelling in the fugitive space. One of these new spaces that students found is a classroom that was willing to be reflective and critical of its practices. Students commented that this class provided them new ways to not only consider this class, but it provided them a model to resist and reimagine other learning spaces.

Pedagogies of Engaged Democracy

The research suggests that in order to facilitate student liberation or thinking outside of normative frameworks that we have to transform the classroom. Liberatory classroom spaces are more than just flipping the classroom or removing certain types of assessments. Critically engaged or participatory driven classrooms place the emphasis and value on the agency and the questions outlined by the students. The students drive the questions asked of the text, and they help to frame the type and tenor of conversations in the classroom. Much of the contemporary literature on Paulo Freire's construct of "problem posing education" starts with the dissolution of customary boundaries between teacher and student, and they highlight that the classroom is a space in which both teachers and students function as learners. Moreover, critically engaged pedagogy begins with identifying classrooms as spaces that have histories of marginalization and oppression. This requires that students and teachers identify their primary work as identifying these carceral practices and logics and begin the work of decarceral practices in the university classroom. As such, this section will engage the expansive literature on democratically engaged work as a response to the carceral nature of the university and the classroom.

While there has been important work on emancipatory education and critically engaged pedagogy, this section will look at the particular impact of a democratically engaged pedagogy. This pedagogical practice posits that the ability to solve a problem rests with the students, teachers, and the broader community. This democratically engaged pedagogy seeks to disrupt the teacher or the university as holding the monopoly on knowledge or theoretical interrogation. Democratically engaged classrooms see the genealogy of the classroom, university, and discipline as essential to the work of the university. Traditional formulations of community-engaged teaching and learning place the university at the center of the solution to public problems. Students and faculty go out to perform tasks as "proto-experts."[16] Within such a pedagogical framework, "student development and social change are often viewed as mutually exclusive."[17] Knowledge and resources flow in a unilateral direction. Prisons or carcerality, therefore, is not a problem or issue exterior to the university.

In democratically engaged pedagogy, the community asks how has the university, the classroom or the discipline contributed to the idea that carcerality is natural and normative. Furthermore, this pedagogy recognizes that most civic problems have been constituted or contorted by the logics of the university.[18] When only one stakeholder is valued as having something to offer, there are no real opportunities for mutual critique or dialogue. This limits possibilities for social transformation because it suspends trust within and across the community. Moreover, left out of the educational experience is attention to power dynamics within the production and valuation of knowledge itself, as well as an effort to examine and transform the institutional culture.[19] By design, courses that look at social problems apart from engaging in serious conversation about their appearance within university life purport a false message of academic elitism and moral purity with the notion being that "we don't have those problems here."

By definition, democratically engaged pedagogy involves community problem-solving. An ideal application of this practice "does not distinguish between the traditional roles of 'student,' 'teacher,' and 'community member'; instead, it assumes that everyone is or will be all three, either simultaneously or in turn."[20] As such, learning and teaching outcomes point outward toward all stakeholders. In this way, civic learning and teaching can become an invaluable source for university and classroom assessment, creating new avenues for reflection, and opening the space for decarceral logics within the university and the classroom.

Furthermore, civic learning can help create a classroom and engaged practices that are based on the idea of full participation. An article on the role of diverse engagement in higher education, "Full Participation: Building the Architecture for Diversity and Public Engagement in Higher Education," builds on efforts on campuses across the country to establish models that link diversity, equity, and community engagement. For the authors, the term "full participation" captures the ways that "the intersections of student and faculty diversity, community engagement, and academic success [can serve] as a nexus for the transformation of communities on and off campus."[21] To put it another way, it is not simply that engagement and diversity are parallel and compatible positives for the university; when linked, each becomes a mechanism for achieving the other. Similarly, full participation sees that student freedom and student learning are necessary outcomes for a democratically engaged university community.

"Full participation is an affirmative value focused on creating institutions that enable people, whatever their identity, background, or institutional position, to thrive, realize their capabilities, engage meaningfully in institutional life, and contribute to the flourishing of others."[22] This concept offers a holistic set of goals that focus attention on (1) the institutional conditions that enable people in different roles to flourish, and (2) the questions designed to mobilize change at the multiple levels and leverage points where change is needed. The goal of full participation in the classroom is to provide opportunities for all students, particularly first generation and BIPOC, students to thrive and flourish in the university. Therefore, the goal of this project is to address the ways in which carceral logics in the classroom, the broader university, and even the discipline prevent students from flourishing and fully participating. So the goal of this intervention is not to fully abolish the classroom or the university but to create spaces where the logic of the university is interrogated or suspended for the benefit of the common good. Students highlighted this attention to the "common good" by discussing the ways this pedagogical intervention shifted their relationship to the broader university. Simply put, students were activated to challenge their professors, transform classrooms, and research other models of the modern university.

Starting with a "Break"

This tactic is intentionally designed to not be a tactic or a normative/required aspect of the classroom experience, but the goal of this intervention is to radically transform the ways that students enter into any classroom space. The hope is that this practice will challenge the larger frame of the university and the university classroom. On the first day of class, students begin the classroom experience by identifying the carceral spaces in the university and this specific class. After participating in the introduction, the students are to identify moments of surveillance, discipline, and control in a typical syllabus (usually one that I've used in previous iterations of this class), the classroom, and the university more broadly. They are also informed that we will collaboratively develop practices, assignments, and a syllabus after the completion of this activity. In order to prime students for this conversation and this nontraditional approach to the first day of class, the students will start off by defining and discussing these terms (surveillance, discipline, and control) in pairs and then watching a brief clip from Ava Duvernay's *13th*. I believe that due to the name of the course (Religion Behind Bars), that the association between these terms and prison will be clear, and that the students will then be able to discuss the ways that these terms and ideas appear in the university. I then ask the students to identify a list of places on campus that they frequent (e.g., cafeteria, library, other classrooms, student center, dorms, etc.) and then ask them to identify the ways in which these ideas appear at those key places.

After the students have completed their engaged research by observing these common student spaces, asking key questions of themselves and other community members, and reporting concepts to the broader community, they will outline the ways in which the practices of surveillance, discipline, and control prevent or mitigate their full participation. Again, all of this activity has preceded any engagement with the reading or even access to the syllabus. The task on the second day of class is to creatively generate ways in which we as a class could reduce carcerality and begin to create practices of full participation. I would articulate that while there are best practices that I could have required or invested in prior to the beginning of class, I explain that full participation and democratically engaged pedagogy are dependent on the voices of the actual participants rather than the idea of some generic set of students or engaged parties. The goal of this opening intervention, therefore, is to suggest that if participation and entry are based upon a normative or assumed set of expectation that "full participation" can never be fully achieved. Furthermore, I remind the students that we are committed to return to this practice of redress as often as we need in order to create a space where all persons can fully participate and challenge the logics of carcerality. Ultimately, as the class progresses, this model of full participation will be applied to the discipline of religious studies, community transformation, and the larger project of civic participation.

When "Religion Behind Bars" began with this "break" rather than the traditional beginning of the class, it provided two important shifts within the classroom. This "break" or the "founding of new space" led to a qualitatively different relationship with the classroom as well as the class. Students noted that rather than the course content being the focus of study that their experience was "bringing their full being," all of their affects, and the broader community into the classroom. Students also articulated that they were more at ease at their radical dissatisfaction with the classroom and the university. The students envisioned themselves as active participants in imagining new possibilities in this classroom as well as the university. They were eager to resist and were now willing to "take apart, dismantle, tear down the structure that, right now, limits our ability to find each other, to see beyond it and to access the places we know lie beyond its walls."[23] They began to imagine themselves as activated citizens and to see the possibilities of not only making themselves present but the broader community.

One of the most compelling insights from this "break" was the demand that more voices be included within the classroom. Students recognized and articulated that the voices allowed in the classroom were arbitrary and a discipling process. As a result, they mandated that other voices be included, especially voices that were not credential or seen as a part of the disciplinary or university canon. Our class at moments became a type of undercommons when students leveraged their "full participation" to introduce new voices and ideas to the larger project of the class. Full participation led to one of my students requesting that their incarcerated brother participate in the course discussions and that we use his letters as a part of the course readings. Another student requested that we reconsider our interaction with the imprisoned who we met at the prisons that we visited. This student suggested that we invite them to participate in the course and ask them what texts and religious traditions to consider in this course. Overall, beginning with the "break" led to a class that was quite different from the one that I initially imagined. Our prison visits changed, our course readings included nontraditional voices, and even our assessments were more attentive to the variety of learning styles and interests in the classroom. Specifically, I allowed for students to create assignments and assessments that were not so focused on the written text and that involved assessment by a broad range of voices. I allowed students to select other members of the university and broader community to assess certain aspects of their assignments. It is not clear if they "broke free," but it is clear that they began to imagine the possibility of doing such.

Conclusion: On Fugitive Preparation

If the larger goal of critical and democratically engaged pedagogy is social transformation, "a revitalized public sphere of public citizens capable of confronting public issues through debate and social action,"[24] then we must acknowledge the import of location and context within educational spaces themselves. Abolition and full participation must not be a project external to the university, but the process of imagining new places of liberation must start within the university and the individual classroom. The goal of this analysis and intervention is to highlight that many religious studies students enter our classrooms and many classrooms with the desire to break free from learning experiences that continue the project of excluding, disciplining, and controlling certain learners and stories. I contend that Religious Studies classrooms provide students with the unique opportunity to engage difference and how that difference is produced and surveilled within colonial contexts. religious studies, at its best, is attempting to use any and all methods to better understand the phenomenon and lived experience of religion. In this way, Religious Studies is unruly and methodologically agnostic, and it can be a space where students, teachers, and community members are tempted to think beyond given categories and frameworks. This model of critical Religious Studies, therefore, points in the direction of full participation, as it encourages us to consider more rigorously and robustly the possibility of making more space for the variety of religious stories. Furthermore, it provides a starting point for the decarceral and democratically engaged pedagogy engaged in this essay.

While this analysis has not "abolished" the classroom or created a fully functioning "undercommons" in line with Moten and Stefano, this project has provided a model to foreground the needs and histories of a diverse cadre of learners. This project has left me, as the professor, and the classroom as uncertain and tentative. A democratically engaged classroom, even one that only slightly gestures in that direction, leaves the professor and the structure of the classroom unmoored from its traditional certainties. I found myself taking on the mantle of a fugitive scholar and teacher who was committed to wait and fully engage the members of my future learning spaces. I realized that my work was to create a space not only for their questions and their critical concerns, but I realized that I was making space for them and myself. As a Black cisgender scholar who had graduated from prestigious universities with the support of parents, who held multiple graduate degrees and one who served as a high-level university administrator, I was consigned to wait before I fully structured the course, the syllabus, the mechanisms of engagement, and to wrestle with unknown possibilities. I too was being pushed to break free and reconsider the radical possibility of learning in and with other restless and broken travelers.

Notes

Introduction

1 For examples of how the term is secularized, one simply has to go to commercial sites like Etsy, and search for Saint candles, with the names of political, artistic, or fictional characters.
2 Anastasia Tsioulcas, "Five Decades on, an Eclectic Church Preaches the Message of John Coltrane." *NPR*. September 23, 2021. https://www.npr.org/2020/09/23/915846867/five-decades-on-an-eclectic-church-preaches-the-message-of-john-coltrane.
3 Tomoko Masuzawa, *The Invention of World Religions: Or, How European Universalism Was Preserved in the Language of Pluralism* (Chicago: University of Chicago Press, 2005).
4 See also Richard King, *Orientalism and Religion: Post-Colonial Theory, India and the Mystic East* (London and New York: Routledge, 1999), 36.
5 Farhad Daftary, "The Study of the Ismailis: Phases and Issues," in *The Study of Shi'i Islam: History, Theology and Law*, eds. Farhad Daftary and Gurdofarid Miskinzoda, (London and New York: Bloomsbury Publishing, 2014), 47–65, esp. 55.
6 See Hussein Rashid, "Plural Voices in the Teaching of Islam," *Thresholds in Education* 41, no. 2 (2018): 87–100, esp. 95–96.
7 William Barylo, *Young Muslim Change-Makers: Grassroots Charities Rethinking Modern Societies* (Abingdon and New York: Routledge, 2018), 13–14.
8 See Rushain Abbasi, "Islam and the Invention of Religion: A Study of Medieval Muslim Discourses on Dīn," *Studia Islamica* 116, no. 1 (2021): 1–106.
9 Gavin Flood, *An Introduction to Hinduism* (New York: Cambridge University Press, 2017), 151.
10 David Chidester, *Empire of Religion: Imperialism and Comparative Religion* (Chicago and London: The University of Chicago Press, 2014).
11 David Chidester, *Authentic Fakes: Religion and American Popular Culture* (Berkeley, CA: University of California Press, 2005), 3.
12 Juliana Hammer, "Islam and Race in American History," in *The Oxford Handbook of Religion and Race in American History*, eds. Paul Harvey and Kathryn Gin Lum, (New York: Oxford University Press, 2018), 205–22; Sylvester Johnson, "Religion, Race, and American Empire," in *The Oxford Handbook of Religion and Race in American History*, eds. Paul Harvey and Kathryn Gin Lum,

(New York: Oxford University Press, 2018), 61–78; Sylvester A. Johnson, *African American Religions, 1500–2000: Colonialism, Democracy, and Freedom* (New York: Cambridge University Press, 2015); K. Merinda Simmons, "Identifying Race and Religion," in *The Oxford Handbook of Religion and Race in American History*, eds. Paul Harvey and Kathryn Gin Lum (New York: Oxford University Press, 2018), 25–39.

13 Judith Weisenfeld, *New World a-Coming: Black Religion and Racial Identity during the Great Migration* (New York: New York University Press, 2016).

14 Chidester, *Empire of Religion*, 52.

15 Dan Hicks, *The Brutish Museums: The Benin Bronzes, Colonial Violence and Cultural Restitution* (London: Pluto Press, 2020), 20.

16 Ronald B. Inden, *Imagining India* (Oxford and Cambridge: Basil Blackwell, 1990).

17 See, for example, Megan Goodwin, *Abusing Religion: Literary Persecution, Sex Scandals, and American Minority Religions* (New Brunswick: Rutgers University Press, 2020).

18 Diane L. Moore, *Overcoming Religious Illiteracy: A Cultural Studies Approach to the Study of Religion in Secondary Education* (New York: Palgrave Macmillan, 2007).

19 Grant Wiggins and Jay McTighe, *Understanding by Design*, 2nd edn (Alexandria: Association for Supervision and Curriculum Development, 2005).

20 "Transparency in Learning and Teaching," TILT Higher Ed, (accessed July 19, 2021), https://tilthighered.com/.

21 Susan A. Ambrose et al., eds., *How Learning Works: Seven Research-Based Principles for Smart Teaching* (San Francisco: Jossey-Bass, 2010).

22 Joshua Eyler, *How Humans Learn: The Science and Stories behind Effective College Teaching* (Morgantown: West Virginia University Press, 2018), 36.

23 Ken Bain, *What the Best College Teachers Do* (Cambridge: Harvard University Press, 2004), 31.

24 Barbara E. Walvoord, "Students' Spirituality and 'Big Questions' in Introductory Religion Courses," *Teaching Theology & Religion* 11 (2008): 3–13.

25 Louis Komjathy, ed., *Contemplative Literature: A Comparative Sourcebook on Meditation and Contemplative Prayer* (New York: SUNY Press, 2015), 11–12; see Religious Studies News' June 18, 2019 Spotlight on Teaching entitled "Contemplative Pedagogy and the Religious Studies Classroom," edited by Sarah Jacoby, which discusses these tensions in greater depth, (accessed July 19, 2021), https://rsn.aarweb.org/spotlight-on-teaching/contemplative-pedagogy/editors-introduction.

26 See the 2004 *Spotlight on Teaching* as well as Carlson, J. "From Site Unseen to Experiential Learning: Religious Studies in the 'Discover Chicago' Model." *Teaching Theology and Religion* 1, no. 2 (1998): 120–7.

27 Beverley McGuire, "Analogous Activities: Tools for Thinking Comparatively in Religious Studies Courses," *Teaching Theology and Religion* 22 (2019): 114–26.
28 Ambrose et al., *How Learning Works*, 83–4.
29 See Eugene V. Gallagher and Joanne Maguire, *Religious Studies Skills Book: Close Reading, Critical Thinking, and Comparison* (New York: Bloomsbury, 2019); Diane L. Moore, "Overcoming Religious Illiteracy: A Cultural Studies Approach," *World History Connected* 4, no. 1 (2015), (accessed August 31, 2021), http://worldhistoryconnected.press.illinois.edu/4.1/moore.html; Eugene V. Gallagher, "Teaching for Religious Literacy," *Teaching Theology and Religion* 12, no. 3 (2009): 208–21; Stephen Prothero, *Religious Literacy: What Every American Needs to Know About Religion and Doesn't* (New York: HarperCollins, 2007); American Academy of Religion, "AAR Religious Literacy Guidelines: What U.S. College Graduates Should Understand about Religion," (accessed August 31, 2021), https://www.aarweb.org/AARMBR/Publications-and-News-/Guides-and-Best-Practices-/Teaching-and-Learning-/AAR-Religious-Literacy-Guidelines.aspx?WebsiteKey=61d76dfc-e7fe-4820-a0ca-1f792d24c06e.
30 Gallagher, "Teaching for Religious Literacy," 208.
31 Karen McCarthy Brown, *Mama Lola: A Vodou Priestess in Brooklyn* (Berkeley: University of California Press, 1991).
32 See Humeira Iqtidar, *Secularizing Islamists?: Jama'at-e-Islami and Jama'at-ud-Da'wa in Urban Pakistan* (Chicago and London: The University of Chicago Press, 2011).

Chapter 1

1 Jennifer Oldstone-Moore, "Sustained Experiential Learning: Modified Monasticism and Pilgrimage," *Teaching Theology and Religion* 12, no. 2 (April 2009): 110.
2 The first amendment of the US Constitution includes two clauses related to religion. The establishment clause prevents creating a government-endorsed religion or religious practice and the free exercise clause allows for choice in the practice of religion, including not being religious at all. Both clauses have been interpreted further through court cases to specify instances in which freedom of religion is restricted (e.g. harm to children) or practices are determined to not be government-neutral (e.g. administratively required engagement in daily Christian prayer in a public school).
3 For example, one of the clearest iterations is found in Manuel Vasquez, *More Than Belief: A Materialist Theory of Religion* (Oxford: Oxford University Press, 2011), 21–41.
4 Caroline Walker Bynum, *Holy Feast and Holy Fast: The Religious Significance of Food to Medieval Women* (Berkeley: University of California Press, 1987); Peter Brown,

The Body and Society: Men, Women, and Sexual Renunciation in Early Christianity (New York: Columbia University Press, 1988); also of note is the first edited volume, including essays from different religious traditions on the topic, Sarah Coakley, ed., *Religion and the Body* (Cambridge: Cambridge University Press, 1997).
5   Marcel Mauss, "Techniques of the Body," *Economy and Society* 2, no. 1 (1973 [1934]): 70–88; and Pierre Bourdieu, *Outline of a Theory of Practice* (Cambridge: Cambridge University Press, 1977).
6   Merleau-Ponty positioned the body-subject as central to perceiving the world, evolving various claims around perception and embodiment across his several publications, including *Phenomenology of Perception*, trans. Colin Smith (New York: Routledge, 1962 [1945]).
7   Notably Michel Foucault, *History of Sexuality*, trans. Robert Hurley (New York: Pantheon, 1978); and Michel Foucault, *Discipline and Punish: The Birth of the Prison*, trans. Alan Sheridan (New York: Vintage, 1995 [1975]).
8   George Lakoff and Mark Johnson, *Metaphors We Live By* (Chicago: University of Chicago Press, 1980), 19 and 57.
9   Ann Taves, *Religious Experience Reconsidered: A Building-Block Approach to the Study of Religion and Other Special Things* (Princeton: Princeton University Press, 2003).
10 Michael Jackson, "Knowledge of the Body," *Man* 18, no. 1 (June 1983): 327–45.
11 Talal Asad, *Genealogies of Religion* (Maryland: Johns Hopkins University Press, 1993), 55–62.
12 Vasudha Narayanan, "Diglossic Hinduism: Liberation and Lentils," *Journal of the American Academy of Religion* 68, no. 4 (2000): 761–79; Chad Bauman and Jennifer Saunders, "Out of India: Immigrant Hindus and South Asian Hinduism in the US," *Religion Compass* 3, no. 1 (2009): 116–35.
13 Thomas Csordas, "Embodiment as a Paradigm for Anthropology," *Ethos* 18, no. 1 (1990): 5–47. In this article, Csordas does not see the body as an object of study, but rather the "existential ground of culture" itself (5); see also his edited volume, *Embodiment and Experience: The Existential Ground of Culture and Self* (Cambridge: Cambridge University Press, 1994).
14 For performance studies intersected with religion, Catherine Bell's *Ritual Theory, Ritual Practice* (Oxford: Oxford University Press, 2009) is a crucial milestone, as well as her chapter, "Performance" in Mark Taylor's *Critical Terms in Religion*, in which she lays out the usual textual and historical approaches to studying Chinese ancestor ritual offerings, and then outlines the ways in which a performance lens changes the analysis to focus more on embodied activities; also Ronald Grimes, *The Craft of Ritual Studies* (Oxford: Oxford University Press, 2013).
15 S. Brent Plate, *A History of Religion in 5 ½ Objects* (New York: Penguin, 2014) and *Material Religion: The Journal of Objects, Art and Belief* that Plate co-founded in 2005.

16 Robert Orsi, *The Madonna of 115th Street: Faith and Community in Italian Harlem, 1880–1950* (New Haven: Yale University, 2010).
17 Sally Promey, ed., *Sensational Religion: Sensory Cultures in Material Practice* (New Haven: Yale University Press, 2014): 1–21. The first footnote in Promey's volume gives an extensive overview of work on the senses and religion including those by David Howes, Constance Klassen, and Kathryn Geurts.
18 Steven Feld, *Sound and Sentiment: Birds, Weeping, Poetics, and Song in Kaluli Expression* (Durham: Duke University Press, 1982).
19 Donovan Schaefer, *Religious Affects: Animality, Evolution and Power* (Durham: Duke University, 2015), 8.
20 As with all of these fully fledged fields, and intersectional approaches, there are multiple scholars to name, but I would highlight Jasbir Puar's *Terrorist Assemblages: Homonationalism in Queer Times* (Durham: Duke University Press, 2007) in conversation with Melissa Wilcox's "Terrorist Assemblages Meets the Study of Religion," *Culture and Religion* 15, no. 2 (2014): 153–7; see also Yvonne Daniel, *Embodied Knowledge in Haitian Vodou, Cuban Yoruba, and Bahian Candomble* (Chicago: University of Illinois Press, 2005).
21 I am using the term discursive in its most basic connection to discourse as spoken and written forms of knowledge. Foucault has expanded on discourse/discursive as connected to knowledge making and power in ways that could include embodied forms of knowing in relation to cultural social codes, although his use of body is often ahistoricized whereas the embodied learning I suggest is particularized to each learner's sensory experiences. I am choosing to not use Foucault's meanings of discursive, although I am addressing power differentials related to knowledge through a different set of lenses.
22 American Academy of Arts & Sciences, Humanities Indicators, "Bachelor's Degrees in Humanities," 2021, https://www.amacad.org/humanities-indicators/higher-education/bachelors-degrees-humanities, (accessed July 31, 2021); Josh Patterson and Rob Townsend, "A Deeper Look at Trends in Undergraduate and Graduate Religion Enrollments and Degree Completions," *Religious Studies News*, January 7, 2021, https://rsn.aarweb.org/trends-religion-enrollments-and-degree-completions, (accessed July 30, 2021).
23 Kimerer L. LaMothe, "What Bodies Know About Religion and the Study of It," *Journal of the American Academy of Religion* 76, no. 3 (2008): 574.
24 Ibid., 593.
25 Ibid., 588–9.
26 When I look at this list of types of pedagogical frameworks, bell hooks comes to mind as a pioneer and influencer on most of these strategies within higher education. See bell hooks, *Teaching to Transgress: Education as a Practice of Freedom* (New York: Routledge, 1994).

27 Diana L. Gustafson, "Embodied Learning: The Body as an Epistemological Site," in *Meeting the Challenge: Innovative Feminist Pedagogies in Action*, eds. Ellen Rose and Maralee Mayberry (New York: Taylor and Francis, 2013), 250.
28 The iceberg model is used to think through culture and/or communication in addition to other adaptations. The range of factors below the surface is often 80–95 percent. See Nigel Thrift, *Spatial Formations* (London: Sage, 1996), 8.
29 Laura I. Rendon, *Sentipensante (Sensing/Thinking) Pedagogy: Educating for Wholeness, Social Justice and Liberation* (Virginia: Stylus Publishing, 2014 [2009]), 14–18; Beth Berila, *Integrating Mindfulness into Anti-Oppression Pedagogy* (New York: Routledge, 2016), 37 and 55.
30 Ibid., 39.
31 Rachel C. Schneider and Sophie Bjork-James, "Whither Whiteness and Religion?: Implications for Theology and the Study of Religion," *Journal of the American Academy of Religion* 88, no. 1 (2020): 175–99.
32 Berila, *Integrating Mindfulness*, 55.
33 Edward Brantmeier and Maria McKenna, "Pedagogy of Vulnerability: Roots, Realities, and the Future," in *Pedagogy of Vulnerability*, eds. E. Brantmeier and M. McKenna (North Carolina: IAP Publishing, 2020), 2.
34 Berila, *Integrating Mindfulness*, 55; Gustafson, "Embodied Learning," 267.
35 Joyce Flueckiger, "Unexpected Learning Opportunities of the Site Visit," Religious Studies News, *Spotlight on Teaching,* 19 (2004). http://rsnonline.org/index7691.html, (accessed February 10, 2022); Jeffrey D. Long, "Site Visits in Interfaith and Religious Studies Pedagogy: Reflections on Visiting A Hindu Temple in Central Pennsylvania," *Teaching Theology & Religion* 21 (2018): 78–91.
36 Becky Kraft, "Engaging the Senses at a Hindu temple in Michigan," Interfaith Center of New York, 2020, https://religiousworldsnyc.org/wp-content/uploads/2020/12/pdfdownload-krafthindutemple.pdf, (accessed July 29, 2021); other site visit curriculum projects posted by the Interfaith Center of New York are available at https://religiousworldsnyc.org/resources/curriculum-projects/#1607619116918-2a61fbb4-7eec.
37 Henry Goldschmidt, "Being There: What do Students Learn by Visiting Houses of Worship?" *Crosscurrents* 68, no. 3 (September 2018): 3.
38 See this tree of contemplative practices circulated by the Center for Contemplative Mind in Society: https://www.contemplativemind.org/practices/tree, (accessed July 30, 2021).
39 See Oldstone-Moore, "Sustained Experiential Learning".
40 Yoga is discussed in Stuart Ray Sarbacker, "Reflections on Theory and Practice: The Case of Modern Yoga", in *Meditation and the Classroom: Contemplative Pedagogy for Religious Studies*, eds. Judith Simmer-Brown and Fran Grace (New York: SUNY, 2011), 147–54; Daniel P. Barbezat and Mirabai Bush, *Contemplative*

Practices in Higher Education (New York: Jossey-Bass, 2014), 168–71; Aikido is the practice discussed in Michelle Mary Lelwica, "Embodying Learning: Post-Cartesian Pedagogy and the Academic Study of Religion," *Teaching Theology & Religion* 12, no. 2 (April 2009): 123–36; Chi gong is the practice discussed in a sociology/Chinese cosmology course on Health, Healing, and Knowledge of the Body by Gustafson, "Embodied Learning," and Roxana Ng, "Decolonizing Teaching and Learning through Embodied Learning: Toward an Integrated Approach," in *Sharing Breath: Embodied Learning and Decolonization*, eds. Sheila Batacharya and Yuk-Lin Renita Wong (Alberta: Athabasca University Press 2018), 33–54; many of these practices have been taught as part of Asian philosophy courses as discussed in Steven Geisz, "Body Practice and Meditation as Philosophy: Teaching Qigong, Taijiquan and Yoga in College Courses," *Teaching Philosophy* 39, no. 2 (June 2016): 115–35.

41 Geisz discusses the issues with perceived advocacy and strategies to avoid this in Geisz, "Body Practice and Meditation," 125–9.
42 Kathleen Fisher, "Look before You Leap: Reconsidering Contemplative Pedagogy," *Teaching Theology and Religion* 20, no. 1 (2017): 4–21.
43 Ibid., 11.
44 Geisz, "Body Practice and Meditation," 119–25.
45 Beverley McGuire, "Analogous Activities: Tools for Thinking Comparatively in Religious Studies Courses," *Teaching Theology and Religion* 22 (2019): 114–26.
46 Elizabeth Perez, *Religion in the Kitchen: Cooking, Talking and the Making of Black Atlantic Traditions* (New York: New York University Press, 2016), 9.
47 Ibid., 98.
48 Megan Watkins, "Gauging the Affective: Becoming Attuned to Its Impact in Education," in *Methodological Advance in Research on Emotion and Education*, eds. M. Zymbalas and P.A. Shultz (New York: Springer, 2016), 71–81; Megan Watkins, "Pedagogic affect/effect: Embodying the desire to learn," *Pedagogies* 1, no. 4 (2006): 269–82.
49 Elspeth Probyn, "Teaching Bodies: Affects in the Classroom," *Body & Society* 10, no. 4 (2004): 33, bracket addition is mine.
50 Eugene Gallagher and Joanne McGuire, *The Religious Studies Skills Book: Close Reading, Critical Thinking, and Comparison* (New York: Bloomsbury, 2019).

Chapter 2

1 Jenna Gray-Hildenbrand and Rebekka King, "Teaching in Contexts: Designing a Competency-based Religious Studies Program," *Teaching Theology and Religion* 22 (2019): 191–204.

2   Presently, I use the textbook: Gary Kessler, *Studying Religion: An Introduction Through Cases* 3rd edn (Boston: McGraw-Hill, 2008); see also: Eugene V. Gallagher and Joanne Maguire, *The Religious Studies Skills Book: Close Reading, Critical Thinking, and Comparison* (London: Bloomsbury Academic, 2018); Stephen Prothero, *Religion Matters: An Introduction to the World's Religions* (New York: W.W. Norton & Co., 2020).

3   For more on legal issues and bracketing see: Eugene V. Gallagher and Joanne Maguire, *The Religious Studies Skills Book: Close Reading, Critical Thinking, and Comparison* (London: Bloomsbury Academic, 2018), 52–4.

4   American Academy of Religion, "AAR Religious Literacy Guidelines: What U.S. College Graduates Need to Understand About Religion," (2019). Available online: https://www.aarweb.org/AARMBR/Publications-and-News-/Guides-and-Best-Practices-/Teaching-and-Learning-/AAR-Religious-Literacy-Guidelines.aspx?WebsiteKey=61d76dfc-e7fe-4820-a0ca-1f792d24c06e.

5   Emily O. Gravett, "Lost in the Great Divide: Motivation in Religious Studies Classrooms," *Teaching Theology and Religion* 21 (2018): 24; see also Eugene V. Gallagher and Joanne Maguire, *The Religious Studies Skills Book: Close Reading, Critical Thinking, and Comparison* (London: Bloomsbury Academic, 2018), 51–8; Russell T. McCutcheon, *Critics Not Caretakers: Redescribing the Public Study of Religion* (Albany: SUNY Press, 2001).

6   Barbara E. Walvoord, *Teaching and Learning in College Introductory Religion Courses* (Malden: Blackwell, 2008), 13–22; see also, Barbara E. Walvoord, "Students' Spirituality and 'Big Questions' in Introductory Religion Courses," *Teaching Theology and Religion* 11, no. 1 (2007): 3–13.

7   Gravett, "Lost in the Great Divide," 25.

8   Ibid., 25.

9   Stephen Prothero, "Belief Unbracketed: A Case for the Religion Scholar to Reveal More of Where He or She Is Coming From," *Harvard Divinity Bulletin* 32, no. 2 (Winter/Spring 2004): 10–11.

10 Prothero, "Belief Unbracketed," 11.

11 Ibid., 11.

12 It should be noted that Stephen Prothero's introductory textbook, *Religion Matters*, provides a discussion on bracketing and the value of empathetic understanding, and then states to students "Of course, this is an impossible task." His answer is to bring knowledge of the world religions in combination with empathy and criticism using a comparative approach. Stephen Prothero, *Religion Matters: An Introduction to the World's Religions* (New York: W.W. Northon & Co., 2020), 8).

13 David Chidester, "Moralizing Noise," *Harvard Divinity Bulletin* 32, no. 3 (Summer 2004): 17.

14 Ibid., 17.

15 R. Marie Griffith, "Maintaining Empathy," *Harvard Divinity Bulletin* 32, no. 3 (Summer 2004): 18.
16 Ibid., 18.
17 Robert A. Orsi, "A 'Bit of Judgment,'" *Harvard Divinity Bulletin* 32, no. 3 (Summer 2004): 16.
18 Ibid., 16–17.
19 Thomas A. Tweed, "On Moving Across: Translocative Religion and the Interpreter's Position," *Journal of the American Academy of Religion* 70, no. 2 (June 2002): 257.
20 Paulo Freire, *Pedagogy of the Oppressed*, 50th anniversary edn (New York: Bloomsbury, 2020), 71–3.
21 Rosemarie Garland-Thomson, "Feminist Disability Studies," *Signs* 30, no. 2 (Winter 2005): 1557–67.
22 Shelly L. Tremain, "Philosophy of Disability as Critical Diversity Studies," *International Journal of Critical Diversity Studies* 1, no. 1. (June 2018): 42.
23 Ben Pitcher and Henriette Gunkel, "Q&A with Jasbir Puar," *Darkmatter Journal* (May 2008). Available online: http://www.darkmatter101.org/site/2008/05/02/qa-with-jasbir-puar/.
24 Ellen Samuels, "Judith Butler's Body Theory and the Question of Disability," *NWSA Journal* 14, no. 3 (Autumn 2002): 65.
25 Cynthia Lewiecki-Wilson and Jen Cellio-Miller, eds., *Disability and Mothering: Liminal Spaces of Embodied Knowledge* (Syracuse: Syracuse University Press, 2011), 7.
26 Walvoord, "Students' Spirituality and 'Big Questions,'" 4.
27 Ibid., 5.
28 Ibid., 5–8.
29 Kristina R. Knoll, "Feminist Disability Studies Pedagogy," *Feminist Teacher* 19, no. 2 (2009): 129.
30 Ibid., 130.
31 Jan H. F. Meyer and Ray Land, "Threshold Concepts and Troublesome Knowledge (2): Epistemological Considerations and Conceptual Framework for Teaching and Learning," *Higher Education* 49, no. 3 (April 2005): 382–5.
32 Ibid., 377.
33 See Jill DeTemple, Eugene Gallagher, Pui-lan Kwok and Thomas Pearson, "Reflective Structured Dialogue: A Conversation with 2018 American Academy of Religion Excellence in Teaching Award Winner Jill DeTemple," *Teaching Theology and Religion* 22 (2019): 223–34.
34 Ibid., 226.
35 Michael Jerryson, "Why 'Do You Believe in God?' Is at the Heart of Our Religious Problem," *Religion Dispatches* (June 3, 2019). Available online https://religiondispatches.org/why-do-you-believe-in-god-is-at-the-heart-of-our-religious-problem/. I provide the short essay in multiple accessible formats based on conversations with students at the start of the semester.

36 Again, building upon Puar's idea of assemblage. Ben Pitcher and Henriette Gunkel, "Q&A with Jasbir Puar," *Darkmatter Journal* (May 2008). Available online: http://www.darkmatter101.org/site/2008/05/02/qa-with-jasbir-puar/.
37 Michael Jerryson died in July 2021. He was forty-seven years old. The groundbreaking scholarship and long-standing friendships he left behind are a testament to his intelligence, compassion, and commitment to both during his life. See "After Michael Jerryson (1974–2021) Nobody Will Ever Look at Buddhism the Same Way", *Religion Dispatches* (July 14, 2021). Available online: https://religiondispatches.org/after-michael-jerryson-1974-2021-nobody-will-ever-look-at-buddhism-the-same-way/.
38 Robert Orsi, *Between Heaven and Earth: The Religious Worlds People Make and the Scholars who Study Them* (Princeton: Princeton University Press, 2005), 198.
39 Ibid., 17.
40 Tweed, "On Moving Across," 260.

Chapter 3

1 Naomi Klein, *The Shock Doctrine: The Rise of Disaster Capitalism* (New York: Picador, 2008).
2 Eugene Gallagher and Joanne Maguire, *Religious Studies Skills Book: Close Reading, Critical Thinking, and Comparison* (London and New York: Bloomsbury, 2018), 43.
3 Ibid., 51.
4 Elizabeth Drescher, *Choosing Our Religion: The Spiritual Lives of Americas Nones* (New York: Oxford University Press, 2016).
5 Sarah Imhoff, "The Creation Story of Religious Studies, or How We Learned to Stop Worrying and Love Schempp," *Journal of the American Academy of Religion* 84, no. 2 (June 2016): 492.
6 Rainer Maria Rilke, "Archaic Torso of Apollo," *All Parting: Selected Poetry and Prose of Rainer Maria Rilke*, trans. Stephen Mitchell (New York: Modern Library, 1995), https://poets.org/poem/archaic-torso-apollo.
7 Stefano Harney and Fred Moten, *The Undercommons: Fugitive Planning and Black Study* (Wivenhoe, New York and Port Watson: Minor Compositions, 2013).
8 Eve Kosofsky Sedgwick, *Touching Feeling: Affect, Pedagogy, Performativity* (Durham and London: Duke University Press, 2003).
9 Rahuldeep Gill, Lecture in South Asian Thought at California Lutheran University, April 29, 2019.
10 Joseph R. Winters, *Hope Draped in Black: Race, Melancholy, and the Agony of Progress* (Durham and London: Duke University Press, 2016).
11 Harney and Moten, *The Undercommons*, 126–7.

12 Jennifer Doyle, *Campus Sex, Campus Security* (South Pasadena: Semiotext(e), 2015), 112.
13 Sedgwick, *Touching Feeling*, 149.
14 Gill, "Lecture in South Asian Thought."
15 Winters, *Hope Draped in Black*, 213.
16 Jeremy N. Bailenson, "Nonverbal Overload: A Theoretical Argument for the Causes of Zoom Fatigue," *Technology, Mind, and Behavior* 2, no. 1 (2021), https://tmb.apaopen.org/pub/nonverbal-overload/release/1.
17 Jill DeTemple and John Sarrouf, "Disruption, Dialogue, and Swerve: Reflective Structured Dialogue in Religious Studies Classrooms," *Teaching Theology and Religion* 20, no. 3 (2017): 283–92.

Chapter 4

1 I dedicate this chapter to Dr. Thomas Pearson, in honor of his inspiring vision, immense labors, and radical hospitality during his two decades at the Wabash Center for Teaching and Learning in Theology and Religion. Moreover, I give thanks to the three Wabash Center cohorts who nurtured me as I crafted these ideas and helped me refine them, amidst multiple crises in our world and in my family.
2 That the learning process inherently depends on emotional factors is strongly suggested by, for example, Chapters 3 and 6 in Susan Ambrose et al., *How Learning Works: 7 Research-Based Principles for Smart Teaching* (Hoboken, NJ: Jossey-Bass, 2010), although they do not give the matter sufficient attention.
3 My pedagogical contentions and conclusions in this chapter do not depend on a strict differentiation between feelings and emotions.
4 See, for example, Antonia Darder, Marta P. Baltodano, and Rodolfo D. Torres, eds., *The Critical Pedagogy Reader*, 3rd edn (New York: Routledge, 2017).
5 See, for instance, Ambrose et al., *How Learning Works*, 174–6.
6 Richard Sennett and John Cobb, *The Hidden Injuries of Class* (New York: Knopf, 1972); also see Barbara Jensen, *Reading Classes: On Culture and Classism in America* (Ithaca: ILR Press, 2012).
7 Readers may find it curious that I do not engage the voluminous literature of affect theory. This is because affect theory is one of several effective models for conceptualizing emotions, and I do not want to suggest that the further conversation within the discipline that I am calling for must be grounded specifically in affect theory.
8 Kathleen Quinlan, *How Higher Education Feels: Commentaries on Poems That Illuminate Emotions in Learning and Teaching* (Boston: Sense Publishers, 2016).

9 These stances are stated throughout the introduction of Quinlan, *How Higher Education Feels*.
10 "Social-emotional learning" (SEL), a model currently having wide reception in K-12 education and beginning to gain more attention in higher education, largely fits with these two stances. The "affective learning" model, derived from work by famed taxonomist Benjamin Bloom and collaborators, emphasizes emotional attitudes and values toward things being encountered in the learning process, in this way blending stances 6 and 3. See "Fundamentals of SEL," Collaborative for Student Academic, Social, and Emotional Learning, (accessed September 16, 2021), https://casel.org/fundamentals-of-sel/what-is-the-casel-framework; Mary Miller, "Teaching and Learning in the Affective Domain," Emerging Perspectives on Learning, Teaching, and Technology (website), 2005, http://epltt.coe.uga.edu/index.php?title=Teaching_and_Learning_in_Affective_Domain.
11 Quinlan, *How Higher Education Feels*, 15.
12 Ibid.
13 There has been some consideration of the emotional labor that instructors perform in teaching. Instructors' dual role as both emotional laborers and structurers of students' emotional labor is an important area for further research.
14 Arlie Russell Hochschild, *The Managed Heart: Commercialization of Human Feeling*, 3rd edn (Berkeley: University of California Press, 2012); Amy Wharton, "The Sociology of Emotional Labor," *Annual Review of Sociology* 35 (2009): 147–65.
15 Julie Beck, "The Concept Creep of 'Emotional Labor,'" *The Atlantic*, November 26, 2018, https://www.theatlantic.com/family/archive/2018/11/arlie-hochschild-housework-isnt-emotional-labor/576637.
16 Dennis Covington, *Salvation on Sand Mountain: Snake Handling and Redemption in Southern Appalachia* (Philadelphia: Da Capo Press, 2009); Sara Miles, *Take This Bread: A Radical Conversion* (New York: Random House, 2007). Covington's portrayal certainly has its problems, but it is sufficient for its primary purpose in the course, which is to compare Covington's (account of his) experiences with Miles'. See the excellent critique raised in Jenna Gray-Hildenbrand, "The Appalachian 'Other': Academic Approaches to the Study of Serpent-Handling Sects," *Religion Compass* 10, no. 3 (2016): 47–57.
17 Before I ask them this, however, I acknowledge that there might be some students in the class who have participated in snake-handling Christianity, so we need to speak respectfully even while answering candidly (although there hasn't yet been—I ask students to let me know privately if they have). This is a way of recognizing that there might be competing emotional experiences among the students.
18 Charles Marsh, *God's Long Summer: Stories of Faith and Civil Rights* (Princeton, NJ: Princeton University Press, 2008).

19 While in other courses there may be pedagogical justification for asking students to read this section, in this course, it is possible pedagogical value is only enough to make it optional.
20 A useful resource for these conversations has been Lisa Landreman, ed., *The Art of Effective Facilitation: Reflections for Social Justice Educators* (Sterling: Stylus Publishing, 2013).
21 When there is a clash between letting students honestly express whatever they feel and upholding my pedagogical (and my institution's) commitments to *equitable* diversity and inclusion, the latter takes priority. I've never had a student openly express pro-segregationist or pro-White supremacist feelings, but if they emerged in class, my inclination is that the most effective response (given my goal of opening the student to challenging their own racist sympathies) would be to not turn the moment into a public shaming but also find a way for the student to hear how others are hurt by such expressions, and then afterward try to engage the student one-on-one in at least trying to see things from another perspective and/or find another aspect of social life that would allow the student to come to empathy by analogy or personal connection. See Diane Goodman, *Promoting Diversity and Social Justice: Educating People from Privileged Groups*, 2nd edn (New York: Routledge, 2011).
22 I explicitly permit students of color to opt out of a given class-session (but not out of the readings and written responses) without penalty if they would find it traumatizing to participate, although no student has ever taken this option.
23 See Derald Wing Sue, *Race Talk and the Conspiracy of Silence: Understanding and Facilitating Difficult Dialogues on Race* (Hoboken: Wiley, 2015).

Chapter 5

1 Robin Le Poidevin, *Arguing for Atheism: An Introduction to the Philosophy of Religion* (New York: Routledge, 1996), 135–46.
2 Garrett Green, "Challenging the Religious Studies Canon: Karl Barth's Theory of Religion", *The Journal of Religion* 75, no. 4 (1995): 473–86. Richard Newton, "Religious Studies LLC and the Question of Canon", *Sowing the Seed* (2015). Available online: https://sowingtheseed.wordpress.com (accessed May 12, 2021); K. Merinda Simmons, "Cannon Fodder", *Method & Theory in the Study of Religion* 28, no. 3 (2016), 297–306; Russel McCutcheon, *Studying Religion: An Introduction* (New York: Routledge, 2018).
3 Sallyann Roth, "Speaking the Unspoken: A Work-Group Consultation to Reopen Dialogue", in *Secrets in Families and Family Therapy*, ed. Evan Imber-Black (New York: W.W. Norton, 1993), 268–9.

4   Dr. Beverley McGuire, editor of this volume, was that colleague. While I can't remember what she said or the question she asked, I am forever grateful that she did. I am also grateful for, and an advocate of, the kinds of teaching and learning communities that spawn conversations like this one. As Phil Fernbach and Steve Sloman have argued, most knowledge is communal, and best supported by communal experiences. See Steven Sloman and Philip Fernbach, *The Knowledge Illusion* (New York: Riverhead Books, 2017).
5   Jill DeTemple, "The Spaces We Make: Dialogic Classrooms and Social Transformation", *Ohio State Journal on Dispute Resolution* 35, no. 5 (2020), 753–79.
6   bell hooks, *Teaching to Transgress: Education as the Practice of Freedom* (New York: Routledge, 1994); Michael Roth, "A Focus on Critical Feeling," *Inside Higher Ed*, March 18, 2021; Carol Dweck, *Self-Theories: Their Role in Motivation, Personality, and Development* (Philadelphia: Psychology Press, 2000); Nel Noddings, *Happiness and Education* (New York: Cambridge University Press, 2003); Jane Fried, *Of Education, Fishbowls and Rabbit Holes: Rethinking Teaching and Liberal Education for an Interconnected World* (Sterling: Stylus Press, 2016); Rita Felski, *The Limits of Critique* (Chicago: University of Chicago Press, 2015); Charles Taylor, *The Ethics of Authenticity* (Cambridge: Harvard University Press, 1991).
7   David Chidester, *Empire of Religion* (Chicago: University of Chicago Press, 2014); Anna Tsing, "The Global Situation", *Cultural Anthropology* 15, no. 3 (2000), 327–60.
8   Joshua Eyler, *How Humans Learn: The Science and Stories Behind Effective College Teaching* (Morgantown: University of West Virginia Press, 2018); Tomoko Masuzawa, *The Invention of World Religions* (Chicago: University of Chicago Press, 2005).
9   Jill DeTemple and John Sarrouf, "Disruption, Dialogue, and Swerve: Reflective Structured Dialogue in Religious Studies Classrooms", *Teaching Theology and Religion* 20, no. 3 (2017), 283–93; Shawna Shapiro, "Inclusive Pedagogy in the Academic Writing Classroom: Cultivating Communities of Belonging", *Journal of Academic Writing* 10, no. 1 (2020), 154–64.
10 "Moments of Dissent" [exercise], Essential Partners, Inc.
11 *Beyond Sacred Documentary* (2015), [Film] Dir. Ping Chong, USA.
12 Robert Kegan, *In Over Our Heads: The Mental Demands of Modern Life* (Cambridge: Harvard University Press, 1994), 185, italics in original.
13 Marcia Baxter Magdola, "Three Elements of Self-Authorship", *Journal of College Student Development* 49, no. 4 (2008), 269–84.
14 Dweck, *Self-Theories*; Jason Baehr, "Educating for Intellectual Virtues: From Theory to Practice", *Journal of the Philosophy of Education* 47, no. 2 (2013): 248–62; Ken Bain, *What the Best College Teachers Do* (Cambridge: Harvard University Press, 2004).
15 Baehr, "Educating for Intellectual Virtues".

16 For an especially useful overview of this concept see Eyler, *How Humans Learn*, 80–2.
17 Mircea Eliade, *The Myth of the Eternal Return or Cosmos and History* (Princeton: Princeton University Press, 1971); Ninian Smart, *Dimensions of the Sacred* (Berkeley: University of California Press, 1986); Huston Smith, *The World's Religions: Our Great Wisdom Traditions* (New York: HarperCollins, 1991).
18 "Course Catalogue", *Graduate Program in Religious Studies, Southern Methodist University* (Dallas: Southern Methodist University, 2020).
19 Masuzawa, *The Invention*; Chidester, *Empire*; McCutcheon, *Studying Religion*.
20 See Goldschimdt, Maguire, Blazer in this volume.
21 Chong, *Beyond Sacred*.
22 Eyler, *How Humans Learn*, 72–4.
23 "Our Method", *Essential Partner, Inc.* https://www.whatisessential.org/our-method
24 DeTemple, *Spaces We Make*, 758–63.

Chapter 6

1 Diane L. Moore, *Overcoming Religious Illiteracy: A Cultural Studies Approach to the Study of Religion in Secondary Education* (New York: Palgrave Macmillan, 2007).
2 Edward W. Said, *Covering Islam: How the Media and the Experts Determine How We See the Rest of the World* (New York: Pantheon Books, 1981), 52.
3 Abū Ḥanīfah ibn Muḥammad Nuʿmān, *The Pillars of Islam: Daʿāʾim Al-Islām*, trans. Ismail Kurban Husein Poonawala (Oxford: Oxford University Press, 2002).
4 Susan L. Douglass, and Ross E. Dunn, "Interpreting Islam in American Schools," *The Annals of the American Academy of Political and Social Science* 588, no. 1 (2003): 52–72.
5 A casual survey of several introductory texts shows they have explicit mentions of the Five Pillars in their table of contents, structure their table of contents around the Five Pillars, or have extended discussions of the Five Pillars in their belief and practices sections. See John L. Esposito, *Islam: The Straight Path* (New York and Oxford: Oxford University Press, 2011); Carole Hillenbrand, *Introduction to Islam: Beliefs and Practices in Historical Perspective* (New York: Thames & Hudson, 2015); Neal Robinson, *Islam: A Concise Introduction* (Richmond, Surrey: Curzon, 1999); Malise Ruthven, *Islam: A Very Short Introduction* (New York: Oxford University Press, 1997); Roberto Tottoli, *Islam: An Advanced Introduction* (Abingdon and New York: Routledge, Taylor & Francis Group, 2021).
6 Susan L. Douglass, and Ross E. Dunn, "Interpreting Islam in American Schools," *The Annals of the American Academy of Political and Social Science* 588, no. 1 (2003): 52–72; Susan L. Douglass, "Teaching About Religion, Islam, and the World

in Public and Private School Curricula," in *Educating the Muslims of America*, eds. Yvonne Yazbeck Haddad, Farid Senzai and Jane I. Smith (Oxford and New York: Oxford University Press, 2009); Abdellatif W. Al Sager and Lisa Zagummy, "Teaching Islam Without the Phobia: What We Can Learn From World History Textbooks," *Thresholds in Education* 41, no. 2 (2018): 75–86.

7   See Moustafa Bayoumi, *This Muslim American Life: Dispatches from the War on Terror* (New York: New York University Press, 2015); Peter Gottschalk, and Gabriel Greenberg, *Islamophobia and Anti-Muslim Sentiment: Picturing the Enemy* (Lanham: Rowman & Littlefield, 2019).

8   Tomoko Masuzawa, *The Invention of World Religions: Or, How European Universalism Was Preserved in the Language of Pluralism* (Chicago: University of Chicago Press, 2005). See also David Chidester, *Empire of Religion: Imperialism and Comparative Religion* (Chicago and London: The University of Chicago Press, 2014).

9   Farhad Daftary, "The Study of the Ismailis: Phases and Issues," in *The Study of Shi'i Islam: History, Theology and Law*, eds. Farhad Daftary and Gurdofarid Miskinzoda (London and New York: Bloomsbury Publishing, 2014), 55.

10 Ilyse Morgenstein Fuerst, "Job Ads Don't Add Up: Arabic + Middle East + Texts ≠ Islam," *Journal of the American Academy of Religion* 88, no. 4 (2020): 915–46.

11 See Panayiota Kendeou and Edward J. O'Brien, "The Knowledge Revision Components (Krec) Framework: Processes and Mechanisms," in *Processing Inaccurate Information: Theoretical and Applied Perspectives from Cognitive Science and the Educational Sciences*, eds. David Rapp and Jason L. G. Braasch (Cambridge: MIT Press, 2014), 353–77.

12 Moore, *Overcoming Religious Illiteracy*. For a more comprehensive overview of how I structure my "Islam 101" class, see Hussein Rashid, "Diverse Muslim Narratives: Rethinking Islam 101," *The Wabash Center Journal on Teaching* 2, no. 1 (2021): 143–58.

13 Moore, *Overcoming Religious Illiteracy*, 79–80.

14 Stuart Hall, Jennifer Daryl Slack and Lawrence Grossberg, *Cultural Studies 1983: A Theoretical History* (Durham and London: Duke University Press, 2016), 8.

15 See also Richard King, *Orientalism and Religion: Post-Colonial Theory, India and the Mystic East* (London and New York: Routledge, 1999), 53.

16 Stuart Hall and David Morley, *Essential Essays* (Durham: Duke University Press, 2019), 38 and 41.

17 See also Carl W. Ernst, *Following Muhammad: Rethinking Islam in the Contemporary World* (Chapel Hill: University of North Carolina Press, 2003), 55.

18 Hall and Morley, *Essential Essays*, 51.

19 Amir Hussain, "Images of Muḥammad in Literature, Art, and Music," in *The Cambridge Companion to Muhammad*, ed. Jonathan E. Brockopp (Cambridge: Cambridge University Press, 2010); Marion Holmes Katz, "The Prophet Muḥammad

in Ritual," in *The Cambridge Companion to Muhammad*, ed. Jonathan E. Brockopp (Cambridge: Cambridge University Press, 2010); Walid A. Saleh, "The Arabian Context of Muḥammad's Life," in *The Cambridge Companion to Muhammad*, ed. Jonathan E. Brockopp (New York: Cambridge University Press, 2010).

20 Christiane J. Gruber, and Frederick Stephen Colby, eds. *The Prophet's Ascension: Cross-Cultural Encounters With the Islamic Mi'rāj Tales* (Bloomington: Indiana University Press, 2010); Kecia Ali, *The Lives of Muhammad* (Cambridge: Harvard University Press, 2014); Ali Sultaan Ali Asani, Kamal Abdel-Malek and Annemarie Schimmel, *Celebrating Muhammad: Images of the Prophet in Popular Muslim Poetry* (Columbia: University of South Carolina Press, 1995); Christiane J. Gruber, *The Praiseworthy One: The Prophet Muhammad in Islamic Texts and Images* (Bloomington: Indiana University Press, 2018); Michael Muhammad Knight, *Muhammad: Forty Introductions* (New York: Soft Skull, 2019).

21 For taking the knowledge of learners seriously, see Paulo Freire, *Pedagogy of the Oppressed* (New York: Continuum, 1993). For considering how to build community through shared knowledge, see bell hooks, *Teaching to Transgress: Education as the Practice of Freedom* (New York: Routledge, 1994).

Chapter 7

1 This phrase was trademarked by Apple in 2010. Doug Gross, "Apple trademarks 'There's an app for that'," *CNN* (October 12, 2010). http://www.cnn.com/2010/TECH/mobile/10/12/app.for.that/index.html, (accessed July 21, 2021).

2 For a discussion and critique of the commercialization and consumption of meditation apps, see Beverley McGuire, "Buddhist-inspired Self-tracking Apps: Tracking Emotions and Values in a Digital Era," *Journal of the Japanese Association for Digital Humanities* 5, no. 2 (2020): 43–60.

3 Jane Naomi Iwamura, *Virtual Orientalism: Asian Religions and American Popular Culture* (New York: Oxford University Press, 2011); Edward Said, *Orientalism* (New York: Vintage, 1979).

4 Kathryn Lofton, *Consuming Religion* (Chicago: The University of Chicago, 2017); Jeff Wilson, *Mindful America* (New York: Oxford University Press, 2014); Jeremy Carrette and Richard King, *Selling Spirituality: The Silent Takeover of Religion* (New York: Routledge, 2004).

5 Susan A. Ambrose et al., *How Learning Works: 7 Research-Based Principles for Smart Teaching* (San Francisco: John Wiley & Sons, 2010).

6 Lofton, *Consuming Religion*, 8.

7 Michael Storper, "Lived Effects of the Contemporary Economy: Globalism, Inequality, and Consumer Society," *Public Culture* 12, no. 2 (Spring 2000): 392.

8   Incidentally, this is the same type of media consumption that Kathryn Lofton describes at the beginning of *Consuming Religion*: she has her readers imagine themselves reading an article in an airline magazine. Lofton, *Consuming Religion*, ix.
9   Ira Shor, *Empowering Education: Critical Teaching for Social Change* (Chicago: The University of Chicago Press, 1992), 15.
10 Peter McLaren, *Life in Schools* (New York: Longman, 1989), 186.
11 George W. Gagnon and Michelle Collay, *Designing for Learning: Six Elements in Constructivist Classrooms* (Thousand Oaks: Corwin Press, Inc., 2001).
12 Henry Giroux, *On Critical Pedagogy* (New York: Continuum, 2011), 3.
13 Paolo Friere, *Pedagogy of the Oppressed*, new revised 20th anniversary edn (New York: Continuum, 1999), 64.
14 Giroux, *On Critical Pedagogy*, 14.
15 hooks, *Teaching to Transgress*, 21.
16 I am grateful to Henry Goldschmidt and Cooper Minister for pointing out this opportunity for student reflection.
17 Ambrose et al., *How Learning Works*.
18 L. Dee, Fink, *Creating Significant Learning Experiences: An Integrated Approach to Designing College Courses* (San Francisco: Jossey-Bass, 2013).

Chapter 8

1   Catherine L. Albanese, *America: Religions and Religion* (United States: Cengage Learning, 2013).
2   Stephen Prothero, *God Is Not One: The Eight Rival Religions That Run the World—and Why Their Differences Matter* (New York: HarperOne, 2010), 3–6.
3   Stephen Prothero, *Religion Matters: An Introduction to the World's Religions* (New York: W.W. Norton & Company, Ltd., 2020), 18.
4   Tomoko Masuzawa, *The Invention of World Religions: Or, How European Universalism Was Preserved in the Language of Pluralism* (Chicago: University of Chicago Press, 2007), 326–7.
5   Lori G. Beaman, "The Myth of Pluralism, Diversity, and Vigor: The Constitutional Privilege of Protestantism in the United States and Canada," *Journal for the Scientific Study of Religion* 42, no. 3 (2003): 313.
6   Ibid., 312.
7   This three-part formula is based on Catherine Albanese's well-known textbook *America: Religions and Religion* (United States: Cengage Learning, 2013). It is my own loose interpretation of her three categories of manyness and oneness: original cast, expansion and contraction, and newmade in America. Instead of an historical lens, I apply a thematic one, organizing along the lines of cultural hegemony.

8   Catherine L. Albanese, *America: Religions and Religion* (United States: Cengage Learning, 2013).
9   Charles H. Long, *Significations Signs, Symbols, and Images in the Interpretation of Religion* (Aurora: Davies Group, 1999), 163.
10 Charles H. Long, "Civil Rights—Civil Religion: Visible People and Invisible Religion," in *American Civil Religion*, eds. Russell E. Richey and Donald G. Jones (San Francisco: Mellen Research University Press, 1990), 211–21; Albert J. Raboteau, *A Fire in the Bones: Reflections on African-American Religious History* (Boston: Beacon Press, 2001); Khyati Joshi, "The Racialization of Hinduism, Islam, and Sikhism in the United States," *Equity & Excellence in Education* 39 (2006): 211–26; Jane Naomi Iwamura, "Critical Faith: Japanese Americans and the Birth of a New Civil Religion," *American Quarterly* 59, no. 3 (2007): 937–68.
11 Including but not limited to: Russell T. McCutcheon, *Studying Religion: An Introduction* (New York: Routledge, 2019); Steven W. Ramey, *Writing Religion: The Case for the Critical Study of Religion* (Tuscaloosa: University Alabama Press, 2015); and David G. Robertson and Christopher R. Cotter, *After "World Religions": Reconstructing Religious Studies* (Basingstoke: Taylor & Francis Ltd, 2016).
12 Jenna Gray-Hildenbrand and Rebekka King, "Teaching in Contexts: Designing a Competency-Based Religious Studies Program," *Teaching Theology and Religion* 22 (2019): 191–204.
13 Eugene V. Gallagher and Joanne Maguire, *The Religious Studies Skills Book: Close Reading, Critical Thinking, and Comparison* (New York: Bloomsbury Academic, 2019).
14 Jonathan Z. Smith, "The Necessary Lie: Duplicity in the Disciplines," in *Studying Religion: An Introduction*, ed. Russell T. McCutcheon (New York: Routledge, 2019), 124.
15 bell hooks, *Teaching Critical Thinking: Practical Wisdom* (London: Routledge, 2010), 59.
16 This assignment is based on an exercise shared with me by Russell T. McCutcheon, when I first began teaching world religions courses many years ago. He suggested using old textbooks to help students think about the world religions paradigm. Here, I have adapted this to the American religion classroom, and added a creative component to the description and analysis of that early activity. Many thanks to Russell for the inspiration for this teaching tactic. Pedagogy is never an isolated endeavor, and I am grateful to all of those who have shared their brilliant ideas with me.
17 This exercise takes place in two class periods.
18 John Corrigan and Lynn S. Neal, *Religious Intolerance in America: A Documentary History* (Chapel Hill: The University of North Carolina Press, 2021); Bret E. Carroll, *The Routledge Historical Atlas of Religion in America* (New York: Routledge, 2000).
19 The parameters and possibilities for this assignment are very flexible. What about a "people's history" format or an open-access online text? What about a social media account? What if the perspectives could center any view of American religions or

any group (like minority racial, ethnic, or religious groups, or gender, sexuality, and other identities)? What if the audience shifted? Giving students freedom to play with these categories can spark imagination and creativity that a "textbook" form may not.

20   David McConeghy, "Narrating the USA's Religious Pluralism," in *After World Religions*, eds. David G. Robertson and Christopher R. Cotter (Basingstoke: Taylor & Francis Ltd., 2016), 139–40.

Chapter 9

1   For more about the Interfaith Center of New York, see https://interfaithcenter.org (accessed June 28, 2021). For our "Religious Worlds of New York" summer institute for teachers, see https://religiousworldsnyc.org (accessed June 28, 2021).

2   Tomoko Masuzawa, *The Invention of World Religions: Or, How European Universalism was Preserved in the Language of Pluralism* (Chicago: The University of Chicago Press, 2005). For other helpful critiques of the "world religions" framework see: Christopher Cotter and David Robertson, eds., *After World Religions: Reconstructing Religious Studies* (London: Routledge, 2016); Timothy Fitzgerald, *The Ideology of Religious Studies* (New York: Oxford University Press, 2004); Jonathan Z. Smith, "A Matter of Class: Taxonomies of Religion," *Harvard Theological Review* 89, no. 4 (1996): 387–403; and the closely related critiques of "pluralism" in Courtney Bender and Pamela Klassen, eds., *After Pluralism: Reimagining Religious Engagement* (New York: Columbia University Press, 2010).

3   My own critiques of world religions pedagogy are developed in more detail in Henry Goldschmidt, "From World Religions to Lived Religion: Towards a Pedagogy of Civic Engagement in Secondary School Religious Studies Curricula," in *Civility, Religious Pluralism, and Education*, eds. Vince Biondo and Andrew Fiala (New York: Routledge, 2014), 177–92.

4   There's no way to survey the world of public, civically engaged scholarship here, but for useful introductions see: Gregory Jay, "The Engaged Humanities: Principles and Practices of Public Scholarship and Teaching," *Journal of Community Engagement and Scholarship* 3, no. 1 (Spring 2010): 51–63; and Svetlana Nikitina, "Applied Humanities: Bridging the Gap between Building Theory and Fostering Citizenship," *Liberal Education* 95, no. 1 (Winter 2009): 36–43. For religious studies perspectives, see Forrest Clingerman and Reid Locklin, eds., *Teaching Civic Engagement* (New York: Oxford University Press, 2016); and Eboo Patel, Jennifer Howe Peace and Noah Silverman, eds., *Interreligious/Interfaith Studies: Defining a New Field* (Boston: Beacon Press, 2018).

5 Interfaith Center of New York, *Policing in Today's Multifaith New York* (2016). Available online at https://www.youtube.com/watch?v=iieScd-bmng (accessed June 28, 2021).
6 Michel Foucault, "Truth and Power," in *Power/Knowledge: Selected Interviews and Other Writings, 1972–1977*, ed. Colin Gordon (New York: Pantheon Books, 1980), 109–33.
7 Foucault, "Truth and Power," 126.
8 Ibid., 126.
9 Ibid., 127.
10 It is important to note that in addition to ICNY's collaborative work with the NYPD, we have also participated in advocacy coalitions pushing for police reform and accountability, including efforts to end NYPD surveillance of Muslim communities and "stop and frisk" policies targeting young men of color. It is also worth noting that *all* of the civic institutions we work with—K-12 schools, social service agencies, police, city government, foundation funders, and faith communities themselves—have served as instruments of both exclusion and inclusion, domination and resistance.
11 Foucault, "Truth and Power," 131.
12 Ibid., 133.
13 Unfortunately, I must admit, our work may also help the NYPD design more effective surveillance plans for local religious communities. ICNY's closest partners in the NYPD are working to develop inclusive strategies for community policing, but as I noted above (n. 10) some of their colleagues engaged in unconstitutional surveillance of New York's Muslim communities in the years following 9/11. For the troubling details, see Muslim American Civil Liberties Coalition, et al., *Mapping Muslims: NYPD Spying and Its Impact on American Muslims* (2013). Available online at https://www.law.cuny.edu/wp-content/uploads/page-assets/academics/clinics/immigration/clear/Mapping-Muslims.pdf (accessed September 9, 2021).
14 Foucault, "Truth and Power," 133.
15 Michel Foucault, "Power and Strategies," in *Power/Knowledge: Selected Interviews and Other Writings, 1972–1977*, ed. Colin Gordon (New York: Pantheon Books, 1980), 141–2.
16 David Chidester, *Empire of Religion: Imperialism and Comparative Religion* (Chicago: The University of Chicago Press, 2014), xiii.
17 Arvind-Pal S. Mandair, *Religion and the Specter of the West: Sikhism, India, Postcoloniality, and the Politics of Translation* (New York: Columbia University Press, 2009). For similar analyses of the histories of other "religions," see for example: Talal Asad, *Formations of the Secular: Christianity, Islam, Modernity* (Stanford: Stanford University Press, 2003), esp. 159–80 and 205–256; Daniel

Boyarin, *Judaism: The Genealogy of a Modern Notion* (New Brunswick: Rutgers University Press, 2019); David Chidester, *Savage Systems: Colonialism and Comparative Religion in Southern Africa* (Charlottesville: University of Virginia Press, 1996); Markus Dressler and Arvind-Pal S. Mandair, eds., *Secularism and Religion-Making* (New York: Oxford University Press, 2011); Mark Elmore, *Becoming Religious in a Secular Age* (Oakland: University of California Press, 2016); John Stratton Hawley, "Naming Hinduism," *The Wilson Quarterly* 15, no. 3 (1991): 20–34; Hent de Vries, ed., *Religion: Beyond a Concept* (New York: Fordham University Press, 2008), esp. 101–279; and arguably Wilfred Cantwell Smith, *The Meaning and End of Religion: A New Approach to the Religious Traditions of Mankind* (Minneapolis: Fortress Press, 1991 [orig. pub. 1962]).

18 Mandair, *Religion and the Specter of the West*, 9.
19 There are important exceptions to this generalization, like when professionals work with people of faith who question familiar categories of identity, such as Messianic Jews and Black Hebrew Israelites. For a concrete example, see James Sonne's discussion of a religious liberty legal clinic's work representing a Messianic Jewish inmate denied kosher food by a prison chaplain who did not consider him Jewish. James Sonne, "Cross-Cultural Lawyering and Religion: A Clinical Perspective," *Clinical Law Review* 25, no. 1 (2018): 255–8.
20 Robert Orsi, "Everyday Miracles: The Study of Lived Religion," in *Lived Religion in America: Toward a History of Practice*, ed. David Hall (Princeton: Princeton University Press, 1997), 3–6. For additional scholarship and reflection on lived religion, see for example: Nancy Ammerman (ed.), *Everyday Religion: Observing Modern Religious Lives* (New York: Oxford University Press, 2007); Hall (ed.), *Lived Religion in America*; Meredith McGuire, *Lived Religion: Faith and Practice in Everyday Life* (New York: Oxford University Press, 2008); Robert Orsi, *The Madonna of 115th Street: Faith and Community in Italian Harlem, 1880-1950* (New Haven: Yale University Press, 1985); Robert Orsi, "Is the Study of Lived Religion Irrelevant to the World We Live In?" *Journal for the Scientific Study of Religion* 42, no. 2 (2003): 169–74; and Robert Wuthnow, *What Happens When We Practice Religion?: Textures of Devotion in Everyday Life* (Princeton: Princeton University Press, 2020).
21 Orsi, "Everyday Miracles," 4.
22 Ibid.. 7.
23 Orsi, "Is the Study of Lived Religion Irrelevant," 172.
24 Chaim Potok, *The Chosen* (New York: Fawcett Publications, 1987 [orig. pub. 1967]). James Baldwin, *Go Tell It on the Mountain* (New York: Vintage Books, 2013 [orig. pub. 1953]). For more on teaching lived religion through literature, and especially *Go Tell it on the Mountain*, see Henry Goldschmidt, "Teaching Lived Religion through Literature: Classroom Strategies for Community-Based

Learning," in *Teaching about Religion in the Social Studies Classroom*, NCSS Bulletin #117, ed. Charles Haynes (Silver Spring: National Council for the Social Studies, 2019), 53–60.

25 For more about the Pluralism Project's case study teaching initiative see https://pluralism.org/case-initiative (accessed July 6, 2021); and Ellie Pierce, "Using the Case Method in Interfaith Studies Classrooms," in *Interreligious/Interfaith Studies: Defining a New Field*, eds. Eboo Patel, Jennifer Howe Peace and Noah Silverman (Boston: Beacon Press, 2018), 72–84.

26 The AAR's 2010 *Guidelines for Teaching about Religion in K-12 Public Schools in the United States* specifically discourage K-12 teachers from inviting religious leaders into the classroom as guest speakers or bringing students to visit houses of worship. Available online at https://www.aarweb.org/AARMBR/Publications-and-News-/Guides-and-Best-Practices-/Teaching-and-Learning-/Teaching-about-Religion-in-K-12-Public-Schools.aspx (accessed July 9, 2021). The 2019 *AAR Religious Literacy Guidelines* for higher education are a bit more open to such community-based, experiential pedagogies, including them on a list of "other approaches" that "can supplement a religious studies approach to religious literacy." Available online at https://www.aarweb.org/AARMBR/Publications-and-News-/Guides-and-Best-Practices-/Teaching-and-Learning-/AAR-Religious-Literacy-Guidelines.aspx (accessed July 9, 2021). I entirely agree with the AAR that conversations with religious leaders cannot be equated with, or take the place of, the academic study of religion. But I would argue that a *civically engaged* study of religion must be both academic and experiential, placing scholarly and faith-based perspectives in conversation.

27 As far as I know, there are no reliable statistics for the number of religious studies faculty members incorporating conversations with religious leaders into their classroom teaching. My claim that this "seem[s] to be increasingly common" is based on anecdotal evidence, as well as the broader trend toward academic civic engagement. For a discussion of guest speakers in the religious studies classroom see Marianne Delaporte, "Giving and Receiving Hospitality During Community Engagement Courses," in *Teaching Civic Engagement*, eds. Forrest Clingerman and Reid Locklin (New York: Oxford University Press, 2016), 61–73.

28 For a detailed description of a specific panel discussion see Goldschmidt, "From World Religions to Lived Religion," 187–90.

29 The church in question is St. Lydia's, which is affiliated with the Evangelical Lutheran Church in America but charts its own path in many ways. For more information see https://stlydias.org (accessed July 11, 2021).

30 For a critique of Five Pillars pedagogy in teaching about Islam and Muslim communities, see Hussein Rashid, "Mustafa: Teaching Beyond the Five Pillars," (this volume).

Chapter 10

1. Barbara E. Walvoord, *Teaching and Learning in College Introductory Religion Courses* (Malden: Blackwell Publishing, 2008).
2. Tomoko Masuzawa, *The Invention of World Religions* (Chicago: University of Chicago Press, 2005); Christopher R. Cotter and David G. Robertson, eds., *After World Religions: Reconstructing Religious Studies* (London: Routledge, 2016).
3. Ian G. Barbour, *Religion and Science: Historical and Contemporary Issues*. Originally published as *Religion in an Age of Science* (San Francisco: HarperSanFrancisco, 1997), 25. See also Ian G. Barbour, *When Science Meets Religion: Enemies, Strangers, or Partners?* (San Francisco: HarperSanFrancisco, 2000).
4. Ronald L. Numbers, ed., *Galileo Goes to Jail and Other Myths about Science and Religion* (Cambridge: Harvard University Press, 2009), 6.
5. Elaine Howard Ecklund, *Science vs. Religion: What Scientists Really Think* (Oxford: Oxford University Press, 2010), 5.
6. Samer Akkach, ed., *'Ilm: Science, Religion and Art in Islam* (Adelaide: University of Adelaide Press, 2019).
7. J. Z. Smith, "Religion, Religions, Religious," in *Critical Terms for Religious Studies*, ed. Mark C. Taylor (Chicago: University of Chicago Press, 1988), 270.
8. Thomas S. Kuhn, *The Structure of Scientific Revolutions* (Chicago: University of Chicago Press, 1962).
9. Michel Foucault, *The Birth of the Clinic: An Archaeology of Medical Perception*, trans. A. M. Sheridan Smith (New York: Vintage Books, 1973).
10. For an introduction to the epistemic issues at the heart of the sociology of scientific knowledge, see Alex Rosenberg and Lee McIntyre, eds., *Philosophy of Science: A Contemporary Introduction*, fifth edition (London: Routledge, 2020).
11. Amanda Behm, Christienna Fryar, Emma Hunter, Elisabeth Leake, Su Lin Lewis and Sarah Miller-Davenport, "Decolonizing History: Enquiry and Practice," *History Workshop Journal* 89 (Spring 2020): 171.
12. Mallory Nye, "Decolonizing the Study of Religion," *Open Library of Humanities* 5, no. 1 (2019): 24.
13. Cyndi Kernahan, *Teaching About Race and Racism in the College Classroom: Notes from a White Professor* (Morgantown: West Virginia University Press, 2019).
14. Ibid., 35.
15. Ibid., 34.
16. Barbour, *Religion and Science,* 77–105.
17. Maurice A. Finocchiaro, ed. and trans., *The Galileo Affair: A Documentary History* (Berkeley: University of California Press, 1989).
18. Ibid., 47–8.

19 Richard J. Blackwell, "Galileo Galilei," in *Science and Religion: A Historical Introduction*, ed. Gary B. Ferngren (Baltimore: Johns Hopkins University Press, 2002), 105.
20 Ibid., 115.
21 Lynn White Jr., "The Historical Roots of Our Ecologic Crisis," *Science* 155, no. 3767 (1967): 1203–7.
22 Noah J. Efron, "Myth 9. That Christianity Gave Birth to Modern Science," in *Galileo Goes to Jail and Other Myths about Science and Religion*, ed. Ronald L. Numbers (Cambridge: Harvard University Press, 2009), 89.
23 Todd LeVasseur, "Reverend Billy and the Church of Stop Shopping: Contemporary Religious Production on a Planet Passing Tipping Points," *Nova Religio: The Journal of Alternative and Emergent Religion* 23, no. 3 (2020): 86–109.
24 Cary Funk and Becka A. Alper, *Religion and Science: Highly Religious Americans Are Less Likely Than Others to See Conflict between Faith and Science* (Washington: Pew Research Center, 2015), 32–41.
25 See Peter Gottschalk, *Religion, Science, and Empire: Classifying Hinduism and Islam in British India* (Oxford: Oxford University Press, 2012).

Chapter 11

1 For example, W&M's entering class in 2021 had an average GPA of 4.3 on a weighted 4.0 scale, and 82 percent of the entering students graduated in the top 10 percent of their high school class.
2 For other explorations of introductory textbooks, see other chapters in this volume.
3 Gary E. Kessler, *Studying Religion: An Introduction Through Cases*, 3rd edn (Boston: McGraw-Hill Higher Education, 2008), 14.
4 Ibid., 16.
5 Ibid., 14.
6 Paul Myhre, *Introduction to Religious Studies* (Winona: Anselm Academic, 2009), 4.
7 Ibid., 13.
8 Malory Nye, *Religion: The Basics*, 2nd edn (New York: Routledge, 2008), 3.
9 Ibid., 5.
10 Jonathan Z. Smith, *Imagining Religion: From Babylon to Jonestown* (Chicago: University of Chicago Press, 1982), xi.
11 Nye, *Religion: The Basics*, 18.
12 Craig Martin, *A Critical Introduction to the Study of Religion* (New York: Taylor and Francis, 2017), 3. A similar approach appears in Russel McCutcheon's *Studying*

Religion: An Introduction in the chapter "What's in a Name?" McCutcheon walks through numerous case studies (the naming of Mount Everest, a court case that hinged on whether a tomato is a vegetable or fruit for tax purposes) to show that "the names we give to things may, instead, tell us more about the namer than they do about the thing being named." McCutcheon, *Studying Religion*, 2nd edn (New York: Routledge, 2019), 16.
13 For exploration of yoga as a consumer practice, see Chapter 8 in this volume.
14 Martin, *A Critical Introduction to the Study of Religion*, 4.
15 Ibid., 5.
16 Ibid., 8.
17 Ibid., 11–12, emphasis in original. For further analysis of American rhetoric and policy leading up to and responding to the 9/11 attacks, see Mahmood Mamdani, *Good Muslim, Bad Muslim: America, the Cold War, and the Roots of Terror* (New York: Doubleday, 2005).
18 Emile Durkheim, *The Elementary Forms of Religious Life*, trans. Karen E. Fields (New York: The Free Press, 1995), 220.
19 David Chidester, "The Church of Baseball, the Fetish of Coca-Cola, and the Potlatch of Rock 'N' Roll," in *Religion and Popular Culture in America*, eds. Bruce David Forbes and Jeffrey H. Mahan (Berkeley: University of California Press, 2005), 221.
20 Rudolf Otto, *The Idea of the Holy*, trans. John W. Harvey (Oxford: Oxford University Press, 1981).
21 Paul Tillich, *Dynamics of Faith* (New York: Harper and Row, 1957).
22 Joan M. Chandler, "Sport Is Not a Religion," in *Sport and Religion*, ed. Shirl Hoffman (Champaign: Human Kinetics Books, 1992), 59.
23 Catherine L. Albanese, *America: Religions and Religion* (Belmont: Wadsworth Publishing Co., 1992), 2.
24 Ibid., 9–10.
25 Ibid., 475–7.
26 See for example David Chidester, *Savage Systems: Colonialism and Comparative Religion in Southern Africa* (Charlottesville: University of Virginia Press, 1996).
27 Donald M. Fisher, *Lacrosse: A History of the Game* (Baltimore: Johns Hopkins University Press, 2002), 14–16.
28 Ibid., 24–34.
29 Brent Nongbri advocates this approach and offers capitalism as a case study. Nongbri, *Before Religion: A History of a Modern Concept* (New Haven: Yale University Press, 2013), 155.
30 H.G. Bissinger, *Friday Night Lights: A Town, a Team, and a Dream* (New York: Perseus Books, 1990); Peter Berg, dir. *Friday Night Lights* (Universal City: Universal Pictures, 2004).

31 Geoff Winningham and Al Reinert, *Rites of Fall: High School Football in Texas* (Austin: University of Texas Press, 1979), 10.
32 Jay Coakley, "Assessing the Sociology of Sport: On Cultural Sensibilities and the Great Sport Myth" *International Review for the Sociology of Sport* 50 (2015): 403.

Chapter 12

1 Tomoko Masuzawa, *The Invention of World Religions* (Chicago: University of Chicago Press, 2005).
2 Lewis R. Gordon, *Disciplinary Decadence: Living Thought in Trying Times* (Boulder: Paradigm Publishers, 2006).
3 Joshua Dubler and Vincent W. Lloyd, *Break Every Yoke: Religion, Justice, and the Abolition of Prisons* (New York: Oxford University Press, 2020), 7.
4 Ibid., 8.
5 Ibid., 9.
6 Ibid., 8.
7 Angela Y. Davis, *Abolition Democracy: Beyond Empire, Prisons, and Torture*, 1st edn (New York: Seven Stories Press, 2005).
8 Dubler and Lloyd, *Break Every Yoke*, 25.
9 Angela Y. Davis, *Are Prisons Obsolete?* (New York: Seven Stories Press, 2003), 13.
10 Ibid., 13.
11 Fred Moten and Stefano Harney, "The University and the Undercommons: Seven Theses", *Social Text* 22, no. 2 (79) (June 1, 2004): 101–15, https://doi.org/10.1215/01642472-22-2_79-101.
12 Stefano Harney and Fred Moten, *The Undercommons: Fugitive Planning & Black Study* (Wivenhoe, New York and Port Watson: Minor Compositions, 2013), 43.
13 Moten and Harney, "The University and the Undercommons," 111.
14 Ibid., 114.
15 Ibid., 106.
16 John Saltmarsh, "Transforming Higher Education Through and For Democratic Civic Engagement: A Model for Change," *Michigan Journal of Community Service Learning* (Fall 2015): 122–7.
17 Corey Dolgon, Tania D. Mitchell and Timothy K Eatman, eds., *The Cambridge Handbook of Service Learning and Community Engagement*, Cambridge Handbooks in Psychology (Cambridge and New York: Cambridge University Press, 2017), 52.
18 Elisabeth T. Vasko, "Civic Learning and Teaching as a Resource for Sexual Justice: An Undergraduate Religious Studies Course Module," *Teaching Theology & Religion* 20, no. 2 (2017): 164, https://doi.org/10.1111/teth.12383.

19 Dolgon, Mitchell, and Eatman, *The Cambridge Handbook of Service Learning and Community Engagement*, 52.
20 Susan Strum et al., "Full Participation: Building the Architecture for Diversity and Community Engagement in Higher Education," *Full Participation*, (2011). Imagining America. 17. https://surface.syr.edu/ia/17.
21 Ibid.
22 Ibid.
23 Harney and Moten, *The Undercommons*, 48.
24 Vasko, "Civic Learning and Teaching as a Resource for Sexual Justice," 164.

Bibliography

Introduction

Abbasi, Rushain. "Islam and the Invention of Religion: A Study of Medieval Muslim Discourses on Dīn." *Studia Islamica* 116, no. 1 (2021): 1–106.

Ambrose, Susan A., Michael W. Bridges, Michele DiPietro, Marsha C. Lovett, and Mari K. Norman. eds. *How Learning Works: Seven Research-Based Principles for Smart Teaching*. San Francisco: Jossey-Bass, 2010.

American Academy of Religion. "AAR Religious Literacy Guidelines: What U.S. College Graduates Should Understand about Religion." https://www.aarweb.org/AARMBR/Publications-and-News-/Guides-and-Best-Practices-/Teaching-and-Learning-/AAR-Religious-Literacy-Guidelines.aspx?WebsiteKey=61d76dfc-e7fe-4820-a0ca-1f792d24c06e, (accessed August 31, 2021).

Bain, Ken. *What the Best College Teachers Do*. Cambridge: Harvard University Press, 2004.

Barylo, William. *Young Muslim Change-Makers: Grassroots Charities Rethinking Modern Societies*. Abingdon and New York: Routledge, 2018.

Brown, Karen McCarthy. *Mama Lola: A Vodou Priestess in Brooklyn*. Berkeley: University of California Press, 1991.

Chidester, David. *Authentic Fakes: Religion and American Popular Culture*. Berkeley: University of California Press, 2005.

Chidester, David. *Empire of Religion: Imperialism and Comparative Religion*. Chicago and London: University of Chicago Press, 2014.

Daftary, Farhad. "The Study of the Ismailis: Phases and Issues." In *The Study of Shi'i Islam: History, Theology and Law*, edited by Farhad Daftary and Gurdofarid Miskinzoda, 47–65. London and New York: Bloomsbury Publishing, 2014.

Eyler, Joshua. *How Humans Learn: The Science and Stories behind Effective College Teaching*. Morgantown: West Virginia University Press, 2018.

Flood, Gavin. *An Introduction to Hinduism*. New York: Cambridge University Press, 2017.

Gallagher, Eugene V. "Teaching for Religious Literacy." *Teaching Theology and Religion* 12, no. 3 (2009): 208–21.

Gallagher, Eugene V., and Joanne Maguire. *Religious Studies Skills Book: Close Reading, Critical Thinking, and Comparison*. New York: Bloomsbury, 2019.

Goodwin, Megan. *Abusing Religion: Literary Persecution, Sex Scandals, and American Minority Religions*. New Brunswick: Rutgers University Press, 2020.

Hammer, Juliana. "Islam and Race in American History." In *The Oxford Handbook of Religion and Race in American History*, edited by Paul Harvey and Kathryn Gin Lum, 205–22. New York: Oxford University Press, 2018.

Hicks, Dan. *The Brutish Museums: The Benin Bronzes, Colonial Violence and Cultural Restitution*. London: Pluto Press, 2020.

Inden, Ronald B. *Imagining India*. Oxford and Cambridge: Basil Blackwell, 1990.

Iqtidar, Humeira. *Secularizing Islamists?: Jama'at-e-Islami and Jama'at-ud-Da'wa in Urban Pakistan*. Chicago and London: University of Chicago Press, 2011.

Jacoby, Sarah, ed. "Contemplative Pedagogy and the Religious Studies Classroom." Spotlight on Teaching. Religious Studies News. https://rsn.aarweb.org/spotlight-on/teaching/contemplative-pedagogy/editors-introduction, (accessed July 19, 2021).

Johnson, Sylvester A. *African American Religions, 1500–2000: Colonialism, Democracy, and Freedom*. New York: Cambridge University Press, 2015.

Johnson, Sylvester A. "Religion, Race, and American Empire." In *The Oxford Handbook of Religion and Race in American History*, edited by Paul Harvey and Kathryn Gin Lum, 61–78. New York: Oxford University Press, 2018.

King, Richard. *Orientalism and Religion: Post-Colonial Theory, India and the Mystic East*. London and New York: Routledge, 1999.

Komjathy, Louis, ed. *Contemplative Literature: A Comparative Sourcebook on Meditation and Contemplative Prayer*. New York: SUNY Press, 2015.

Masuzawa, Tomoko. *The Invention of World Religions: Or, How European Universalism Was Preserved in the Language of Pluralism*. Chicago: University of Chicago Press, 2005.

McGuire, Beverley. "Analogous Activities: Tools for Thinking Comparatively in Religious Studies Courses." *Teaching Theology and Religion* 22 (2019): 114–26.

Moore, Diane L. *Overcoming Religious Illiteracy: A Cultural Studies Approach to the Study of Religion in Secondary Education*. New York: Palgrave Macmillan, 2007.

Moore, Diane L. "Overcoming Religious Illiteracy: A Cultural Studies Approach." *World History Connected* 4, no. 1 (2015). http://worldhistoryconnected.press.illinois.edu/4.1/moore.html, (accessed August 31, 2021).

Prothero, Stephen. *Religious Literacy: What Every American Needs to Know about Religion and Doesn't*. New York: HarperCollins, 2007.

Rashid, Hussein. "Plural Voices in the Teaching of Islam." *Thresholds in Education* 41, no. 2 (2018): 87–100.

Simmons, K. Merinda. "Identifying Race and Religion." In *The Oxford Handbook of Religion and Race in American History*, edited by Paul Harvey and Kathryn Gin Lum, 25–39. New York: Oxford University Press, 2018.

TILT Higher Ed. "Transparency in Learning and Teaching." https://tilthighered.com/, (accessed July 19, 2021).

Tsioulcas, Anastasia. "Five Decades on, an Eclectic Church Preaches the Message of John Coltrane." *NPR*. September 23, 2021, https://www.npr.org/2020/09/23/915846867/five-decades-on-an-eclectic-church-preaches-the-message-of-john-coltrane

Weisenfeld, Judith. *New World a-Coming: Black Religion and Racial Identity during the Great Migration.* New York: New York University Press, 2016.

Wiggins, Grant and Jay McTighe. *Understanding by Design.* 2nd edn. Alexandria: Association for Supervision and Curriculum Development, 2005.

Walvoord, Barbara E. "Students' Spirituality and 'Big Questions' in Introductory Religion Courses." *Teaching Theology & Religion* 11 (2008): 3–13.

Chapter 1

American Academy of Arts & Sciences, Humanities Indicators. "Bachelor's Degrees in Humanities." 2021, https://www.amacad.org/humanities-indicators/higher-education/bachelors-degrees-humanities, (accessed July 31, 2021).

Asad, Talal. *Genealogies of Religion.* Maryland: Johns Hopkins University Press, 1993.

Barbezat, Daniel and Mirabai Bush. *Contemplative Practices in Higher Education.* New York: Jossey-Bass, 2014.

Bauman, Chad and Jennifer Saunders. "Out of India: Immigrant Hindus and South Asian Hinduism in the USA." *Religion Compass* 3, no. 1 (2009): 116–35.

Bell, Catherine. "Performance". In *Critical Terms for Religious Studies*, edited by Mark Taylor, 205–24. Chicago: University of Chicago Press, 1998.

Bell, Catherine. *Ritual Theory, Ritual Practice.* Oxford: Oxford University Press, 2009.

Berila, Beth. *Integrating Mindfulness into Anti-Oppression Pedagogy.* New York: Routledge, 2016.

Bourdieu, Pierre. *Outline of a Theory of Practice.* Cambridge: Cambridge University Press, 1977.

Brantmeier, Edward and Maria McKenna. "Pedagogy of Vulnerability: Roots, Realities, and the Future." In *Pedagogy of Vulnerability*, edited by E. Brantmeier and M. McKenna, 1–21. North Carolina: IAP Publishing, 2020.

Brown, Peter. *The Body and Society: Men, Women, and Sexual Renunciation in Early Christianity.* New York: Columbia University Press, 1988.

Bynum, Caroline W. *Holy Feast and Holy Fast: The Religious Significance of Food to Medieval Women.* Berkeley: University of California Press, 1987.

Coakley, Sarah, ed. *Religion and the Body.* Cambridge: Cambridge University Press, 1997.

Csordas, Thomas, ed. *Embodiment and Experience: The Existential Ground of Culture and Self.* Cambridge: Cambridge University Press, 1994.

Csordas, Thomas. "Embodiment as a Paradigm for Anthropology." *Ethos* 18, no. 1 (1990): 5–47.

Daniel, Yvonne. *Embodied Knowledge in Haitian Vodou, Cuban Yoruba, and Bahian Candomble.* Chicago: University of Illinois Press, 2005.

Feld, Steven. *Sound and Sentiment: Birds, Weeping, Poetics, and Song in Kaluli Expression*. Durham: Duke University Press, 1982.
Fisher, Kathleen. "Look before You Leap: Reconsidering Contemplative Pedagogy." *Teaching Theology and Religion* 20, no. 1 (2017): 4–21.
Flueckiger, Joyce. "Unexpected Learning Opportunities of the Site Visit." *Religious Studies News, Spotlight on Teaching* 19 (2004): 1–4.
Foucault, Michel. *Discipline and Punish: The Birth of the Prison*. Translated by Alan Sheridan. New York: Vintage, 1995 [1975].
Foucault, Michel. *History of Sexuality*. Translated by Robert Hurley. New York: Pantheon, 1978.
Gallagher, Eugene and Joanne McGuire. *The Religious Studies Skills Book: Close Reading, Critical Thinking, and Comparison*. New York: Bloomsbury, 2019.
Geisz, Steven. "Body Practice and Meditation as Philosophy: Teaching Qigong, Taijiquan and Yoga in College Courses." *Teaching Philosophy* 39, no. 2 (June 2016): 115–35.
Goldschmidt, Henry. "Being There: What Do Students Learn by Visiting Houses of Worship?" *Crosscurrents* 68, no. 3 (September 2018): 394–411.
Grimes, Ronald. *The Craft of Ritual Studies*. Oxford: Oxford University Press, 2013.
Gustafson, Diana L. "Embodied Learning: The Body as an Epistemological Site." In *Meeting the Challenge: Innovative Feminist Pedagogies in Action*, edited by Ellen Rose and Maralee Mayberry, 249–73. New York: Taylor and Francis, 2013.
hooks, bell. *Teaching to Transgress: Education as a Practice of Freedom*. New York: Routledge, 1994.
Jackson, Michael. "Knowledge of the Body." *Man* 18, no. 1 (June 1983): 327–45.
Kraft, Becky. "Engaging the Senses at a Hindu Temple in Michigan." *Interfaith Center of New York*, 2020, https://religiousworldsnyc.org/wp-content/uploads/2020/12/pdfdownload-krafthindutemple.pdf, (accessed July 29, 2021).
Lakoff, George and Mark Johnson. *Metaphors We Live By*. Chicago: University of Chicago Press, 1980.
LaMothe, Kimerer L. "What Bodies Know about Religion and the Study of It." *Journal of the American Academy of Religion* 76, no. 3 (2008): 573–601.
Lelwica, Michelle M. "Embodying Learning: Post-Cartesian Pedagogy and the Academic Study of Religion." *Teaching Theology & Religion* 12, no. 2 (April 2009): 123–36.
Long, Jeffrey D. "Site Visits in Interfaith and Religious Studies Pedagogy: Reflections on Visiting a Hindu Temple in Central Pennsylvania." *Teaching Theology & Religion* 21 (2018): 78–91.
Mauss, Marcel. "Techniques of the Body." *Economy and Society* 2, no. 1 (1973 [1934]): 70–88.
McGuire, Beverley. "Analogous Activities: Tools for Thinking Comparatively in Religious Studies Courses." *Teaching Theology and Religion* 22 (2019): 114–26.
Merleau-Ponty, Maurice. *Phenomenology of Perception*. Translated by Colin Smith. New York: Routledge, 1962 [1945].

Narayanan, Vasudha. "Diglossic Hinduism: Liberation and Lentils." *Journal of the American Academy of Religion* 68, no. 4 (2000): 761–79.

Ng, Roxana. "Decolonizing Teaching and Learning through Embodied Learning: Toward an Integrated Approach." In *Sharing Breath: Embodied Learning and Decolonization*, edited by Sheila Batacharya and Yuk-Lin Renita Wong, 33–54. Alberta: Athabasca University Press, 2018.

Oldstone-Moore, Jennifer. "Sustained Experiential Learning: Modified Monasticism and Pilgrimage." *Teaching Theology and Religion* 12, no. 2 (April 2009): 109–22.

Orsi, Robert. *The Madonna of 115th Street: Faith and Community in Italian Harlem, 1880–1950*. New Haven: Yale University, 2010.

Patterson, Josh and Rob Townsend. "A Deeper Look at Trends in Undergraduate and Graduate Religion Enrollments and Degree Completions." *Religious Studies News*, January 7, 2021, https://rsn.aarweb.org/trends-religion-enrollments-and-degree-completions, (accessed July 30, 2021).

Perez, Elizabeth. *Religion in the Kitchen: Cooking, Talking and the Making of Black Atlantic Traditions*. New York: New York University Press, 2016.

Plate, S. Brent. *A History of Religion in 5 ½ Objects*. New York: Penguin, 2014.

Probyn, Elspeth. "Teaching Bodies: Affects in the Classroom." *Body & Society* 10, no. 4 (2004): 21–43.

Promey, Sally, ed. *Sensational Religion: Sensory Cultures in Material Practice*. New Haven: Yale University Press, 2014.

Puar, Jasbir. *Terrorist Assemblages: Homonationalism in Queer Times*. Durham: Duke University Press, 2007.

Rendon, Laura I. *Sentipensante (Sensing/Thinking) Pedagogy: Educating for Wholeness, Social Justice and Liberation*. Virginia: Stylus Publishing, 2014 [2009].

Sarbacker, Stuart Ray. "Reflections on Theory and Practice: The Case of Modern Yoga." In *Meditation and the Classroom: Contemplative Pedagogy for Religious Studies*, edited by Judith Simmer-Brown and Fran Grace, 147–54. New York: SUNY, 2011.

Schaefer, Donovan. *Religious Affects: Animality, Evolution and Power*. Durham: Duke University, 2015.

Schneider, Rachel C. and Sophie Bjork-James. "Whither Whiteness and Religion?: Implications for Theology and the Study of Religion." *Journal of the American Academy of Religion* 88, no. 1 (2020): 175–99.

Taves, Ann. *Religious Experience Reconsidered: A Building-Block Approach to the Study of Religion and Other Special Things*. Princeton: Princeton University Press, 2003.

Thrift, Nigel. *Spatial Formations*. London: Sage, 1996.

Vasquez, Manuel. *More Than Belief: A Materialist Theory of Religion*. Oxford: Oxford University Press, 2011.

Watkins, Megan. "Pedagogic Affect/Effect: Embodying the Desire to Learn." *Pedagogies* 1, no. 4 (2006): 269–82.

Watkins, Megan. "Gauging the Affective: Becoming Attuned to Its Impact in Education." In *Methodological Advance in Research on Emotion and Education*, edited by M. Zymbalas and P.A. Shultz, 71–81. New York: Springer, 2016.

Wilcox, Melissa. "*Terrorist Assemblages* Meets the Study of Religion." *Culture and Religion* 15, no. 2 (2014): 153–7.

Chapter 2

American Academy of Religion, "AAR Religious Literacy Guidelines: What U.S. College Graduates Need to Understand about Religion." (2019). Available online: https://www.aarweb.org/AARMBR/Publications-and-News-/Guides-and-Best-Practices-/Teaching-and-Learning-/AAR-Religious-Literacy-Guidelines.aspx?WebsiteKey=61d76dfc-e7fe-4820-a0ca-1f792d24c06e

Chidester, David. "Moralizing Noise." *Harvard Divinity Bulletin* 32, no. 3 (Summer 2004): 17.

DeTemple, Jill, Eugene Gallagher, Pui-lan Kwok, and Thomas Pearson, "Reflective Structured Dialogue: A Conversation with 2018 American Academy of Religion Excellence in Teaching Award Winner Jill DeTemple." *Teaching Theology and Religion* 22 (2019): 223–34.

Freire, Paulo. *Pedagogy of the Oppressed*. 50th anniversary edn. New York: Bloomsbury, 2020.

Gallagher, Eugene V., and Joanne Maguire. *The Religious Studies Skills Book: Close Reading, Critical Thinking, and Comparison*. London: Bloomsbury Academic, 2018.

Garland-Thomson, Rosemarie. "Feminist Disability Studies." *Signs* 30, no. 2 (Winter 2005): 1557–87.

Gravett, Emily O. "Lost in the Great Divide: Motivation in Religious Studies Classrooms." *Teaching Theology and Religion* 21 (2018): 21–32.

Gray-Hildenbrand, Jenna and Rebekka King. "Teaching in Contexts: Designing a Competency-based Religious Studies Program." *Teaching Theology and Religion* 22 (2019): 191–204.

Griffith, R. Marie. "Maintaining Empathy." *Harvard Divinity Bulletin* 32, no. 3 (Summer 2004): 18.

Jerryson, Michael. "Why 'Do You Believe in God?' Is at the Heart of Our Religious Problem." *Religion Dispatches*. (June 3, 2019). Available online: https://religiondispatches.org/why-do-you-believe-in-god-is-at-the-heart-of-our-religious-problem/.

Kessler, Gary. *Studying Religion: An Introduction through Cases*. 3rd edn. Boston: McGraw-Hill, 2008.

Knoll, Kristina R. "Feminist Disability Studies Pedagogy." *Feminist Teacher* 19, no. 2 (2009): 122–33.

Lewiecki-Wilson, Cynthia and Jen Cellio-Miller. eds. *Disability and Mothering: Liminal Spaces of Embodied Knowledge*. Syracuse: Syracuse University Press, 2011.

McCutcheon, Russell T. *Critics Not Caretakers: Redescribing the Public Study of Religion*. Albany: SUNY Press, 2001.

Meyer, Jan H. F. and Ray Land. "Threshold Concepts and Troublesome Knowledge (2): Epistemological Considerations and Conceptual Framework for Teaching and Learning." *Higher Education* 49, no. 3 (April 2005): 373–88.

Orsi, Robert. "A 'Bit of Judgment.'" *Harvard Divinity Bulletin* 32, no. 3 (Summer 2004): 16–17.

Orsi, Robert. *Between Heaven and Earth: The Religious Worlds People Make and the Scholars Who Study Them*. Princeton: Princeton University Press, 2005.

Pitcher, Ben and Henriette Gunkel. "Q&A with Jasbir Puar," *Darkmatter Journal* (May 2008). Available online: http://www.darkmatter101.org/site/2008/05/02/qa-with-jasbir-puar/.

Prothero, Stephen. "Belief Unbracketed: A Case for the Religion Scholar to Reveal More of Where He or She Is Coming from." *Harvard Divinity Bulletin* 32, no. 2 (Winter/Spring 2004): 10–11.

Prothero, Stephen. *Religion Matters: An Introduction to the World's Religions*. New York: W. W. Norton & Company, 2020.

Samuels, Ellen. "Judith Butler's Body Theory and the Question of Disability." *NWSA Journal*, 14, no. 3 (Autumn 2002): 58–76.

Tremain, Shelly L. "Philosophy of Disability as Critical Diversity Studies." *International Journal of Critical Diversity Studies* 1, no. 1 (June 2018): 30–44.

Tweed, Thomas A. "On Moving across: Translocative Religion and the Interpreter's Position." *Journal of the American Academy of Religion* 70, no. 2 (June 2002): 253–77.

Walvoord, Barbara E. "Students' Spirituality and 'Big Questions' in Introductory Religion Courses." *Teaching Theology and Religion* 11, no. 1 (2007): 3–13.

Walvoord, Barbara E. *Teaching and Learning in College Introductory Religion Courses*. Malden: Blackwell, 2008.

Chapter 3

Bailenson, Jeremy N. "Nonverbal Overload: A Theoretical Argument for the Causes of Zoom Fatigue." *Technology, Mind, and Behavior* 2, no. 1 (2021). Available online: https://tmb.apaopen.org/pub/nonverbal-overload/release/1.

DeTemple, Jill and John Sarrouf. "Disruption, Dialogue, and Swerve: Reflective Structured Dialogue in Religious Studies Classrooms." *Teaching Theology and Religion* 20, no. 3 (2017): 283–92.

Doyle, Jennifer. *Campus Sex, Campus Security*. South Pasadena: Semiotext(e), 2015.
Drescher, Elizabeth. *Choosing Our Religion: The Spiritual Lives of Americas Nones*. New York: Oxford University Press, 2016.
Gallagher, Eugene and Joanne Maguire. *Religious Studies Skills Book: Close Reading, Critical Thinking, and Comparison*. London and New York: Bloomsbury, 2018.
Gill, Rahuldeep. Lecture in South Asian Thought at California Lutheran University. April 29, 2019.
Harney, Stefano and Fred Moten. *The Undercommons: Fugitive Planning and Black Study*. Wivenhoe, New York and Port Watson: Minor Compositions, 2013.
Klein, Naomi. *The Shock Doctrine: The Rise of Disaster Capitalism*. New York: Picador, 2008.
Imhoff, Sarah. "The Creation Story of Religious Studies, or How We Learned to Stop Worrying and Love Schempp." *Journal of the American Academy of Religion* 84, no. 2 (June 2016): 466–97.
Rilke, Rainer Maria. "Archaic Torso of Apollo." In *All Parting: Selected Poetry and Prose of Rainer Maria Rilke*. Translated by Stephen Mitchell, 67–8. New York: Modern Library, 1995. Available online: https://poets.org/poem/archaic-torso-apollo.
Sedgwick, Eve Kosofsky. *Touching Feeling: Affect, Pedagogy, Performativity*. Durham and London: Duke University Press, 2003.
Winters, Joseph R. *Hope Draped in Black: Race, Melancholy, and the Agony of Progress*. Durham and London: Duke University Press, 2016.

Chapter 4

Ambrose, Susan, Michael Bridges, Michele DiPietro, Marsha Lovett, and Marie Norman. *How Learning Works: 7 Research-Based Principles for Smart Teaching*. Hoboken: Jossey-Bass, 2010.
Beck, Julie. "The Concept Creep of 'Emotional Labor.'" *The Atlantic*. November 26, 2018. https://www.theatlantic.com/family/archive/2018/11/arlie-hochschild-housework-isnt-emotional-labor/576637.
Collaborative for Student Academic, Social, and Emotional Learning. "Fundamentals of SEL." https://casel.org/fundamentals-of-sel/what-is-the-casel-framework, (accessed September 16, 2021).
Covington, Dennis. *Salvation on Sand Mountain: Snake Handling and Redemption in Southern Appalachia*. Philadelphia: Da Capo Press, 2009.
Darder, Antonia, Marta P. Baltodano, and Rodolfo D. Torres. eds. *The Critical Pedagogy Reader*. 3rd edn. New York: Routledge, 2017.
Goodman, Diane. *Promoting Diversity and Social Justice: Educating People from Privileged Groups*. 2nd edn. New York: Routledge, 2011.

Gray-Hildenbrand, Jenna. "The Appalachian 'Other': Academic Approaches to the Study of Serpent-Handling Sects." *Religion Compass* 10, no. 3 (2016): 47–57.
Hochschild, Arlie Russell. *The Managed Heart: Commercialization of Human Feeling*. 3rd edn. Berkeley: University of California Press, 2012.
Jensen, Barbara. *Reading Classes: On Culture and Classism in America*. Ithaca: ILR Press, 2012.
Landreman, Lisa, ed. *The Art of Effective Facilitation: Reflections for Social Justice Educators*. Sterling: Stylus Publishing, 2013.
Marsh, Charles, *God's Long Summer: Stories of Faith and Civil Rights*. Princeton: Princeton University Press, 2008.
Miles, Sara. *Take This Bread: A Radical Conversion*. New York: Random House, 2007.
Miller, Mary. "Teaching and Learning in the Affective Domain." *Emerging Perspectives on Learning, Teaching, and Technology* (website). 2005. http://epltt.coe.uga.edu/index.php?title=Teaching_and_Learning_in_Affective_Domain.
Quinlan, Kathleen. *How Higher Education Feels: Commentaries on Poems That Illuminate Emotions in Learning and Teaching*. Boston: Sense Publishers, 2016.
Sennett, Richard and John Cobb. *The Hidden Injuries of Class*. New York: Knopf, 1972.
Sue, Derald Wing. *Race Talk and the Conspiracy of Silence: Understanding and Facilitating Difficult Dialogues on Race*. Hoboken: Wiley, 2015.
Wharton, Amy. "The Sociology of Emotional Labor." *Annual Review of Sociology* 35 (2009): 147–65.

Chapter 5

Baehr, Jason. "Educating for Intellectual Virtues: From Theory to Practice." *Journal of the Philosophy of Education* 47, no. 2 (2013): 248–62.
Bain, Ken. *What the Best College Teachers Do*. Cambridge: Harvard University Press, 2004.
Beyond Sacred Documentary [film]. Dir. Ping Chong. USA: Whistle Films Production, 2015. Available online: https://www.youtube.com/watch?v=XktjcpGnacM, (accessed July 30, 2021).
Chidester, David. *Empire of Religion: Imperialism and Comparative Religion*. Chicago: University of Chicago Press, 2014.
"Course Catalogue." *Graduate Program in Religious Studies*. Dallas: Southern Methodist University, 2020. https://catalog.smu.edu/preview_program.php?catoid=52&poid=13383.
DeTemple, Jill. "The Spaces We Make: Dialogic Classrooms and Social Transformation." *Ohio State Journal on Dispute Resolution* 35, no. 5 (2020): 753–79.

DeTemple, Jill and John Sarrouf. "Disruption, Dialogue, and Swerve: Reflective Structured Dialogue in Religious Studies Classrooms." *Teaching Theology and Religion* 20, no. 3 (2017): 283–93.
Dweck, Carol. *Self-Theories: Their Role in Motivation, Personality, and Development*. Philadelphia: Psychology Press, 2000.
Eliade, Mircea. *Myth of the Eternal Return or Cosmos and History*. Princeton: Princeton University Press, 1971.
Eyler, Joshua. *How Humans Learn: The Science and Stories behind Effective College Teaching*. Morgantown: West Virginia University Press, 2018.
Felski, Rita. *The Limits of Critique*. Chicago: University of Chicago Press, 2015.
Fitzpatrick, Kathleen. *Generous Thinking: A Radical Approach to Saving the University*. Baltimore: Johns Hopkins University Press, 2019.
Freire, Paulo. *Pedagogy of the Oppressed*. New York: Bloomsbury Academic, 2018 [1970].
Fried, Jane. *Of Education, Fishbowls and Rabbit Holes: Rethinking Teaching and Liberal Education for an Interconnected World*. Sterling: Stylus Press, 2016.
Green, Garrett. "Challenging the Religious Studies Canon: Karl Barth's Theory of Religion." *The Journal of Religion* 75, no. 4 (1995): 473–86.
hooks, bell. *Teaching to Transgress: Education as the Practice of Freedom*. New York: Routledge, 1994.
Kegan, Robert. *In Over Our Heads: The Mental Demands of Modern Life*. Cambridge: Harvard University Press, 1994.
Magdola, Marcia Baxter. "Three Elements of Self-Authorship." *Journal of College Student Development* 49, no. 4 (2008): 269–84.
Masuzawa, Tomoko. *The Invention of World Religions*. Chicago: University of Chicago Press, 2005.
McCutcheon, Russel. *Studying Religion: An Introduction*. New York: Routledge, 2018.
"Moments of Dissent." Essential Partners, Inc. https://whatisessential.org/resources/moments-dissent
Newton, Richard. "Religious Studies LLC and the Question of Canon." *Sowing the Seed*, 2015. Available online: https://sowingtheseedwordpress.com, (accessed May 12, 2021).
Noddings, Nel. *Happiness and Education*. New York: Cambridge University Press, 2003.
"Our Method." Essential Partners, Inc. Available online: https://whatisessential.org/our-method, (accessed July 30, 2021).
Le Poidevin, Robin. *Arguing for Atheism: An Introduction to the Philosophy of Religion*. New York: Routledge, 1996.
Roth, Michael. "A Focus on Critical Feeling." *Inside Higher Ed*, 2021. Available online: https://www.insidehighered.com/views/2021/03/18/colleges-should-teach-critical-feeling-well-critical-thinking-opinion, (accessed March 18, 2021).
Roth, Sallyann. "Speaking the Unspoken: A Work-Group Consultation to Reopen Dialogue." In *Secrets in Families and Family Therapy*, edited by Evan Imber-Black, 268–91. New York: W. W. Norton & Company, 1993.

Imber-Black, Evan, ed. *Secrets in Families and Family Therapy.* New York: W. W. Norton & Company, 1993.

Shapiro, Shawna. "Inclusive Pedagogy in the Academic Writing Classroom: Cultivating Communities of Belonging." *Journal of Academic Writing* 10, no. 1 (2020): 154–64.

Simmons, K. Merinda. "Cannon Fodder." *Method & Theory in the Study of Religion* 28, no. 3 (2016): 297–306.

Sloman, Steven and Phillip Fernbach. *The Knowledge Illusion: Why We Never Think Alone.* New York: Riverhead Books, 2017.

Smart, Ninian. *Dimensions of the Sacred.* Berkeley: University of California Press, 1986.

Smith, Huston. *The World's Religions: Our Great Wisdom Traditions.* New York: HarperCollins, 1991.

Taylor, Charles. *The Ethics of Authenticity.* Cambridge: Harvard University Press, 1991.

Taylor, Mark C., ed. *Critical Terms in Religious Studies.* Chicago: University of Chicago Press, 1998.

Tsing, Anna. "The Global Situation." *Cultural Anthropology* 15, no. 3 (2000): 327–60.

Chapter 6

Al Sager, Abdellatif W. and Lisa Zagummy. "Teaching Islam without the Phobia: What We Can Learn from World History Textbooks." *Thresholds in Education* 41, no. 2 (2018): 75–86.

Ali, Kecia. *The Lives of Muhammad.* Cambridge: Harvard University Press, 2014.

Asani, Ali Sultaan Ali, Kamal Abdel-Malek, and Annemarie Schimmel. *Celebrating Muhammad: Images of the Prophet in Popular Muslim Poetry.* Columbia: University of South Carolina Press, 1995.

Bayoumi, Moustafa. *This Muslim American Life: Dispatches from the War on Terror.* New York: New York University Press, 2015.

Chidester, David. *Empire of Religion: Imperialism and Comparative Religion.* Chicago and London: The University of Chicago Press, 2014.

Daftary, Farhad. "The Study of the Ismailis: Phases and Issues." In *The Study of Shi'i Islam: History, Theology and Law*, edited by Farhad Daftary and Gurdofarid Miskinzoda, 47–65. London and New York: Bloomsbury Publishing, 2014.

Douglass, Susan L. "Teaching about Religion, Islam, and the World in Public and Private School Curricula." In *Educating the Muslims of America*, edited by Yvonne Yazbeck Haddad, Farid Senzai and Jane I. Smith, 85–108. Oxford and New York: Oxford University Press, 2009.

Douglass, Susan L. and Ross E. Dunn. "Interpreting Islam in American Schools." *The Annals of the American Academy of Political and Social Science* 588, no. 1 (2003): 52–72.

Ernst, Carl W. *Following Muhammad: Rethinking Islam in the Contemporary World.* Chapel Hill: University of North Carolina Press, 2003.

Esposito, John L. *Islam: The Straight Path*. New York and Oxford: Oxford University Press, 2011.

Freire, Paulo. *Pedagogy of the Oppressed*. New York: Continuum, 1993.

Gottschalk, Peter and Gabriel Greenberg. *Islamophobia and Anti-Muslim Sentiment: Picturing the Enemy*. Lanham: Rowman & Littlefield, 2019.

Gruber, Christiane J. *The Praiseworthy One: The Prophet Muhammad in Islamic Texts and Images*. Bloomington: Indiana University Press, 2018.

Gruber, Christiane J., and Frederick Stephen Colby. eds. *The Prophet's Ascension: Cross-Cultural Encounters with the Islamic Mi'rāj Tales*. Bloomington: Indiana University Press, 2010.

Hall, Stuart and David Morley. *Essential Essays*. Durham: Duke University Press, 2019.

Hall, Stuart, Jennifer Daryl Slack, and Lawrence Grossberg. *Cultural Studies 1983: A Theoretical History*. Durham and London: Duke University Press, 2016.

Hillenbrand, Carole. *Introduction to Islam: Beliefs and Practices in Historical Perspective*. New York: Thames & Hudson, 2015.

hooks, bell. *Teaching to Transgress: Education as the Practice of Freedom*. New York: Routledge, 1994.

Hussain, Amir. "Images of Muḥammad in Literature, Art, and Music." In *The Cambridge Companion to Muhammad*, edited by Jonathan E. Brockopp, 274–92. Cambridge: Cambridge University Press, 2010.

Katz, Marion Holmes. "The Prophet Muḥammad in Ritual." In *The Cambridge Companion to Muhammad*, edited by Jonathan E. Brockopp, 139–57. Cambridge: Cambridge University Press, 2010.

Kendeou, Panayiota and Edward J. O'Brien. "The Knowledge Revision Components (Krec) Framework: Processes and Mechanisms." In *Processing Inaccurate Information: Theoretical and Applied Perspectives from Cognitive Science and the Educational Sciences*, edited by David Rapp and Jason L. G. Braasch, 353–77. Cambridge: MIT Press, 2014.

King, Richard. *Orientalism and Religion: Post-Colonial Theory, India and the Mystic East*. London and New York: Routledge, 1999.

Knight, Michael Muhammad. *Muhammad: Forty Introductions*. New York: Soft Skull, 2019.

Masuzawa, Tomoko. *The Invention of World Religions: Or, How European Universalism Was Preserved in the Language of Pluralism*. Chicago: University of Chicago Press, 2005.

Moore, Diane L. *Overcoming Religious Illiteracy: A Cultural Studies Approach to the Study of Religion in Secondary Education*. New York: Palgrave Macmillan, 2007.

Morgenstein Fuerst, Ilyse. "Job Ads Don't Add Up: Arabic + Middle East + Texts ≠ Islam." *Journal of the American Academy of Religion* 88, no. 4 (2020): 915–46.

Nuʿmān, Abū Ḥanīfah ibn Muḥammad. *The Pillars of Islam: Daʿā'Im Al-Islām*. Translated by Ismail Kurban Husein Poonawala. Oxford: Oxford University Press, 2002.

Rashid, Hussein. "Diverse Muslim Narratives: Rethinking Islam 101." *The Wabash Center Journal on Teaching* 2, no. 1 (2021): 143–58.

Robinson, Neal. *Islam: A Concise Introduction*. Richmond, Surrey: Curzon, 1999.

Ruthven, Malise. *Islam: A Very Short Introduction*. New York: Oxford University Press, 1997.

Said, Edward W. *Covering Islam: How the Media and the Experts Determine How We See the Rest of the World*. New York: Pantheon Books, 1981.

Saleh, Walid A. "The Arabian Context of Muḥammad's Life." In *The Cambridge Companion to Muḥammad*, edited by Jonathan E. Brockopp, 21–38. New York: Cambridge University Press, 2010.

Tottoli, Roberto, ed. *Islam: An Advanced Introduction*. Abingdon, Oxon and New York: Routledge, Taylor & Francis Group, 2021.

Chapter 7

Ambrose, Susan A., Michael W. Bridges, Michele DiPietro, Marsha C. Voett, and Marie K. Norman. *How Learning Works: 7 Research-Based Principles for Smart Teaching*. San Francisco: John Wiley & Sons, 2010.

Carrette, Jeremy and Richard King. *Selling Spirituality: The Silent Takeover of Religion*. New York: Routledge, 2004.

Dewey, John. *How We Think*. Amherst: Prometheus Books, 1991.

Fink, L. Dee. *Creating Significant Learning Experiences: An Integrated Approach to Designing College Courses*. San Francisco: Jossey-Bass, 2013.

Gagnon, George W. and Michelle Collay. *Designing for Learning: Six Elements in Constructivist Classrooms*. Thousand Oaks: Corwin Press, Inc., 2001.

Giroux, Henry A. *On Critical Pedagogy*. New York: Continuum, 2011.

Iwamura, Jane Naomi. *Virtual Orientalism: Asian Religions and American Popular Culture*. New York: Oxford University Press, 2011.

Lofton, Kathryn. *Consuming Religion*. Chicago: University of Chicago Press, 2017.

Macrine, Sheila L. *Critical Pedagogy in Uncertain Times: Hope and Possibilities*. Cham: Palgrave Macmillan, 2020.

McLaren, Peter. *Life in Schools*. New York: Longman, 1989.

Pelech, James and Gail Piper. *The Comprehensive Handbook of Constructivist Teaching*. Charlotte: Information Age Publishing, 2010.

Piaget, Jean. *To Understand Is to Invent: The Future of Education*. Translated by G-A Roberts. New York: Penguin, 1976.

Piaget, Jean and Barbel Inhelder. *The Psychology of the Child*. New York: Basic Books, 1969.

Said, Edward. *Orientalism*. New York: Vintage, 1979.

Sandlin, Jennifer A. and Peter McLaren. eds. *Critical Pedagogies of Consumption: Living and Learning in the Shadow of the "Shopocalypse"*. New York: Routledge, 2010.

Sandlin, Jennifer A. and Peter McLaren. "Exploring Consumption's Pedagogy and Envisioning a Critical Pedagogy of Consumption—Living and Learning in the Shadow of the 'Shopocalypse.'" In *Critical Pedagogies of Consumption: Living and Learning in the Shadow of the "Shopocalypse"*, edited by Jennifer A. Sandlin and Peter McLaren, 1–19. New York: Routledge, 2010.

Shor, Ira. *Empowering Education: Critical Teaching for Social Change*. Chicago: University of Chicago Press, 1992.

Storper, Michael. "Lived Effects of the Contemporary Economy: Globalism, Inequality, and Consumer Society." *Public Culture* 12, no. 2 (Spring 2000): 375–409.

Vygotsky, Lev S. *Thought and Language*. Translated by A. Kozulin. Cambridge: MIT Press, 1986.

Wilson, Jeff. 2014. *Mindful America*. New York: Oxford University Press. https://libcat.uncw.edu/record=b3367288~S4

Chapter 8

Albanese, Catherine L. *America: Religions and Religion*. United States: Cengage Learning, 2013.

Beaman, Lori G. "The Myth of Pluralism, Diversity, and Vigor: The Constitutional Privilege of Protestantism in the United States and Canada." *Journal for the Scientific Study of Religion* 42, no. 3 (2003): 311–25.

Carroll, Bret E. *The Routledge Historical Atlas of Religion in America*. New York: Routledge, 2000.

Corrigan, John and Lynn S. Neal. *Religious Intolerance in America: A Documentary History*. Chapel Hill: The University of North Carolina Press, 2021.

Gallagher, Eugene V. and Joanne Maguire. *The Religious Studies Skills Book: Close Reading, Critical Thinking, and Comparison*. New York: Bloomsbury Academic, 2019.

Gray-Hildenbrand, Jenna and Rebekka King. "Teaching in Contexts: Designing a Competency-Based Religious Studies Program." *Teaching Theology and Religion* 22 (2019): 191–204.

hooks, bell. *Teaching Critical Thinking: Practical Wisdom*. London: Routledge, 2010.

Iwamura, Jane Naomi. "Critical Faith: Japanese Americans and the Birth of a New Civil Religion." *American Quarterly* 59, no. 3 (2007): 937–68. Project MUSE, doi:10.1353/aq.2007.0058.

Iwamura, Jane Naomi. *Virtual Orientalism: Asian Religions and American Popular Culture*. New York: Oxford University Press, 2011.

Long, Charles H. "Civil Rights–Civil Religion: Visible People and Invisible Religion." In *American Civil Religion*, edited by Richey, Russell E. and Donald G. Jones, 211–21. San Francisco: Mellen Research University Press, 1990.

Long, Charles H. *Significations Signs, Symbols, and Images in the Interpretation of Religion*. Aurora: Davies Group, 1999.

Masuzawa, Tomoko. *The Invention of World Religions: Or, How European Universalism Was Preserved in the Language of Pluralism*. Chicago: University of Chicago Press, 2007.

McConeghy, David. "Narrating the USA's Religious Pluralism." In *After World Religions*, edited by David G. Robertson and Christopher R. Cotter, 139–40. Basingstoke: Taylor & Francis Ltd., 2016.

McCutcheon, Russell T. *Studying Religion: An Introduction*. New York: Routledge, 2019.

Prothero, Stephen R. *God Is Not One: The Eight Rival Religions That Run the World*. New York: HarperOne, 2010.

Prothero, Stephen R. *Religion Matters: An Introduction to the World's Religions*. New York: W. W. Norton & Company, Ltd., 2020.

Raboteau, Albert J. *A Fire in the Bones: Reflections on African-American Religious History*. Boston: Beacon Press, 2001.

Ramey, Steven W. *Writing Religion: The Case for the Critical Study of Religion*. Tuscaloosa: University of Alabama Press, 2015.

Robertson, David G. and Christopher R. Cotter. *After "World Religions". Reconstructing Religious Studies*. Basingstoke: Taylor & Francis Ltd., 2016.

Smith, Jonathan Z. "The Necessary Lie: Duplicity in the Disciplines." In *Studying Religion: An Introduction*, edited by Russell T. McCutcheon, 124–9. New York: Routledge, 2019.

Chapter 9

Ammerman, Nancy, ed. *Everyday Religion: Observing Modern Religious Lives*. New York: Oxford University Press, 2007.

Asad, Talal. *Formations of the Secular: Christianity, Islam, Modernity*. Stanford: Stanford University Press, 2003.

Baldwin, James. 1953. *Go Tell It on the Mountain*. New York: Vintage Books, 2013.

Bender, Courtney and Pamela Klassen. eds. *After Pluralism: Reimagining Religious Engagement*. New York: Columbia University Press, 2010.

Boyarin, Daniel. *Judaism: The Genealogy of a Modern Notion*. New Brunswick: Rutgers University Press, 2019.

Chidester, David. *Savage Systems: Colonialism and Comparative Religion in Southern Africa*. Charlottesville: University of Virginia Press, 1996.

Chidester, David. *Empire of Religion: Imperialism and Comparative Religion*. Chicago: University of Chicago Press, 2014.

Clingerman, Forrest and Reid Locklin. eds. *Teaching Civic Engagement*. New York: Oxford University Press, 2016.

Cotter, Christopher and David Robertson. eds. *After World Religions: Reconstructing Religious Studies*. London: Routledge, 2016.

Delaporte, Marianne. "Giving and Receiving Hospitality during Community Engagement Courses." In *Teaching Civic Engagement*, edited by Forrest Clingerman and Reid Locklin, 61–73. New York: Oxford University Press, 2016.

Dressler, Markus and Arvind-Pal S. Mandair. eds. *Secularism and Religion-Making*. New York: Oxford University Press, 2011.

Elmore, Mark. *Becoming Religious in a Secular Age*. Oakland: University of California Press, 2016.

Fitzgerald, Timothy. *The Ideology of Religious Studies*. New York: Oxford University Press, 2004.

Foucault, Michel. "Power and Strategies." In *Power/Knowledge: Selected Interviews and Other Writings, 1972–1977*, edited by Colin Gordon, 134–45. New York: Pantheon Books, 1980.

Foucault, Michel. "Truth and Power." In *Power/Knowledge: Selected Interviews and Other Writings, 1972–1977*, edited by Colin Gordon, 109–33. New York: Pantheon Books, 1980.

Goldschmidt, Henry. "From World Religions to Lived Religion: Towards a Pedagogy of Civic Engagement in Secondary School Religious Studies Curricula." In *Civility, Religious Pluralism, and Education*. edited by Vince Biondo and Andrew Fiala, 177–92. New York: Routledge, 2014.

Goldschmidt, Henry. "Teaching Lived Religion through Literature: Classroom Strategies for Community-Based Learning." In *Teaching about Religion in the Social Studies Classroom*, NCSS Bulletin #117, edited by Charles Haynes, 53–60. Silver Spring: National Council for the Social Studies, 2019.

Hall, David, ed. *Lived Religion in America: Toward a History of Practice*. Princeton: Princeton University Press, 1997.

Hawley, John Stratton. "Naming Hinduism." *The Wilson Quarterly* 15, no. 3 (1991): 20–34.

Jay, Gregory. "The Engaged Humanities: Principles and Practices of Public Scholarship and Teaching." *Journal of Community Engagement and Scholarship* 3, no. 1 (Spring 2010): 51–63.

Mandair, Arvind-Pal S. *Religion and the Specter of the West: Sikhism, India, Postcoloniality, and the Politics of Translation*. New York: Columbia University Press, 2009.

Masuzawa, Tomoko. *The Invention of World Religions: Or, How European Universalism Was Preserved in the Language of Pluralism*. Chicago: University of Chicago Press, 2005.

McGuire, Meredith. *Lived Religion: Faith and Practice in Everyday Life*. New York: Oxford University Press, 2008.

Muslim American Civil Liberties Coalition, Creating Law Enforcement Accountability & Responsibility Project, and Asian American Legal Defense and Education Fund. *Mapping Muslims: NYPD Spying and Its Impact on American Muslims* (2013). Available online: https://www.law.cuny.edu/wp-content/uploads/page-assets/academics/clinics/immigration/clear/Mapping-Muslims.pdf, (accessed July 5, 2021).

Nikitina, Svetlana. "Applied Humanities: Bridging the Gap between Building Theory and Fostering Citizenship." *Liberal Education* 95, no. 1 (Winter 2009): 36–43.

Orsi, Robert. *The Madonna of 115th Street: Faith and Community in Italian Harlem, 1880–1950*. New Haven: Yale University Press, 1985.

Orsi, Robert. "Everyday Miracles: The Study of Lived Religion." In *Lived Religion in America: Toward a History of Practice*, edited by David Hall, 3–21. Princeton: Princeton University Press, 1997.

Orsi, Robert. "Is the Study of Lived Religion Irrelevant to the World We Live In?" *Journal for the Scientific Study of Religion* 42, no. 2 (2003): 169–74.

Patel, Eboo, Jennifer Howe Peace, and Noah Silverman. eds. *Interreligious/Interfaith Studies: Defining a New Field*. Boston: Beacon Press, 2018.

Pierce, Ellie. "Using the Case Method in Interfaith Studies Classrooms." In *Interreligious/Interfaith Studies: Defining a New Field*, edited by Eboo Patel, Jennifer Howe Peace and Noah Silverman, 72–84. Boston: Beacon Press, 2018.

Potok, Chaim. 1967. *The Chosen*. New York: Fawcett Publications, 1987.

Rashid, Hussein. "Mustafa: Teaching beyond the Five Pillars." In *Teaching Critical Religious Studies*, edited by Jenna Gray-Hildenbrand, Beverley McGuire and Hussein Rashid, 129–48. London: Bloomsbury Academic, 2022.

Smith, Jonathan Z. "A Matter of Class: Taxonomies of Religion." *Harvard Theological Review* 89, no. 4 (1996): 387–403.

Smith, Wilfred Cantwell. 1962. *The Meaning and End of Religion: A New Approach to the Religious Traditions of Mankind*. Minneapolis: Fortress Press, 1991.

Sonne, James. "Cross-Cultural Lawyering and Religion: A Clinical Perspective." *Clinical Law Review* 25, no. 1 (2018): 223–68.

de Vries, Hent, ed. *Religion: Beyond a Concept*. New York: Fordham University Press, 2008.

Wuthnow, Robert. *What Happens When We Practice Religion?: Textures of Devotion in Everyday Life*. Princeton: Princeton University Press, 2020.

Chapter 10

Akkach, Samer, ed. *'Ilm: Science, Religion and Art in Islam*. Adelaide: University of Adelaide Press, 2019.

Barbour, Ian G. *Religion and Science: Historical and Contemporary Issues*. San Francisco: HarperSanFrancisco, 1997

Barbour, Ian G. *When Science Meets Religion: Enemies, Strangers, or Partners?* San Francisco: HarperSanFrancisco, 2000.

Behm, Amanda, Christienna Fryar, Emma Hunter, Elisabeth Leake, Su Lin Lewis, and Sarah Miller-Davenport. "Decolonizing History: Enquiry and Practice." *History Workshop Journal* 89 (2020): 169–91, doi: http://doi.org/10.1093/hwj/dbz052.

Blackwell, Richard J. "Galileo Galilei." In *Science and Religion: A Historical Introduction*, edited by Gary B. Ferngren, 105–16. Baltimore: Johns Hopkins University Press, 2002.

Bratton, Susan Power. "Ecology and Religion." In *The Oxford Handbook of Religion and Science*, edited by Philip Clayton and Zachary Simpson, 207–25. Oxford: Oxford University Press, 2006.

Clayton, Philip and Zachary Simpson. eds. *The Oxford Handbook of Religion and Science*. Oxford: Oxford University Press, 2006.

Ecklund, Elaine Howard. *Science vs. Religion: What Scientists Really Think*. Oxford: Oxford University Press, 2010.

Efron, Noah J. "Myth 9. That Christianity Gave Birth to Modern Science." In *Galileo Goes to Jail and Other Myths about Science and Religion*, edited by Ronald L. Numbers, 79–89. Cambridge: Harvard University Press, 2009.

Finocchiaro, Maurice A., ed. and trans. *The Galileo Affair: A Documentary History*. Berkeley: University of California Press, 1989.

Funk, Cary and Becka A. Alper. *Religion and Science: Highly Religious Americans Are Less likely than Others to See Conflict between Faith and Science*. Washington: Pew Research Center, 2015.

Gottschalk, Peter. *Religion, Science, and Empire: Classifying Hinduism and Islam in British India*. Oxford: Oxford University Press, 2012.

Kuhn, Thomas S. *The Structure of Scientific Revolutions*. Chicago: University of Chicago Press, 1962.

Kernahan, Cyndi. *Teaching about Race and Racism in the College Classroom: Notes from a White Professor*. Morgantown: West Virginia University Press, 2019.

LeVasseur, Todd. "Reverend Billy and the Church of Stop Shopping: Contemporary Religious Production on a Planet Passing Tipping Points." *Nova Religio: The Journal of Alternative and Emergent Religion* 23, no. (3) (2020): 86–109, doi: https://doi.org/10.1525/nr.2020.23.3.86.

Numbers, Ronald L. ed. *Galileo Goes to Jail and Other Myths about Science and Religion*. Cambridge: Harvard University Press, 2009.

Nye, Mallory. "Decolonizing the Study of Religion." *Open Library of Humanities* 5, no. 1 (2019): 1–45, doi: https://doi.org/10.16995/olh.421.

Smith, Jonathan Z. "Religion, Religions, Religious." In *Critical Terms for Religious Studies*, edited by Mark C. Taylor, 269–84. Chicago: University of Chicago Press, 1988.

Walvoord, Barbara E. *Teaching and Learning in College Introductory Religion Courses*. Malden: Blackwell Pub, 2008.

White, Lynn, Jr. "The Historical Roots of Our Ecologic Crisis." *Science* 155, no. 3767 (1967): 1203–7, doi: https://doi.org/10.1126/science.155.3767.1203.

Chapter 11

Albanese, Catherine L. *America: Religions and Religion*. Belmont: Wadsworth Publishing Co., 1992.

Berg, Peter, dir. *Friday Night Lights*. Universal City: Universal Pictures, 2004.

Bissinger, H.G. *Friday Night Lights: A Town, a Team, and a Dream*. New York: Perseus Books, 1990.
Chandler, Joan M. "Sport Is Not a Religion." In *Sport and Religion*, edited by Shirl Hoffman, 55–62. Champaign: Human Kinetics Books, 1992.
Chidester, David. *Savage Systems: Colonialism and Comparative Religion in Southern Africa*. Charlottesville: University of Virginia Press, 1996.
Chidester, David. "The Church of Baseball, the Fetish of Coca-Cola, and the Potlatch of Rock 'N' Roll." In *Religion and Popular Culture in America*, edited by Bruce David Forbes and Jeffrey H. Mahan, 213–31. Berkeley: University of California Press, 2005.
Coakley, Jay. "Assessing the Sociology of Sport: On Cultural Sensibilities and the Great Sport Myth." *International Review for the Sociology of Sport* 50 (2015): 402–6.
Durkheim, Émile. *The Elementary Forms of Religious Life*. Translated by Karen E. Fields. New York: The Free Press, 1995.
Fisher, Donald M. *Lacrosse: A History of the Game*. Baltimore: Johns Hopkins University Press, 2002.
Kessler, Gary E. *Studying Religion: An Introduction through Cases*. 3rd edn. Boston: McGraw-Hill Higher Education, 2008.
Mamdani, Mahmood. *Good Muslim, Bad Muslim: America, the Cold War, and the Roots of Terror*. New York: Doubleday, 2005.
Martin, Craig. *A Critical Introduction to the Study of Religion*. New York: Taylor and Francis, 2017.
McCutcheon, Russell. *Studying Religion: An Introduction*. 2nd edn. New York: Routledge, 2019.
Myhre, Paul. *Introduction to Religious Studies*. Winona: Anselm Academic, 2009.
Nongbri, Brent. *Before Religion: A History of a Modern Concept*. New Haven: Yale University Press, 2013.
Nye, Malory. *Religion: The Basics*. 2nd edn. New York: Routledge, 2008.
Otto, Rudolf. *The Idea of the Holy*. Translated by John W. Harvey. Oxford: Oxford University Press, 1981.
Smith, Jonathan Z. *Imagining Religion: From Babylon to Jonestown*. Chicago: University of Chicago Press, 1982.
Tillich, Paul. *Dynamics of Faith*. New York: Harper and Row, 1957.
Winningham, Geoff and Al Reinert. *Rites of Fall: High School Football in Texas*. Austin: University of Texas Press, 1979.

Chapter 12

Davis, Angela Y. *Are Prisons Obsolete?* New York: Seven Stories Press, 2003.
Davis, Angela Y. *Abolition Democracy: Beyond Empire, Prisons, and Torture*. 1st edn. New York: Seven Stories Press, 2005.

Dolgon, Corey, Tania D. Mitchell, and Timothy K. Eatman. eds. *The Cambridge Handbook of Service Learning and Community Engagement*. New York: Cambridge University Press, 2017.

Dubler, Joshua and Vincent W. Lloyd. *Break Every Yoke: Religion, Justice, and the Abolition of Prisons*. New York: Oxford University Press, 2020.

Gordon, Lewis R. *Disciplinary Decadence: Living Thought in Trying Times*. The Radical Imagination Series. Boulder: Paradigm Publishers, 2006.

Harney, Stefano and Fred Moten. *The Undercommons: Fugitive Planning & Black Study*. Wivenhoe, New York and Port Watson: Minor Compositions, 2013.

Masuzawa, Tomoko. *The Invention of World Religions, or, How European Universalism Was Preserved in the Language of Pluralism*. Chicago: University of Chicago Press, 2005.

Moten, Fred and Stefano Harney. "The University and the Undercommons: SEVEN THESES." *Social Text* 22, no. 2 (79) (June 1, 2004): 101–15. https://doi.org/10.1215/01642472-22-2_79-101.

Saltmarsh, John. "Transforming Higher Education through and for Democratic Civic Engagement: A Model for Change." *Michigan Journal of Community Service Learning* (Fall 2015): 122–7.

Strum, Susan; Eatman, Timothy; Saltmarch, John; and Bush, Adam, "Full Participation: Building the Architecture for Diversity and Community Engagement in Higher Education" (2011). *Imagining America*. 17. https://surface.syr.edu/ia/17.

Vasko, Elisabeth T. "Civic Learning and Teaching as a Resource for Sexual Justice: An Undergraduate Religious Studies Course Module." *Teaching Theology & Religion* 20, no. 2 (2017): 162–70. https://doi.org/10.1111/teth.12383.

Index

Locators followed by "n." indicate endnotes

abolition 12, 163–4
    fugitivity and 164, 166–7
    and full participation 164, 172
    history and haunting of 165
    and university classroom 164–6
academic criticism 47
academic objectivity 44
Acro-yoga 100
Adi Granth (Sikh) 26
adult education 18, 23
affective learning model 185 n.10
ahimsa, studying 26
aikido 25, 180 n.40
Akkach, Samer, *'ilm* 136–7, 140
Albanese, Catherine 105, 109
    America: Religions and Religion 106, 191 n.7
    American code of living 154
    features of religious system 154
Al-Biruni 141
Ali, Kecia 89
Alien Religion 38, 40
Alpetragius 141
American Academy of Religion (AAR) 32, 125, 177 n.4, 196 n.26
American cultural language 109
American Protestantism 111
American religions, teaching
    classroom 192 n.16
    myth-making work 105
    problem 106–8
    solutions 108–10
    teaching tactic 110–12
    textbook tables of contents 113–14
Asad, Talal, *Genealogies of Religion* 20
Asian culture 95
Asian religions class 95
    findings 99–103
    problem 96
    relevant literature 96–7
    teaching tactic 97–9
    works, tactic 103–4
Asian religious practices 11, 25, 95

Baehr, Jason 74
Bain, Ken 74
Baldwin, James, *Go Tell it on the Mountain* 125, 195 n.24
Barbour, Ian G. 135
    four-part model 141
Barylo, William 4
Beaman, Lori 107–8
Beers, George 155
bell hooks 69, 110, 178 n.26
Bhagavad Gita 20, 124
Birmingham School 86–7
Blackwell, Richard 141–2
Blazer, Annie 12
Bloom, Benjamin 185 n.10
bodied religion 21, 27
bodiless religion 19–22
Bourdieu, Pierre 19
Bowie, David 2
bracketing 10, 19, 31–33, 181 n.12. See also pre-bracketing
    limitations 44–5
    problematic aspects of 33–5
Brahma (Hinduism) 4, 20
Brantmeier, Edward, *Pedagogy of Vulnerability* 24
breaking free (pedagogical imperative) 163–4
Brown, Karen, *Mama Lola* 13
Brown, Peter 19
Buddhism 38, 49, 121, 124, 144
Buddhist meditation techniques 95
Burrows, Mark 46–7
Butler, Judith 20
Bynum, Caroline Walker 19

capitalism 97, 163, 199 n.29
carcerality 162–3, 166, 168, 170
Castelli, Benedetto 141
Catholicism 4, 123, 151
Central Conference of American Rabbis (United States) 144
Chandler, Joan, "Sport is Not a Religion" 154
Chidester, David 4–5, 34, 153
  Empire of Religion 69
  "European and indigenous cocreations" 121
chi gong 25, 180 n.40
Chong, Ping, *Beyond Sacred* 71, 76
Christianity/Christians 3, 19, 44, 58–60, 135, 137, 140, 150, 152, 155
  anti-/pro-segregation 59
  Christian-centric conflict narrative 135–7
  dinner church (Brooklyn) 126–7
  and environmentalism 142–3
  hegemony and cultural imperialism 121
  language of 1, 163
  religious rituals 31, 43, 158
  snake-handling 58, 60, 185 n.17
  white supremacy *vs*. Christian resistance 61–2
civically engaged study (religion) 8, 128, 196 n.26
civic learning and teaching 168–9
clapping game 70, 76–7
classrooms (religious studies) 6, 10, 18, 43, 75, 109, 126, 148, 171, 172
  American religions 106–7, 192 n.16
  bodied learning 29
  bracketing (*see* bracketing)
  civically engaged 8, 128, 196 n.26
  community-building 24
  creativity and imagination 110
  critically engaged 167–8, 172
  democratically engaged 8, 12, 164, 168, 170, 172
  dialogic 68–70
  example from 142–4
  "Exploring, Inquiring, and Questioning Religion" 38
  normalizing neutrality 43–6
  practicing interdependency 9, 37

RSD 79
space for affect in 46–50
teaching tactic 38–40, 50–1
as undercommons 166–7, 171
university 12, 164, 166, 168–70
The Climate Crisis and New York Faith Communities (conference) 124
Coakley, Jay, "great sport myth" 159, 161
colonizing voyeurism 25
commercialization and consumption 11, 95–6, 99, 190 n.2
Comparative Theology 3–5, 85
Confucianism 99
constructivism 97
Constructivist Learning Design 97
consumerism 96, 98, 101, 104
contemplative practices 25, 179 n.38
Copernican model 141
Cortés, Hernán 138
COVID-19 pandemic 42
Covington, Dennis 58, 185 n.16
  Salvation on Sand Mountain 58–60
critically engaged pedagogy 167–8, 172
critical pedagogy 97
critical thinking skills 7, 22, 25, 33, 69, 78, 96, 107, 109, 112, 148
cultural appreciation and appropriation 99–100
cultural imperialism 115, 121
Cultural Studies 87–8, 92
culture, religion and 87–8, 91–2

Daftary, Farhad 4
Daoism 99
Davis, Angela 165–6
  Are Prisons Obsolete 166
democratically engaged pedagogy 8, 12, 164, 168, 170, 172
DeTemple, Jill 10, 51. *See also* graduate theory and method seminar
devotional life (Muslims) 86
dialogic classrooms 68–70
diasporic identity 13
dinner church (Brooklyn) 126–7
disabled students 54
Doyle, Jennifer, "university's soft flesh" 48
Drescher, Elizabeth, *Choosing Our Religion: The Spiritual Lives of America's Nones* 44

Dubler, Joshua, *Break Every Yoke* 163–5
Du Bois, W. E. B. 5
Durga/Kali (Hindu goddess) 28
Durkheim, Emile 153
　effervescence 75, 153
　Elementary Forms of the Religious Life 153
Dweck, Carol 69, 74

Eck, Diana
　A New Religious America: How a "Christian Country" Has Become the World's Most Religiously Diverse Nation 106
　Pluralist Project 106
Ecklund, Elaine Howard 136
Efron, Noah J. 143
embodied pedagogy/learning 8, 18–19, 23, 30, 178 n.21
　benefits 23–4
　interdisciplinary 19–22
　model for sensory and affective education 26–9
　in Religious Studies 24–6
　and vulnerability 24
emotional dimension of learning 10, 59
　acknowledging 53–5
　conceptualizing 55–7
　ethos of responsibility 63–4
emotional disorientation 55
emotional intelligence 55
emotionalizing education 55
emotional labor 53, 56–8, 60–2, 185 n.13. *See also* emotional dimension of learning
environmentalism, religion and 142–4
Essential Partners, Inc. 68, 70, 79
European Christian 115, 121
European colonialism 118
European Enlightenment 18–19, 155
Evangelicalism 142
experiential learning 7
Eyler, Joshua 78
　How Humans Learn 69

Faith-Based Perspectives on Trauma and Healing (conference) 124
Feminist Disability Studies 10, 36
Fernbach, Phil 187 n.4
Fiasco, Lupe, *Muhammad Walks* 91

Fisher, Donald 155
Fisher, Kathleen 25
Foucault, Michel 19, 178 n.21
　Birth of a Clinic 138
　"Power and Strategies" 120
　regime of truth 119–20
　universal and specific intellectuals 117–18, 128–9
Freire, Paulo 8, 97, 167. *See also* problem-posing education
Freud, Sigmund 75, 150
Friday Night Lights (Bissinger) 156–61
Fuerst, Ilyse Morgenstein 85
full participation 162, 164, 169–70, 172
　and democratically engaged pedagogy 164, 170
　goals 169

Galileo 134, 141–2, 145
　Affair 141
　and Roman Catholic Church 142
Gallagher, Eugene V. 46, 109
　Religious Studies Skills Book 43–4
Geisz, Steven 25–6
Gill, Rahuldeep 47–9
Giroux, Henry 8, 97
God in America 112
Goldschmidt, Henry 11, 25
Gordon, Lewis, *Disciplinary Decadence* 163
government-endorsed religion 176 n.2
graduate theory and method seminar 10, 66–7
　"The Clapping Game" 70, 76–7
　communication agreements 70
　course evaluations 73
　Fall 2020 Core Seminar, agreements 71
　"Five Questions" game 74
　"Five Things" game 70, 72, 77
　"No Weasles" Cookie Cake 67
　political polarization 68
Gravett, Emily 33
Gray-Hildenbrand, Jenna 10, 109
great sport myth (GSM) 159, 161
Griffith, R. Marie 34
Guidelines for Teaching about Religion in K-12 Public Schools in the United States (2010, AAR) 196 n.26
Guru Nanak 48
Gustafson, Diana 23

hadith 90
Hajj 88
Halima 90
Hall, Stuart 87–8
Hamer, Fannie Lou 59
Haraway, Donna 138
Harney, Stefano 47, 166–7, 172
Headspace app 95, 100
heliocentrism 141
Hicks, David 5–6
higher education 18, 23, 54, 185 n.10
   AAR Religious Literacy Guidelines (2019) 196 n.26
   diverse engagement 169
   Islam 85
   race and racism in 139
Hinduism 4, 20, 98
   Keisha program 68
   and Sikhism 121
Hindu trinity 4
Hitchhiker game 77–8
Hochschild, Arlie Russell 56–7. *See also* emotional labor
homogenous religions 122
Hoover, Heidi 125
humanity of people 14

iceberg model 23, 179 n.28
Imhoff, Sarah, discipline of religious studies 45–6
Indonesian Council of Ulama 143
instructors 9, 11–12, 48, 55, 62, 74, 95, 97, 103–4, 133–4, 136, 141, 185 n.13
   backward design 7
   cognitive tasks 57
   need 37, 144–5
   question-centered approach 37
   teaching 45
   voice 36–7
interdisciplinarity 21
Interfaith Center of New York (ICNY)
   education programs 11, 115, 128, 179 n.36
   effects of power 119
   and NYPD 116–17, 122, 194 n.10, 194 n.13
   pedagogic principles 120–4
   Policing in Today's Multifaith New York 116
intra-faith diversity 122, 126

intrinsically motivated students 74
Islam 4, 49, 86, 152
   "Five Pillars of Islam" 4, 11, 81–2, 85, 93, 127, 137, 188 n.5, 196 n.30
   as heterodoxy 4
Islam class 81
   literature 86–8
   Muslim and non-Muslim 82
   Muslim heritage 81
   problem, identify 82–4
   solution 91–3
   teaching tactic 88–91
Islamophobia 6
Iwamura, Jane 109
   "Oriental monk" 102

Jackson, Michael D., "Knowledge of the Body" 20
Jerryson, Michael 39–40, 183 n.37
Johnson, Mark, *Metaphors We Live By* 19
Joshi, Khyati 109
Judaism 121, 143, 150, 152
juxtapose religion/juxtapositions 12, 32

K-12 education 18, 23, 118, 185 n.10
Kegan, Robert 73. *See also* self-authorship
Kernahan, Cydni 139–42
Kessler, Gary, *Studying Religion: An Introduction Through Cases* 149–50
King, Rebekka 109
Klein, Naomi, *The Shock Doctrine: The Rise of Disaster Capitalism* 42
Knoll, Kristina 37
knowledge making and power 178 n.21
knowledge transmission and creation 66
Kraft, Becky 25
Kuhn, Thomas S. 138

Lakoff, George, *Metaphors We Live By* 19
LaMothe, Kimerer, sensory education 22–3, 25–9
Land, Ray 37
language(s) 18, 92
   American cultural 109
   of Christianity/Christians 1, 163
   of pluralism 115
   prescriptive and descriptive 32, 35
   of sect and heresy 4
Latour, Bruno 138

Learning Community (Yoga and
  Mindfulness) 99
learning outcomes 38, 40, 48, 52, 61, 63,
  69, 74, 111, 146
learning process 10, 21, 24–5, 30, 47, 50–2,
  60, 96–7, 184 n.2, 185 n.10
  blended 22–3, 27
  emotional tasks 54
Le Poidevin, Robin 65–6, 76
Lesches, Avi 125
Lewis, Su Lin, decolonizing history 138–9
linguistic hybridity 6
liturgical manual 20
lived religion 9, 20, 24, 122, 124, 195 n.24
Lloyd, Vincent, *Break Every Yoke* 163
Lofton, Kate 96
Lofton, Kathryn, media consumption
  191 n.8
Long, Charles, American Civil Religion 109

Magdola, Marcia Baxter 73, 75
Maguire, Joanne 45–6, 109
  Religious Studies Skills Book 43–4
Mandair, Arvind-Pal S. 123
  Religion and the Specter of the West 121
mandala 17–18
Marsh, Charles, *God's Long Summer: Stories
  of Faith and Civil Rights* 59–61
Martin, Craig
  9/11 attacks, example 152
  *A Critical Introduction to the Study of
    Religion* 151
  primitives 152
mass literacy 92
Masuzawa, Tomoko 3, 85
  *The Invention of World Religions:
    Or, How European Universalism
    was Preserved in the Language of
    Pluralism* 69, 107, 163
Mauss, Marcel 19
McConeghy, David 112–13
McCutcheon, Russell 192 n.16
  Studying Religion: An Introduction
    199 n.12
McGinn, Sean 116
McGuire, Beverley 11, 26, 187 n.4
McKenna, Maria, *Pedagogy of
  Vulnerability* 24
McLaren, Peter 96
Mercury, Freddie 2, 91

Merleau-Ponty, Maurice 19, 177 n.6
Meyer, Jan 37
Middle Tennessee State University
  (MTSU) 31–32, 109
Minister, M. Cooper 10
Moore, Diane 6, 81, 86–7
  religious literacy, principles of 86–7
  situated knowledge 87
Moten, Fred 47–8, 167
  *The Undercommons: Fugitive Planning
    and Black Study* 163–4, 166
Muhammad, Prophet 89–94
Myhre, Paul, *Introduction to Religious
  Studies* 150
myths 139–42
  alternative narratives 140
  of conflict 135–6, 142
  confronting 139–40

naming affects (classroom) 50–2
naming gaps 13
Native American, sport 155
neoliberalism 98
Nhat Hanh, Thich 124
nirvana 100
Noddings, Nel 69
Nongbri, Brent 199 n.29
Numbers, Ronald L. 135
Nye, Mallory 139
  Religion: The Basics 150–1

Occidental religions 143
Odessa, religion 158
Oldstone-Moore, Jennifer 25
Oppenheimer, Robert 118
Orientalism 93, 98–9, 102
Orientalist depictions of Muslims 11, 82
orientation, time problem and lessons for
  65–6. *See also* reorientation
Orsi, Robert 34, 124
  "Bronx Lourdes" grotto 122–3
  in-between space 40–1
Otto, Rudolf, "the holy" 153

patron saint 2
Pearson, Thomas 184 n.1
pedagogic principles (ICNY) 117, 120–1,
  125
  faith-based personal stories and
    political projects 122–3

internal diversity, faith traditions/
  communities 120–1
pedagogy 18, 61, 65, 115–16, 120, 167, 192
    n.16. *See also* embodied pedagogy/
    learning
  critical 97
  of embodied questioning 10, 41
  of engaged democracy 167–9
  theory and 3, 6, 12
  world religions 115–16, 120, 122, 128,
    193 n.3
Pedestrianism 40
Pérez, Elizabeth, micropractices 27
personal and collective learning 97
Piaget, Jean 97
pluralism 11, 112, 193 n.2
  in the American religions 106–7
  European universalism 115
Pluralism Project's Case Initiative 125,
  196 n.25
Posadas, Jeremy 10
Potok, Chaim, *The Chosen* 125
practice of religion 21–2, 24–5, 176 n.2
practice to refuse (classroom) 47–8
Prayer Song (Mos Def/Yasiin Bey and
  K'naan) 91
pre-bracketing. *See also* bracketing
  embodied questioning 40–1
  questioning bodies 36–7
  teaching tactic (classroom) 38–9
problem-posing education 97, 167
Probyn, Elspeth 29
Protestant Christianity/Christian 1, 3, 9,
    18, 20, 24, 85, 108, 115, 123, 135–7,
    140, 151
  Protestantism to pluralism 106–7
  public Protestantism 109
Protestant Reformation 151
Prothero, Stephen 33–4
  God is Not One 106
  Religion Matters 106, 181 n.12
Puar, Jasbir 36
Purity and Danger 69

qawwali 90
queer students 54
question-centered approach 37
Quinlan, Kathleen, *How Higher Education
  Feels* 55–6
Qur'an 90, 92

Raboteau, Albert 109
race/racism, religion and 2, 5, 59, 62, 138
Raihan 90
Rashid, Hussein 11
reflective structured dialogue (RSD) 8,
    38–9, 51, 68–9, 79
  as in-class assignments 71
religion 2, 34, 38, 66, 121, 145, 149, 151
  in American culture 5
  changed over time 151–2, 154–5
  clauses 176 n.2
  and coloniality 163
  and culture 87–8, 91–2
  and environmentalism 142–4
  as orientations 75
  performance studies 177 n.14
  rationality and 71
  reductive disciplinary rubrics 163
  reification of religions 137–9
  and science (*see* science, religion and)
  sports and (*see* sports, religion and)
  as *sui generis* 13
  theories of 137
Religion and Sports in the US (course)
  148, 157
Religion Behind Bars: Religion and
  Mass Incarceration in US Society
  (course) 162–3, 171
Religion & Society 31–2
religious diversity 107–8, 116–17, 119
  education programs 11, 115, 128
religious experience 8, 11, 163
religious festival 28–9
religious leaders 117, 196 n.26
  panel discussions with 122–6
religious literacy 6–7, 11, 32, 81, 91, 115
  and cultural studies 89, 93
  principles of 86–7, 90
religious practices 7, 11, 18, 25–6, 28, 45,
    93, 95, 122, 127, 176 n.2
religious-spiritual healing practices 146
Religious Studies 1, 3, 10, 34, 163, 172
  as academic discipline 18
  courses 7, 66
  goals of (Venn diagram) 144–6
  imperium 3–4
  prior knowledge 7–8, 95, 97–8, 101, 103
  reorientation as paradigm 75–6
religious traditions 1, 5, 10, 86, 93, 106,
    116, 122, 134, 171

reorientation 68–71
  analysis 71–4
  as paradigm for religious studies 75–6
  tools for 76–9
reparative reading, practice of 48
Rhapsody, Bohemian 3–9
rice-krispie treats (goddess) 28
Rilke, Rainer Maria, "Archaic Torso of Apollo" 46–7
rituals 20, 25, 154, 156
  Christian religious 31, 43, 158
Roberts, Martha Smith 11
Roth, Michael, critical feeling 69
Rumi, "Qur'an in Persian" 92

Said, Edward 143
saint 1
  patron 2
  secularized 2
Samuels, Ellen 36
Sarrouf, John 51
Sartre, Jean-Paul 118
Schaefer, Donovan 20
scholars 21, 41, 62, 121, 133, 142, 145, 151, 154
  of religion 9, 19–20, 38, 43, 45, 66, 128, 135–8, 143
  and students, reembodying 22–6
Scholarship of Teaching and Learning (SoTL) 6, 9–10, 12–13
science, religion and 12, 133–4
  classroom, example 142–4
  insurmountable hostility 136
  myths 139–42
  problem 135–7
  reification of religions, challenge 137–9
  students and instructors, needs 144–7
Scopes, John 134, 139, 145
Sedgwick, Eve 47
  paranoia 48
  practice of reparative reading 48
self-authorship 73, 79
self-fulfilling/-amplifying paradigm 135–6
sensory education 22–3, 26–9
shahada 89, 91
Sheloush, Lea 116
Shi'ism 4, 94

Shiva (Hinduism) 4
Sikhism 117, 121
Sloman, Steve 187 n.4
Smith, Jonathan Z. 151
  "The Necessary Lie: Duplicity in the Disciplines" 109–10
  "Religion, Religions, Religious" 137–8
social constructivism 134
social-emotional learning (SEL) 185 n.10
social workers, conference 124
sociology of scientific knowledge (SSK) 134, 137
  hard and soft programme 138
space for affect (classroom) 46–50
spiritual capitalism 98–9, 103–4
spirituality 99, 101–2, 104
sports
  civilization and savagery 156
  Friday Night Lights 156–61
  GSM 159
  high-school football 157–8
  lacrosse games (Canada) 155–6
  problem of defining religion 149–50
  religion and 148, 160
  religion, defining 153
  religious devotion 158
  religious rituals and 154
  teaching tactic 156–7
St. John Coltrane 2
stereotype threat 54
Storper, Michael 96
student(s) 7, 18, 68, 72–3, 76, 85, 92, 94, 110, 139, 167, 170, 185 n.17
  American Religion, narratives 110–12
  bracketing 33, 35, 41, 44–6
  communication agreements 70
  emotional learning (*see* emotional dimension of learning)
  emotional regulation 56
  ethos of responsibility 63–4
  faith tradition 127
  full participation 169
  intrinsically motivated 74
  need 144–7
  Orientalism 100
  prior knowledge 8, 11, 95, 97, 101, 103

pro-segregationist/White supremacist
  feelings 186 n.21
racial discrimination 158–9
reembodying scholars and 22–6
religion and science classroom 133–4,
  140
sensory awareness 29
sports 152, 156, 158–9
textbooks 111–12
student-centered approach 8
Study of Religion. *See* Religious Studies
Sufism 92
Sunni Islam 4, 85, 126

tabula rasa 93
tabu/totem 5
Taves, Ann, *Religious Experience Reconsidered* 19
Taylor, Mark C., *Critical Terms* 69, 177 n.14
teaching and learning (religion) 6, 24, 34, 40, 44, 55, 65–6, 69, 75, 168. *See also* learning process
  American religions 105–7, 112
  of Islam (*see* Islam class)
  lived religion 195 n.24
  practice, examples 57–62
  race and racism 139
  religion and science (*see* science, religion and)
  scholarship of 61
  themes 9
theory and pedagogy 3, 6, 12
Tillich, Paul, ultimate concern 153–4
time
  problem and lessons for orientation 65–6
  theories of 65–6
tools (reorientation)
  Beyond Sacred play 76
  clapping game 76–7
  Five Things game 77
  hitchhiker game 77–8
  playlist game 78
  reflective structured dialogue (RSD) 79
Transparency in Learning and Teaching project (TILT) 7
trauma and affect theories 42–3, 184 n.7
Tsing, Anna 69

Tucker Edmonds, Joseph, university classroom 12
Tweed, Thomas 35, 41

undocumented students 54
The United States
  carcerality 162–3
  Central Conference of American Rabbis 144
  language of Christianity 1
  modernity 163
  public Protestantism 109
  religious freedom in 106
  religious language and imagery 92
  religious marketplace 2
  Study of Religion in 4–5
university classroom 12, 168, 170
  abolition and 164–6
Upanisads 20

Vedas 20
virtual orientalism 98
Vishnu (Hinduism) 4
Vygotsky, Lev 97
  zone of proximal development 74

Wabash Center for Teaching and Learning 1, 184 n.1
Walvoord, Barbara 7, 33, 134
  voice instructors 36–7
Watkins, Megan 29
Western Christianity 134, 136, 144
White, Lynn, Jr., "White thesis" 143
white supremacy 5, 24, 61–2
William & Mary (W&M, Williamsburg) 148, 198 n.1
Winters, Joseph 47
  Hope Draped in Black 49
working-class students 54
world religions 3, 38, 107, 115, 128, 134, 145–6, 181 n.12, 193 n.2
  compatriot of power 117–20
  pedagogy, critiques of 193 n.3
  public sphere 116
World Religions Paradigm 1, 3, 85, 107, 134, 145, 192 n.16
  civilizing mission of Enlightenment 6
  colonialism and 93
  critiques of 2–3, 6, 11, 13, 87–8, 93

Ya Mustafa 90, 92, 94
yoga and meditation 11, 25, 43, 95, 100–1, 103–4, 151, 179 n.40
Yoga Journal 98–100
Yusuf Islam (Cat Stevens) 90

Zeller, Benjamin 12
Zoom (video-chatting technology) 50–1
Zubko, Katherine, belief-centered approaches 9

www.ingramcontent.com/pod-product-compliance
Lightning Source LLC
Chambersburg PA
CBHW062140300426
44115CB00012BA/1992